'A valuable addition to any maths teacher's bookshelf, this contains clear, strategic advice on a range of strategies to support learners, depending on the obstacles they face. It also contains approaches for specific key topics, meaning learners can dip into the sections as they need to support their learning. This book is just what neurodiverse learners, their families and teachers need!'

– **Heather Davis,** independent mathematics education consultant

'I highly recommend this comprehensive book for every neurodiverse learner working towards GCSE Maths. It provides valuable insight (for the learner and those working with them) into the challenges being neurodiverse can have on the acquisition of maths, but then offers essential tips on overcoming these challenges to achieve success. The study guide covers fundamental topics in a straightforward, easy to follow way with useful visual images and practical examples to aid understanding. A "must-have" resource.'

– **Catherine Eadle,** The Dyscalculia Network

'This is a wonderful textbook. Packed to the brim with useful strategies and practical tips, it is aimed at those overlooked by more traditional styles of teaching. The focus on readers learning how and why a method works and the positive "can do" attitude that permeates the whole text make the book an absolute boon to anyone who feels that maths is not for them.'

– **Sophie Goldie,** textbook author, examiner and online learning resources developer

★ ★ ★ ★ ★

GCSE MATHS FOR NEURODIVERGENT LEARNERS

GCSE MATHS
FOR
NEURODIVERGENT
LEARNERS

Build Your Confidence in
Number, Proportion and Algebra

Judy Hornigold
and **Rose Jewell**

Illustrated by Sophie Kennedy
Foreword by Steve Chinn

Jessica Kingsley Publishers
London and Philadelphia

First published in Great Britain in 2022 by Jessica Kingsley Publishers
An imprint of Hodder & Stoughton Ltd
An Hachette UK Company

1

A CIP catalogue record for this title is available from the British Library
and the Library of Congress

ISBN 978 1 78775 700 4
eISBN 978 1 78775 701 1

Printed and bound in China by Leo Paper Products Ltd

Jessica Kingsley Publishers' policy is to use papers that are natural,
renewable and recyclable products and made from wood grown
in sustainable forests. The logging and manufacturing processes
are expected to conform to the environmental regulations
of the country of origin.

Jessica Kingsley Publishers
Carmelite House
50 Victoria Embankment
London EC4Y 0DZ

www.jkp.com

Contents

Foreword

This truly comprehensive book covers everything from the basics of maths through to algebra, anxiety, revision and examination strategies. Judy and Rose offer an abundance of advice and examples in basic maths topics and maths problems.

They also propose choices in the methods you can use, including the Singapore bar model, in a way that will not overwhelm or confuse you! They encourage something called metacognition, the process of reflecting and appraising your own thinking.

The book starts with a description of some common learning differences. It explains how these neurodiverse conditions can affect your maths learning.

Importantly, this study guide completely takes you away from the old-school idea that maths is simply about rote learning!

You will find a big range of memorable visualisations and materials to support your understanding; you can choose from these and find out which suit you best. This book will help you if you think differently, not just if you are neurodiverse or have difficulties with maths.

I particularly like the sunshine diagrams for factors.

Dealing with operations involving negative numbers is often a challenge. Once again, the authors use more than one way of explaining this seemingly difficult topic so you have every chance of success when tackling questions that involve negative numbers.

The final part of this very useful book offers tips for revising for and actually taking those maths examinations that many find utterly daunting.

This is such a comprehensive and supportive book!

Steve Chinn

Preface

We all have to take GCSE Maths, but we don't all find it easy. If you are struggling with maths, and even hating maths, then this is the book for you!

There are many reasons why you may be finding maths hard. It may go back to the maths you did in primary school. Maybe you never really understood some of the fundamentals back then, like place value, or maybe you found it hard to work with fractions or percentages. Or maybe you weren't taught them in ways that worked for you.

Most people find algebra very hard to begin with, and these more challenging areas of maths can make us feel that we can't do any maths at all.

There can be many different reasons we find maths difficult, which we will go into in a bit more detail later on.

Some of you may even feel that you dislike maths, and your heart might even sink at the thought of ploughing through a maths book.

If that is the case, then this book is specifically for you. It will show you new ways of learning maths. It will build your confidence with number, proportion and even algebra. This book will show you that you can do maths.

While you may never be a person who totally loves maths, we've designed this book with a different approach from traditional maths books. You may find you even enjoy some of the strategies and ideas in it and, through trying out these new methods and approaches, you can become a more confident mathematician.

Judy and Rose

How to Use this Book

This book is designed to help you improve your maths skills and understand how you learn best. After working through it, you may also enjoy maths a bit more! The book is in three parts.

PART 1

Part 1 explains why some people find maths difficult and talks about specific learning differences that may impact on your learning in maths. It includes some general strategies that may help you and gives some insight into how your brain works and why you may be experiencing difficulties with maths. If you read Part 1 first, it will be a good introduction to the more practical, second part of the book. But we have written the book so you can read it in any order that suits you best.

PART 2

Part 2 is split into 14 chapters covering a range of GCSE Maths topics for number, proportion and algebra. It does not cover everything that is in the curriculum. We focus instead on areas that learners, especially those with learning differences, commonly have difficulty with.

We have also deliberately not arranged the topics by school year. Learners of different ages are often at very different stages in their learning. You may find that in a chapter there are questions that you have not yet covered in school. That's fine; just work through what you can. You can come back to those questions when you get to them in school.

The important thing is for you to find strategies that work for you and to build on those. Throughout the chapters you will see that we ask you to reflect on which of the methods shown you prefer and why. This is to help you identify your individual strengths as a learner and to help you develop a range of methods and strategies that really work for you.

At the end of each chapter, think about what you have learned. Do you feel that there are areas where you need more practice? Can you now go back to your school textbooks and apply your new approaches to some of the exercises there?

CONCRETE MATERIALS

One of the most important things you can do to help you in maths is to use concrete materials and to develop your ability to visualize maths. People who can picture the maths in their head have a much easier time than those who cannot.

> **Concrete materials** are physical manipulatives, such as cubes and counters, used to model maths concepts.

You will have used concrete materials in primary school, but they are just as applicable to secondary school. We know that countries that are very successful in maths encourage the use of concrete materials all the way up to GCSE level and beyond. So, concrete materials are in no way 'babyish' and can really help you to understand the maths. You don't need lots of equipment. Two-sided coloured counters and coloured card can be very versatile, and we show you in this book how to use these resources. A series of counters for you to download, print out and stick onto coloured card can be found in the 'Resources' section of this book (see page 278), or you can buy two-sided coloured counters from educational suppliers, such as www.learningresources.co.uk

There are also some excellent virtual manipulatives, such as www.mathsbot.com (click on the manipulatives tab), where you can model the maths with images of the concrete materials.

PART 3

Part 3 of this book includes advice on preparing for your GCSE Maths exams, a glossary of the keywords that appear in Part 2, templates for some useful maths resources, and answers to the questions in Part 2. All of the templates from the 'Resources' chapter are available to download and print from www.jkp.com/catalogue/book/9781787757004.

Part 1

Introduction

There are many reasons you might find maths difficult, and why this book might be right for you. For some people, their struggles with maths are the result of a specific learning difference, such as dyslexia, dyscalculia, dyspraxia, autism (ASD) or attention deficit hyperactivity disorder (ADHD). It may be that you have issues with memory, or a combination of difficulties. Your difficulties may be due to maths anxiety or even a fear of maths.

This book will help you to understand why you are struggling with maths and will help you to find strategies that will work for you. You will discover what kind of learner you are and how you learn best. This book will help you to understand what works for you and what doesn't, so you will be able to work more effectively and productively.

People with **dyslexia** have difficulty with reading, writing and spelling.

People with **dyscalculia** have difficulty with understanding numbers.

People with **dyspraxia** have difficulties with movements and coordination.

People with **ASD** may have difficulty with communication and social interaction.

People with **ADHD** have difficulty with focusing and holding their attention.

NEURODIVERSITY

Neurodiversity refers to the range of differences in the way that the human brain works.

We are all different and we all have our own strengths and weaknesses. Some people may have a specific difference in the way that they learn. It can be very helpful to understand what these differences are and how they can affect the way that we learn. You will probably have heard of some of these differences but maybe not all of them. As you read through Part 1, think about whether some of these difficulties apply to you. If you can recognize areas that you find challenging, then it can be easier to find solutions and strategies that will help. Tips are given throughout Part 1 to provide practical strategies that may help you. They are presented in the text with red vertical side bars and star-shaped bullet points (the first example is on page 16). Understanding how you learn best is going to make a huge difference to the progress that you can make. It will also help your teachers to understand what works for you and what doesn't.

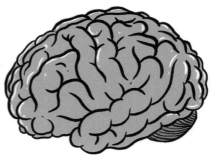

Neurodiversity refers to differences in the human brain.

The elements of neurodiversity

Adapted from AchieveAbility (2011)[1]

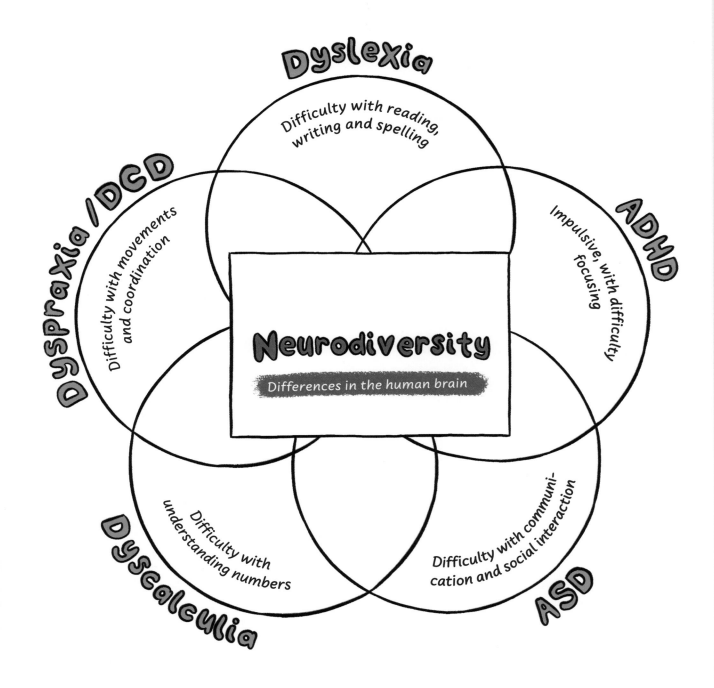

Let's look at some of the more common learning differences.

Dyslexia

The word 'dyslexia' originates from Greek and literally means 'difficulty with words'. Dyslexia affects around 10% of the population and is a life-long condition. Having dyslexia is not related to your intelligence. Alarmingly, for many years, at school or even in their families, learners with dyslexia were made to feel 'stupid' or were told that they were 'lazy'. This is not the case. Dyslexic learners are often highly intelligent, hardworking and highly creative. In fact, some employers actively seek dyslexic employees because of the skill set that they have.

DEFINITIONS OF DYSLEXIA

There is no single definition of dyslexia, but many people choose to refer to this definition.

> 'Dyslexia is a learning difficulty that primarily affects the skills involved in accurate and fluent word reading and spelling. Characteristic features of dyslexia are difficulties in phonological awareness, verbal memory and verbal processing speed. Dyslexia occurs across the range of intellectual abilities. It is best thought of as a continuum, not a distinct category, and there are no clear cut-off points.
>
> Co-occurring difficulties may be seen in aspects of language, motor co-ordination, mental calculation, concentration and personal organisation, but these are not, by themselves, markers of dyslexia. A good indication of the severity and persistence of dyslexic difficulties can be gained by examining how the individual responds or has responded to well founded intervention.'
>
> Rose Review (2009)[2]

Phonological awareness is how well we can process individual sounds in words.

Verbal memory is how well we can remember what we have heard.

Verbal processing speed is how long it takes us to make sense of the information that we hear.

If you are a dyslexic learner, you will have difficulty with reading and spelling, and perhaps have weak memory in some areas; for example, you may find it hard to hold lots of pieces of information in your head at one time. Or you may find it tricky getting information to stick in your long-term memory.

Long-term memory is used for storing information over an extended period.

The British Dyslexia Association (BDA) added to the Rose Review's definition of dyslexia to include difficulties of a visual-processing nature that some people with dyslexia can experience.

Some people with dyslexia experience visual disturbances, such as words or letters moving around on the page. If this is true for you, it can make reading very hard indeed.

For this reason, we have made the text and layout of this book as dyslexia-friendly as we can.

There are many positive aspects of dyslexia, which the BDA also emphasizes. Dyslexic people have significant strengths as well as difficulties.

'Individuals who experience dyslexia have learning differences and can show a combination of abilities and difficulties that affect the learning process.
Some learners have strengths in other areas, such as design, problem solving, creative skills, interactive skills and oral skills.'

BDA (2010)³

If you are dyslexic, then this book is designed to support you to learn how to use your strengths when you approach maths learning.

HOW DOES DYSLEXIA AFFECT OUR ABILITY TO LEARN MATHS AND WHAT CAN WE DO ABOUT IT?

Difficulty learning to read

Most dyslexic learners will find it hard to learn to read, and this is the main area of difficulty that is associated with dyslexia. Many people with dyslexia overcome this problem with time and practice. Technology, such as text-to-speech software, can help you, as well as reading a hardcopy of a book alongside an audio book. If you can understand your learning differences, then it will be easier for you to find strategies that will help.

So, when you learn maths, it is often the language of maths – the reading – that can stop you from being able to learn maths in the best way for you.

Even if you can do the maths, reading and understanding word problems can be challenging. Words with multiple meanings can also cause confusion, such as 'product' and 'table'.

★ Build up a dictionary of words that you find hard to read or words that are confusing because they have multiple meanings. You can illustrate the meaning of the words if that helps.
★ Use text-to-speech software on your electronic device.
★ You could try printing or copying materials onto buff-coloured paper or selecting a different background on a computer screen.

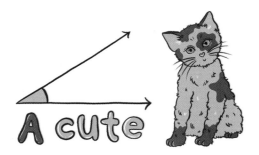

Numberless word problems

Numberless word problems are a great technique to help you understand what a problem is about without being distracted by context and numbers.

When you tackle word problems, take all the numbers out of the problem. Then, simplify context references, such as names and places.

Look at this word problem.

Problem	Change to
Madeleine and Jean-Christopher need £30 to spend on an anniversary present for their parents.	M and J need money for a present.
They have already saved £25.75. How much more money do they need to save to buy the present?	They already have some money. How much more do they need?

What is this problem about?

Are we adding or subtracting? Could we do either operation?

Now let's put in one of the numbers.

Problem	Change to	With one number written in
Madeleine and Jean-Christopher need £30 to spend on an anniversary present for their parents.	M and J need money for a present.	M and J need £30 for a present.
They have already saved £25.75. How much more money do they need to save to buy the present?	They already have some money. How much more do they need?	They already have some money. How much more do they need?

There are two possible ways to solve this word problem.

Option 1: Add to the money Madeleine and Jean-Christopher have until you reach £30.

Option 2: Subtract the money Madeleine and Jean-Christopher have from £30.

Both options should give you the same answer!

Now let's put in the last number.

Problem	Change to	With all numbers written in
Madeleine and Jean-Christopher need £30 to spend on an anniversary present for their parents.	M and J need money for a present.	M and J need £30 for a present.
They have already saved £25.75. How much more money do they need to save to buy the present?	They already have some money. How much more do they need?	They already have £25.75. How much more do they need?

OPTION 1

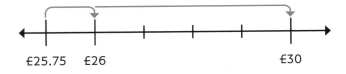

£25.75   £26   £30

They need another 25p + £4 = £4.25

OPTION 2

```
  30.00
- 25.75
───────
   4.25
```

You can find out more about numberless word problems at https://bstockus.wordpress.com/numberless-word-problems

Difficulty processing information at speed

If you are dyslexic, it can take you a lot longer to process information, and this can be a big issue in a maths class. There is often a strong emphasis on speed in maths, where you and your classmates are expected to answer quickly and finishing quickly is encouraged almost as if it's a race to the finish line.

If you are great at maths, but you have a slow processing speed, then working fast can be challenging as you need more time to process the information and to do the mental and written calculations. You may find that you lose your train of thought when doing multi-step problems. It may be that you rarely finish the tasks that have been set in class or perhaps your homework seems to take hours to complete.

★ Make sure that your teachers know that you have difficulty processing information quickly. Make sure that they give you extra time to respond in class.

★ Ask for an assessment to find out if you are entitled to extra time in tests.

★ Ask your teacher to give you a sample selection of homework questions that cover each important topic or type of problem. You do not need to complete the whole set of questions as long as you have done, and understood, some examples of each.

★ Write down each stage of a calculation. You can use multiplication squares or Napier's bones (see page 279) so that you don't have to store lots of information in your head.

> **Napier's bones** are a tool for multiplying. They are made from a multiplication square cut into vertical strips; each vertical strip is a 'bone'.

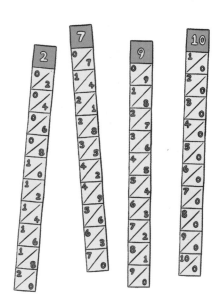

★ Ask your teacher to give you the information about the homework tasks at the beginning of the lesson. Explain to them that at the end of the lesson, you may not have enough time to copy the information into your planner or homework diary.

★ Ask your teacher to give you short, clear instructions. No more than three things at a time.

Difficulty retaining information in your short-term/working memory or long-term memory

For many dyslexic learners, storing and retrieving information can be very problematic. You may have difficulty with:

- holding information in your short-term or working memory
- transferring the information to your long-term memory or
- retrieving the information from your memory.

Short-term memory is used to hold information in the mind for a short period of time.

Working memory is the ability to manipulate information being held in the short-term memory.

When you learn something, a pathway is made in the brain. You can have many different pathways to the same bit of information. This is especially true when you are trying to remember a particular spelling. You may have spelt a word in lots of different ways and sometimes your brain locates the correct spelling from your memory and sometimes not!

Short-term and working memory

Most people can store around seven pieces of unrelated information in their head, for about 30 seconds. This is because we all have a limited capacity for our short-term and working memory. This is sometimes referred to as our 'memory shelf'. If too many items are put onto the memory shelf, then something will fall off.

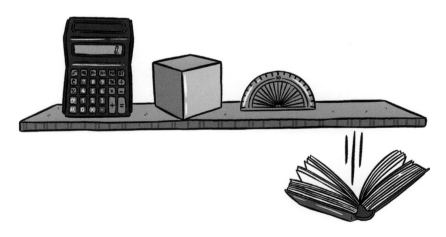

For example, if you were going shopping, you could probably remember three or four things that you needed to buy without writing a list. If you were shopping for a lot more items, it would be a good idea to write a list, so that you don't forget something.

If you are a dyslexic learner, then your memory shelf can be small, with maybe capacity for only three or four items. Also, for some dyslexic learners, if your memory shelf is over-loaded, then it will collapse completely. Everything will be forgotten. This is because your brain works differently.

When you are working on a complex problem or one with many parts to it, then you may find it very difficult to keep hold of all the information that you need in order to complete the problem. In Part 3 of this book, we include some suggestions for things that can help with this.

Distractions and stress can affect our short-term and working memory. When you are at school, or at home doing your homework or revision, try to limit distractions and stress as much as possible.

Distractions include:

- being tired, thirsty or hungry
- sitting by the window and being preoccupied by what is going on outside
- noise from other learners or from outside
- flickering lights.

Causes of stress include:

- time pressure
- being in a test situation
- having to answer a question in front of other people
- being given too much information too quickly.

If you feel that any of the things in these lists are distracting or stressful for you, talk to your teacher or parents about ways you could reduce them.

Long-term memory

Another aspect of memory which can be extremely frustrating for you if you're dyslexic is that you may find it difficult to transfer information into your long-term memory. You may have understood the maths in the lesson, but when you get home or revisit that topic later, you might feel as if your understanding has disappeared. You may struggle to recall your times tables or other number facts, despite having practised them for hours on end.

When information comes into our short-term memory, we have a choice to discard it or to transfer it to our long-term memory. For many people, the transfer to long-

Over-learning involves revisiting information again and again.

term memory can be hard. If you are a dyslexic learner, one of the most effective strategies is over-learning. This means revisiting the information again and again. It is a 'little and often' approach.

Imagine that you are walking through a field of long grass. As you walk, you are crushing the long grass, but by the next day that grass will have bounced back again. Imagine that you walk the same path every day. After a while, the grass will not bounce back. There will be a permanent path.

This is the same way that your memory works. The more often you revisit something, the more likely it is that there will be a permanent path in your long-term memory to that information.

To help you with this over-learning, it can be a good idea to make a set of memory cards. You can use presentation software or simply write the information that you need to remember onto small cards. Look at the cards every day, for 5–10 minutes.

You can put whatever you want on the cards. Pick something that you are working on in maths or that you are having trouble remembering.

Here are some examples:

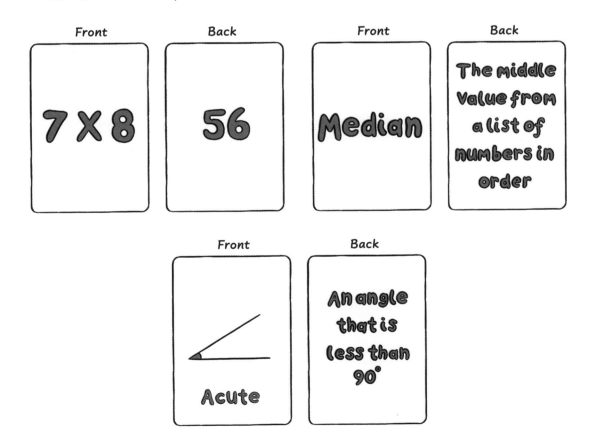

★ Think about what strategies work for you. If you are trying to remember a phone number or directions, do you repeat the information over and over again, or do you visualize it in your head? Do you use your fingers and imagine a number on each finger?

★ Colour-coding your revision can really help. Highlighting maths terms and numbers in word problems can also be useful.

★ Some people learn better while they are physically doing something. In Part 2 of this book, you will see ideas for using your body movements to help you understand topics like algebra and negative numbers.

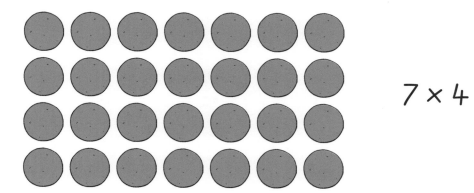

★ Another useful way to remember something is to transform it in some way. You could draw a picture to show the maths. You could model it with maths equipment. Or you could explain it in writing or speech to someone else. Think about what would work best for you.

7×4

★ There are some old-fashioned games that can really help. You may have played them on car journeys or on rainy days on holiday. One such game involves creating a long list of things to buy at the shop. Players take it in turns to add an item to the shopping list. See the suggested games on page 278.

Tracking difficulties and visual problems

Some, but not all, dyslexic learners may have tracking difficulties. This means that your eyes are not focused together as they move over words on a page. It can make it hard for you to keep track of which calculation on the page you are working on.

Poor visual perception can lead to difficulties in discriminating between similar letters, such as 'b' and 'd' or 'p' and 'q', or between symbols used in maths, such as '+' and '×'.

Some people see this as a separate issue from dyslexia, whereas others see it as part of a dyslexic profile. Indications that you might be experiencing tracking difficulties and visual problems include:

- letters or numbers that move or jump around the page as you read
- blurred or fuzzy letters/numbers
- headaches when reading
- double vision or gaps between letters in words
- difficulty reading small, tightly spaced text, or elaborate scripts
- easily losing your place on a page and difficulty tracking across a page
- over-sensitivity to bright lights or to black text on a white background.

Visual processing difficulties can make it hard to read numerical information from tables and graphs.

★ Simply changing the background colour on your screen or the colour of paper may make all the difference. Dark blue text on a cream background is much easier to read than black text on a white background.

★ Aperture cards can also help. These are cards with a window cut out. Put an aperture card on a page of calculations and only one line can be seen.

★ If you have trouble reading from maths tables, for example from a multiplication table, you might prefer to use Napier's bones (see page 279), or you could try 'flexitables' www.flexitable.co.uk

★ Flexitables are plastic multiplication tables that can be folded horizontally and vertically. If you fold along the lines of the numbers you are multiplying, the product of the numbers will appear in the bottom right corner.

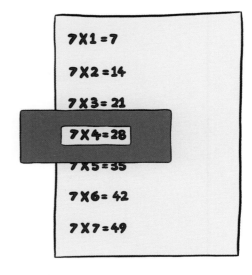

$7 \times 1 = 7$

$7 \times 2 = 14$

$7 \times 3 = 21$

$7 \times 4 = 28$

$7 \times 5 = 35$

$7 \times 6 = 42$

$7 \times 7 = 49$

★ If you have a table with a lot of information, for example, a train timetable, you can use an L-shaped piece of card to isolate the row and column that you need.

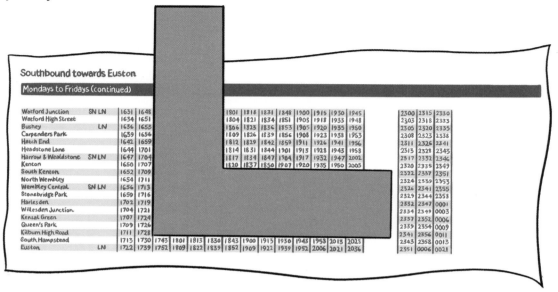

Southbound towards Euston

Mondays to Fridays (continued)

Watford Junction	SN LN	1631	1648		1801	1818	1831	1848	1900	1915	1930	1945		2300	2315	2330
Watford High Street		1634	1651		1804	1821	1834	1851	1903	1918	1933	1948		2303	2318	2333
Bushey	LN	1636	1653		1806	1823	1836	1853	1905	1920	1935	1950		2305	2320	2335
Carpenders Park		1639	1656		1809	1826	1839	1856	1908	1923	1938	1953		2308	2323	2338
Hatch End		1642	1659		1812	1829	1842	1859	1911	1926	1941	1956		2311	2326	2341
Headstone Lane		1644	1701		1814	1831	1844	1901	1913	1928	1943	1958		2313	2328	2343
Harrow & Wealdstone	SN LN	1647	1704		1817	1834	1847	1904	1917	1932	1947	2002		2317	2332	2346
Kenton		1650	1707		1820	1837	1850	1907	1920	1935	1950	2005		2320	2335	2349
South Kenton		1652	1709											2322	2337	2351
North Wembley		1654	1711											2324	2339	2353
Wembley Central	SN LN	1656	1713											2326	2341	2355
Stonebridge Park		1659	1716											2329	2344	2358
Harlesden		1702	1719											2332	2347	0001
Willesden Junction		1704	1721											2334	2349	0003
Kensal Green		1707	1724											2337	2352	0006
Queen's Park		1709	1726											2339	2354	0009
Kilburn High Road		1711	1728											2341	2356	0011
South Hampstead		1713	1730	1743	1801	1813	1830	1843	1900	1913	1930	1943	1958	2013	2028	2343	2358	0013
Euston	LN	1722	1739	1752	1809	1822	1839	1852	1909	1922	1939	1952	2006	2021	2036	2351	0006	0021

Letter/digit reversal

If you're dyslexic, you may reverse certain letters. The most common letters dyslexic learners reverse are ones where the lowercase versions are very similar, namely, p/q, b/d, m/n and i/j. You might like to substitute the capital forms of these letters within words, as it is easier to distinguish the capital form. For example, writing 'I went to BeD' instead of 'I went to bed'. The same is true of digits, which can also be reversed. The reversal often occurs because some digits are formed by writing them in a clockwise direction and some in an anticlockwise direction.

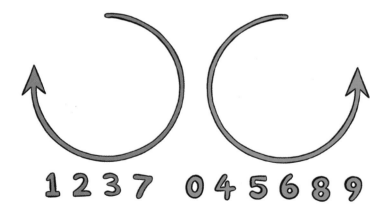

1 2 3 7   0 4 5 6 8 9

You may find that you are writing digits the wrong way round. This may be because writing some digits requires a left to right movement, while writing other digits requires a right to left movement. Try colour-coding the digits, so you can practise writing:

★ the clockwise digits (1, 2, 3, 7) in blue
★ the anticlockwise digits (0, 4, 5, 6, 8, 9) in red.

Time management – organization and sequencing

If you're dyslexic, as you get older it can be organization that becomes the issue rather than reading or spelling. The demands on personal organization and time management are high in secondary schools and you may find that you always seem to have the wrong books on the wrong day or have not left enough time to complete your assignments.

★ If you find that you're always forgetting books or equipment or missing deadlines for homework, then your smartphone can be a real help. Set reminders, but make sure that you set them so that you have enough time to get organized. So, if you have to hand in some work on a Friday, set a reminder for Monday and Wednesday. That way, you won't be left in a panic on Thursday evening!

★ There are also lots of useful apps that can help you to get organized. Here are a couple of weblinks to some great ideas:

www.additudemag.com/mobile-apps-for-adhd-minds

www.peoplescout.co.uk/insights/30-x-apps-to-help-neurodiverse-students

Left/right confusion

This is a common indicator of dyslexia, and again is something that many young learners struggle with. The difference for a dyslexic learner is that left/right confusion persists. This is often coupled with letter reversals or mirror writing.

Another thing to look out for here is cross laterality. Generally speaking, if you are left-handed, then you will be left-footed, left-eyed and left-eared, but people with cross laterality have a mixture of left and right. It is straightforward to find out whether you have cross laterality with a few simple props.

To test for footedness, put a football on the ground and see which foot you naturally kick it with.

To test for which eye is dominant, look through a cardboard tube and note which eye you put the tube to.

To test for the dominant ear, place a ticking watch on the table and pick it up to hear it and note which ear you hold it to.

Learners with cross laterality are more likely to have left/right confusion and may struggle in maths, as some procedures go from left to right and others from right to left.

$$23\overline{)460}$$

→

left to right

$$\begin{array}{r} 236 \\ 460 \\ \hline \\ \hline \end{array}$$

←

right to left

★ Use coloured arrows to highlight the direction that you need to work in.
★ Keep a set of worked examples handy so that you don't have to remember which direction to go in.

Low self-esteem

Many dyslexic teenagers suffer from low self-esteem and a lack of self-confidence. This is particularly the case if you're not aware of your dyslexia or if you have not had appropriate support. It is very easy for one harsh comment from a teacher or another learner to destroy your self-esteem. Or it may be that you have struggled for so long that you truly believe that you can't do maths.

Learners who are confident in maths are much more likely to attempt difficult questions and are more likely to work at the edge of their comfort zone. In contrast, learners who have no confidence in their maths ability will be reluctant to take risks and will tend to work well within their comfort zone, and therefore will be less likely to make good progress in maths.

★ Your school may already be promoting a growth mindset.
This can be useful in helping you to believe that you will be able to improve in maths. There is a whole section on growth mindset on page 55.

Copying from the board

Dyslexic learners will find it hard to copy from the board and this should be avoided at all costs. A dyslexic learner will frequently lose their place and will constantly be looking up to the board and back to the paper, much more than other people in the class. This can be a huge issue in maths, where many calculations may be displayed on the board at once. The dyslexic learner will find it difficult to keep track of which question they are answering and will often mix up parts of different questions.

★ Ask your teacher if you can have copies of any slides in advance, so that you don't have to copy from the board. If you are allowed to have a smartphone or tablet in school, then you can use your device to photograph any information on the board as well.

STRENGTHS

The good news is that as well as some weaknesses, dyslexic learners have many strengths, and these are being much more widely recognized in the workplace. Employers in fields such as architecture and computing actively seek to recruit people with dyslexia because they have superb problem-solving skills and excellent 3D and spatial awareness.

Creativity

Dyslexic people learn in a different way because they think in a different way, and it is this difference that can make them so creative. They also often have to find different ways of overcoming their difficulties, so can be very original and creative in their approach to learning.

Problem solving

Dyslexic learners are often excellent problem solvers. They look at things from a different perspective. They are also very good at finding 'best fit' solutions to problems.

Being able to see the 'big picture'

Dyslexic brains are structured differently, and dyslexic learners often excel at seeing the gist or essence of a situation. They don't get bogged down by the detail and can spot the larger context behind ideas and situations, viewing things holistically rather than in minute detail.

Innovation

This can be a great strength for dyslexic learners as they can see new or unusual connections, which can help them to be more innovative and creative in their thinking.

3D spatial ability and visualization

Many dyslexic learners are particularly good at thinking in three dimensions and make very good architects, mechanics, engineers and designers as a result of this ability. They tend to see the world in pictures in their heads rather than in words, and have great visualization skills.

Does any of this sound familiar to you? If it does, then this does not necessarily mean that you are dyslexic! You can discuss these issues with your parents and with your school SENCo to see if they feel that you need to have this investigated further.

Dyscalculia

Dyscalculia is a specific learning difficulty in maths, particularly in how we understand numbers and the four operations (addition, subtraction, multiplication and division). The word 'dyscalculia' comes from Greek and Latin and means 'counting badly'.

Dyscalculia has nothing to do with our IQ. It is simply a difference in the way that the brain processes numerical information. People with dyscalculia may struggle with many day-to-day activities, such as managing their finances and finding the best value items when shopping. They can often be isolated as they find it difficult to understand the scoring systems of games and sports. Time management can be problematic, and many dyscalculic adults have trouble using public transport as they can't extract the relevant information from timetables, or they have difficulty planning the time required for journeys.

DEFINITION

The British Dyslexia Association (BDA) and the SpLD Assessment Standards Committee (SASC) defined dyscalculia as follows:

'Dyscalculia is a specific and persistent difficulty in understanding numbers which can lead to a diverse range of difficulties with mathematics. It will be unexpected in relation to age, level of education and experience and occurs across all ages and abilities.

Mathematics difficulties are best thought of as a continuum, not a distinct category, and they have many causal factors. Dyscalculia falls at one end of the spectrum and will be distinguishable from other mathematics issues due to the severity of difficulties with number sense, including subitizing, symbolic and non-symbolic magnitude comparison, and ordering. It can occur singly but can also co-occur with other specific learning difficulties, mathematics anxiety and medical conditions.'

BDA/SASC (2019)[4]

Number sense is the ability to understand our number system and the relationships between numbers and number operations.

Subitizing is the ability to state how many items are in a set without counting them.

THE MAIN INDICATORS OF DYSCALCULIA

The inability to subitize small quantities

The word 'subitize' comes from the Latin word 'subito', which means suddenly. It refers to our ability to immediately (almost automatically, without consciously thinking about it) recognize the number of items in a set without having to count them. Most people can subitize up to six or seven items.

If you're dyscalculic, then you may have difficulty subitizing just three items.

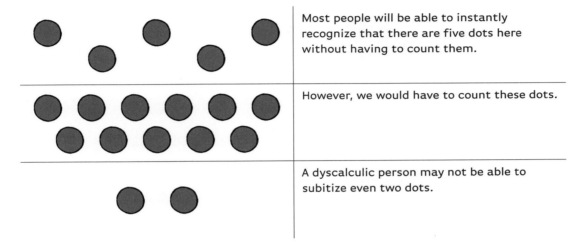

Most people will be able to instantly recognize that there are five dots here without having to count them.

However, we would have to count these dots.

A dyscalculic person may not be able to subitize even two dots.

Look at these sets of dots. Are there sets where you just know how many dots there are without counting?

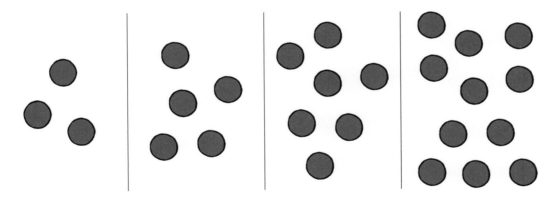

Which sets did you have to count?

Why is this important?

You may be wondering what this has to do with GCSE Maths, but if you are unable to subitize, it is an indicator that your brain is not processing numerical information in a typical way. It may be that you find it hard to visualize quantities; for example, imagining how much space 200 books would take up. A dyscalculic brain finds it hard to match the number symbols to the number quantity, so it is hard to have a 'feel' for number.

Poor number sense

Number sense refers to our ability to understand numbers and how they relate to each other. Someone with good number sense will know what they can and can't do with numbers and will be able to manipulate numbers and use them flexibly. For example, if you are multiplying 54 × 99, you may decide to use 54 × 100 to help you.

Having good number sense helps you to see connections in maths and to find more efficient ways of solving problems.

Let's look at this example:

$$36 × 25 ÷ 9$$

Now, this does not look like a particularly easy problem to solve without a calculator, but can number sense make the calculation more accessible?

Let's look for connections.

36 is a multiple of 9, so we can rewrite 36 × 25 ÷ 9 as 25 × 36 ÷ 9

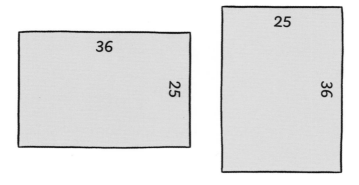

$$36 ÷ 9 = 4$$

So now we have 25 × 4, which equals 100.

Or if that doesn't work well for you, let's try this...

36 × 25 = 18 × 50 (we have halved the first number and doubled the second number).

Let's do this again – halve the first number and double the second number.

$$18 × 50 = 9 × 100 = 900$$

Now we can divide 900 by 9 to give us 100.

One way to visualize this method is to think of multiplication as an array. When we multiply two numbers together, we will make a rectangle.

So, if we multiply 4 × 5, we get this...

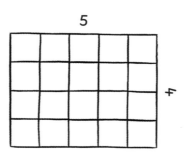

The area of the rectangle is 20.

If we halve one side and double the other side, the rectangle changes but the area stays the same.

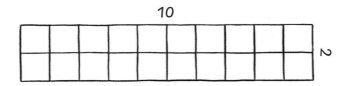

So, developing our number sense is a way to make the maths that we do easier.

An inability to estimate whether a numerical answer is reasonable

Learners with dyscalculia find it hard to assess whether an answer is reasonable or not; they don't have a 'ballpark' figure for what the answer should be. Consequently, they don't spot mistakes easily.

An inability to notice patterns

Our brains are wired up to notice patterns; it is the way that we make sense of the world. Learners with dyscalculia are unable to easily spot patterns in maths. If we are able to see patterns in maths, then it makes it much easier for us to generalize and to predict solutions. By spotting patterns and connections, we can reduce the number of things that we need to remember. For example, multiples of 5 always end in a 5 or a 0, so we can recognize the pattern without having to remember them all.

1	2	3	4	5	6	7	8	9	10
11	12	13	14	15	16	17	18	19	20
21	22	23	24	25	26	27	28	29	30
31	32	33	34	35	36	37	38	39	40
41	42	43	44	45	46	47	48	49	50
51	52	53	54	55	56	57	58	59	60
61	62	63	64	65	66	67	68	69	70
71	72	73	74	75	76	77	78	79	80
81	82	83	84	85	86	87	88	89	90
91	92	93	94	95	96	97	98	99	100

Difficulty with generalizing

Generalizing is all about being able to transfer acquired knowledge to a new and unfamiliar situation. The ability to do this helps us to make sense of maths and to understand the connections and patterns. Dyscalculic learners struggle with generalization of ideas and concepts and find it hard to transfer information from one area of maths to another. This means that maths is a multitude of individual pieces of information that have to be stored and remembered or calculated from scratch each time.

Difficulty in recalling times tables and number facts

Dyscalculic learners have great difficulty remembering arithmetical facts, such as times tables and number bonds. This makes it much harder for them to carry out simple calculations, particularly if they have to do them mentally.

Having dyscalculia doesn't mean that you will never be able to do any maths, but it will make life harder for you. However, knowing that you have a different way of learning can be very powerful as now you can seek out strategies and ways that work for you so that you will learn better and understand more.

WAYS TO HELP

Now that we have some understanding of the difficulties you may have, we can look at some strategies to help. The strategies are grouped under the following headings:

- Core number and reasoning
- Memory
- Visual spatial awareness

Core number and reasoning

- Difficulty in understanding number and our number system
- Inability to estimate
- Difficulty in comparing numbers
- Not understanding place value
- Difficulty in understanding concepts and relationships
- Difficulty in problem solving and in choosing the most appropriate method
- Not being able to see connections and patterns

One of the main ways to address difficulty with core number and reasoning is to develop number sense.

If you have good number sense, then you will be able to manipulate numbers to make calculations easier and will be flexible in your approach to solving problems. You will have a good feel for the reasonableness of an answer and will routinely estimate answers before calculating. You look for connections and spot patterns in number, using this information to help you to predict future outcomes. You may have several approaches to calculating and problem solving and know when to use them and how to adapt them to meet new situations. Learners with good number sense enjoy playing with and exploring numbers and number relationships.

If you have poor number sense, then you will be very procedure focused and will tend to rely on a few methods that you feel happy with. You will often apply inefficient and immature strategies to calculations and will find it hard to spot connections that could get you to the answer more quickly. You prefer using pen and paper rather than working things out in your head. You will avoid estimating an answer before working it out and will generally accept whatever answer you get, without considering whether it is reasonable or not.

Learners with poor number sense don't enjoy maths and won't spend time playing around with and exploring numbers.

If you feel that you have poor number sense, what can you do about it?

Ways to develop number sense

Don't be afraid to play around with numbers. Find out what works and what doesn't, and don't worry about making mistakes.

Make sure that you use concrete materials to help you to see the maths. In Part 2, in Chapter 6, we show you how to use double-sided two-coloured counters to make sense of different concepts in maths.

Try out different methods for solving problems and then practise the ones that work best for you. You may be stuck in a rut using a certain procedure that is actually making maths harder for you.

Try to look for connections before you start calculating.

Let's consider:

$$4 + 7 + 6 + 3$$

You could add the 4 and 7 to make 11, then add on the 6 to make 17 and then add the 3 to make 20

OR

You could look for an easier way.

When we add it doesn't matter which order we add up the numbers, so we can change the order here to this:

$$4 + 6 + 7 + 3$$

Can you spot that 4 + 6 = 10 and 3 + 7 = 10?

Is that easier than the first way we tried to find the answer?

TRY TO MAKE CONNECTIONS

Addition and subtraction are inverse operations.

Multiplication and division are also inverse operations.

You can set out the relationship between three numbers in a multiplication fact by using a triangle.

Inverse *means the opposite. In maths, the inverse of an operation reverses the effect of another operation.*

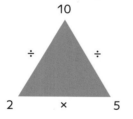

$$10 \div 2 = 5$$
$$10 \div 5 = 2$$
$$2 \times 5 = 10$$
$$5 \times 2 = 10$$

AREA AND MULTIPLICATION

Linking area and multiplication can really help you to understand written methods, such as the grid method, and can help you to 'see' the connections.

Let's look at 16 × 14. We can show this as the area of a rectangle that is 16 cm by 14 cm.

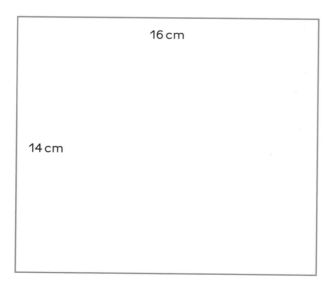

Now, let's imagine a 10 cm by 10 cm square hiding inside the rectangle.

If we now divide the rectangle into four parts, we can represent it like this.

Can you see how the diagram links to the grid method for multiplication?

×	10	6
10	100	60
4	40	24

We can even extend this thinking to link to how we multiply out brackets in quadratic equations.

$$(x + 6)(x + 4) = x^2 + 6x + 4x + 24$$

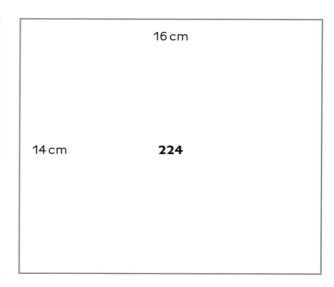

From this diagram we can see that $224 \div 16 = 14$ or $16\overline{)224} = 14$ and that $224 \div 14 = 16$ or $14\overline{)224} = 16$

Let's try a different problem: How would you solve 9×16 mentally?

Spend a few minutes trying out different methods.

Now have a look at these methods. Which one do you prefer? Why?

Is there a method that you don't understand? Can you explain which part you don't understand?

Method 1: breaking a factor into smaller factors	**Method 2:** using partial products
9×16 $= 9 \times (8 \times 2)$ $= 72 \times 2$ $= 144$	$9 \times 10 = 90$ $9 \times 6 = 54$ $90 + 54 = 144$
Method 3: using numbers that are easier to work with	**Method 4:** doubling and halving
9×16 Use 10×16 instead $10 \times 16 = 160$ Subtract 1×16 $160 - 16 = 144$	9×16 18×8 36×4 72×2 $144 \times 1 = 144$

Memory

- Not being able to remember number facts and times tables
- Difficulty with mental maths
- Forgetting procedures
- Losing track when doing multi-step calculations

Many learners' problems in maths stem from difficulties that they have with memory, whether it be short-term, long-term or working memory. Memory is a really complex issue, so let's just spend some time looking at the memory system.

Memory is an umbrella term that is used to describe the complex system of encoding, storing and retrieving information. This information can be received through any of the five senses. The figure below shows how we deal with the information that is bombarding our senses all of the time. We filter much of it out and then decide what we need to attend to. This then feeds into the short-term memory, where we again filter out what we don't need to remember and transfer what we do need to remember to our long-term memory, which is akin to a filing cabinet storage system in the brain.

The memory system

Adapted from Richards (2003)[5]

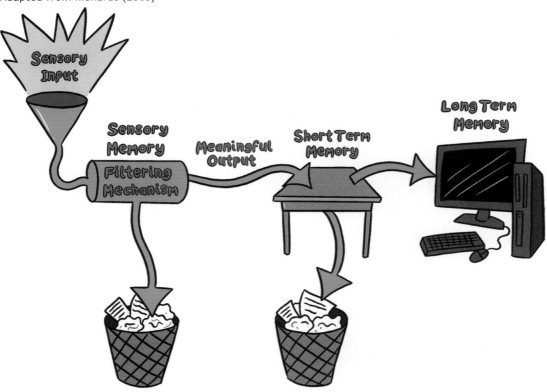

In this model, we can divide memory into a series of stores and view memory as information flow between these stores.

Sensory memory lasts between 0.25 and 0.5 seconds and has a very large capacity for all our sensory experience. There are different stores in the sensory memory for each of the senses.

Short-term memory is available for up to 18 seconds and has a much more limited capacity, usually around seven items. We use it for storing information without manipulating it mentally or doing something else at the same time.

There are two types of short-term memory, verbal short-term memory and visual spatial short-term memory. Remembering a telephone number uses verbal short-term memory, as it is to do with recalling information that we have perceived aurally. Picking out a top to match the trousers you have just bought uses visuo-spatial memory as it is to do with recalling information that has been perceived visually.

When the information is no longer needed in the short-term memory it is discarded. Information in short-term memory is very fragile and is easily lost through distraction.

However, if we want to use the information, then we need to store it in the short-term working memory. This allows us to hold on to the information while we work with it or manipulate it in some way; for example, while carrying out a mental calculation, such as 12×25. In this instance we may think of this as $(10 \times 25) + (2 \times 25)$. We would need to hold 10×25 in our working memory while we calculate 2×25 and then add the two products together to give us the answer to 12×25.

Indicators of memory difficulties

Working memory difficulties can be shown in a wide range of behaviours. You may find it hard to concentrate and your teachers may think that you are simply not listening. This is particularly true if you have been given multiple instructions. Your working memory may have been completely overloaded and has effectively collapsed. You may be easily distracted, impulsive, or display 'immediate forgetfulness'. You can't keep information in your working memory for very long so will just flit from one thing to the next as information comes into, and almost immediately leaves, your working memory. You may be very fidgety, always moving in an attempt to stay alert, and this can lead to tiredness and irritability.

All of these difficulties can make you feel very frustrated and anxious about your learning and may affect your self-esteem.

You may have problems with how much information you can remember and for how long. Most people can retain up to seven separate items in their working memory, but for people with poor working memory capacity this can be as few as three items.

Time refers to how long the information can be stored. If individual pieces of information are presented too far apart, then it can be very hard to retain that information completely and in the correct sequence.

In addition to this working memory system there is also a long-term area of memory. We can choose to select information from our working memory to store in our long-term memory. The long-term memory is where we store information that we need to keep and refer to later on. Often, people may have difficulty in transferring information from their short-term to their long-term memory. Or they may have difficulty in retrieving information from their long-term memory. So how can we try to improve our ability to do this?

Ways to improve memory

Just spend a moment thinking about things that you find easier to remember. What is it about them that makes them memorable?

TAKE BREAKS WHEN REVISING

Research has shown that we remember most information given at the beginning and at the end of a lesson or talk. Information given in the middle of a session is less likely to be remembered. When you are revising for a test or doing your homework, try to work in short sessions of around 20–25 minutes and build in short breaks in between sessions. These breaks only need be a few minutes, maybe just fetching a glass of water or walking around the house. In this way you will have more beginnings and endings and will be able to focus for longer. You will retain more information.

MAKE LINKS TO THINGS YOU ALREADY KNOW

We are much more likely to remember something if we can link it to something that we already know. In terms of maths, try to link the new learning to a mathematical concept or fact that you already know.

TURN THE MUNDANE INTO THE EXTRAORDINARY

Anything that is out of the ordinary is easier for us to remember. If we have had a period of time at school or at home, say, when one day is pretty much the same as another, it can be hard to recall when or where a particular event happened, because there is so much similarity between the days. But then, something extraordinary happens, such as the fire alarm going off, and everyone has to evacuate the building. It is much more likely that you will be able to recall the day that that happened for a long time after the event as it is so extraordinary.

So, for maths learning, we need to try and turn the dull into the exciting. Imagery and visualization can help here. Instead of using pizzas and cakes for fraction work, why not illustrate the fractions with something more unusual, such as a circular multi-coloured alien planet.

REPEAT, REPEAT

Over-learning is a key strategy in supporting memory. We talked earlier about over-learning and how the more you practise and repeat something, the easier it will be to remember it. This means that 10 minutes of revision every day is much better than one full hour once a week.

MATCH THE MATHS TO YOUR INTERESTS

We are much more likely to remember something if we are interested in it. So, if you have a word problem that is about flowers and you are more interested in football, then change the context of the problem to football. It will keep you motivated for longer.

The four Ms

Another way that might help you is to think about the four Ms.

Make the information:

- manageable
- multisensory
- memorable
- meaningful.

MAKE THE INFORMATION MANAGEABLE

A **multisensory** approach uses more than one sense at a time.

- Break down information into smaller chunks.
- Give yourself time to process the information.
- Read a question for meaning, then read it again for detail and then read it again to decide on a strategy.
- Discard irrelevant information in word problems (see 'Simplifying word problems' box).
- Learn how to write out the multiplication square or Napier's bones (see 'Multiplication square' box).
- Learn to use a calculator.

★ Dyscalculator is a calculator app specifically for dyscalculic learners. The app includes options to help learners who have trouble identifying numbers, finding the difference between numbers, ordering numbers or deciding which operations to use. Numbers are displayed in symbolic, written and audio format. The app is free to download.

★ The calculator that we recommend you use with this book is the Casio FX-83GTX as it is an excellent all-round calculator with a very clear display. You probably have this calculator in school, but if not, you can find it in most large supermarkets.

Simplifying word problems

You can often get bogged down by the detail in a word problem, most of which has no bearing on the maths at all.

For example, consider the following word problem.

Sarah, Amir and Joanna all enjoy collecting football cards of their favourite team, Manchester United. They have 60 cards all together. If they share the cards equally, how many will each child have?

Most of the words in this problem are irrelevant.

The key information here is that there are 3 people, sharing 60 cards equally. So, we need to think about 60 divided by 3.

Multiplication square

With practice, most people can master the multiplication square quite quickly, and you should aim to write out the complete grid in less than 5 minutes. Begin by drawing the grid, either 10 × 10 or 12 × 12. Then, fill in the 'key' facts. These are the 1 × , 2 × , 5 × and 10 × tables.

Multiplication is commutative, so once you have filled out 2 × 5 you can also fill out 5 × 2.

Now choose which table to complete next. You might choose the 9 × table, because it has such distinct patterns, or maybe the 4 × table as this is double the 2 × table.

Carry on in this way and soon you will see that there are only a few facts left to fill in and these can be derived from other facts if you can't remember them.

×	1	2	3	4	5	6	7	8	9	10
1	1	2	3	4	5	6	7	8	9	10
2	2	4	6	8	10	12	14	16	18	20
3	3	6		12	15				27	30
4	4	8	12	16	20	24	28	32	36	40
5	5	10	15	20	25	30	35	40	45	50
6	6	12		24	30				54	60
7	7	14		28	35				63	70
8	8	16		32	40				72	80
9	9	18	27	36	45	54	63	72	81	90
10	10	20	30	40	50	60	70	80	90	100

Usually the multiplication facts that are left are:

7 × 8 = 56

8 × 8 = 64

7 × 7 = 49

If you write 7 × 8 = 56 with the 56 first, you get

56 = 7 × 8

Can you see the sequence 5, 6, 7, 8?

One way to remember 8 × 8 = 64, is to say 'I ate and ate until I was sick on the floor!'

So now we only have to remember 7 × 7 = 49, so that's not so bad after all!

Remember that when you multiply two odd numbers together, the answer will always be an odd number. All the other numbers on the multiplication square are even.

Learning to write out your multiplication table is a really good thing to be able to do. It means that when you go into exam, you can write this out before you do anything else. This will help to calm your nerves and also means that you don't have to worry about remembering or working out tables facts during the test as they are all there for you.

MAKE THE INFORMATION MULTISENSORY

Information is received into the brain through our senses: sight, sound, touch, smell and taste. Most people prefer to have information presented in a certain way. Think about a time when you have visited a museum. Do you always go for the audio guide? Do you prefer to read all the information rather than listen to it or would you prefer to go around pressing all the buttons and being more actively involved?

Many learners with a specific learning difficulty have a weakness in one or more of these ways of learning. If you can learn by using all three ways at once it will help your stronger ways support your weaker ones.

VISUAL STRATEGIES

You can make information more memorable by using colour to highlight key information or by enlarging key numbers and operations so that they stand out.

NUMerator = NUMber of parts

Drawing a bar model can really help with understanding. Bar models are explained more on page 115.

Look at this word problem.

Sam has saved some money. His father gives Sam twice the amount that he has saved.

When he goes shopping, Sam spends £45 on a pair of trainers and a third of the remaining money on a book that costs £15.

How much had Sam saved originally?

This seems like quite a tricky word problem, but it can be greatly simplified by drawing a mathematical model.

The amount that Sam has saved can be shown using a rectangle.

Sam's savings

His father gave him twice that amount, so now Sam has:

Sam's savings	Father's gift

Sam spends £45 on trainers. Then, he spends one third of his remaining money on a book. Therefore, the final section of the diagram can be split into thirds, with each third worth £15.

Sam's savings	Father's gift		
45	15	15	15

We can see from the diagram that Sam has spent £90 all together, so he must have had £30 saved (and £60 given to him by his father).

AUDITORY STRATEGIES

Mnemonics are memory devices that help learners recall pieces of information. For example, 'Cherry pie is delicious' is a mnemonic that can help with recall of the formula for the circumference of a circle: $C = \pi d$

This can then be followed by 'Apple pies are square', which can be used to help with recall of the formula for the area of a circle: $A = \pi r^2$

It is a good idea to use mnemonics sparingly, because if you have too many of them, you will end up needing a mnemonic to remember all your mnemonics!

KINAESTHETIC STRATEGIES

You need to be doing, feeling and touching as much as possible when you are working on maths problems. So, the use of concrete materials is really important. There is a resources section at the end of this book on page 278. If you don't have these materials, then virtual ones are a good alternative. See www.mathsbot.com (click on the manipulatives tab).

Kinaesthetic learning is learning through physical activity.

MAKE THE INFORMATION MEMORABLE

For information to stay in the memory, it must be clearly and firmly registered.

Your teachers should make sure that information they give is clear and unambiguous. Long, multi-step instructions should be broken down into smaller steps that will be easier to remember.

You will need to repeat and rehearse the information daily to make the most of 'over-learning'. It will help if you can connect the new information to something that you already know. Make sure that you are really listening, that you are actively trying to understand and remember the information.

Another strategy that can help you to remember information is to change the way that you record it. One of the most inefficient ways of learning something is to read it and copy it out, yet this is the approach that most people take when they are revising for exams. A much more effective way of revising is to do something with the information and to transform it in some way. This could be in the form of drawing a mind map, acting something out, creating a picture, explaining it to someone else, making up a song.

MAKE THE INFORMATION MEANINGFUL

Try to relate the information to something that you are interested in or have experience of. When you are working on a maths calculation, try to think of a real-life context where you would need to do this calculation. This will help you to see the purpose of the maths and will keep your motivation levels up.

For example, think about a Netflix series you really like! The calculation is 6 divided by $\frac{3}{4}$. Rethink it!

'I have 6 hours of free time today! How many episodes of a series can I binge-watch in 6 hours, if each episode lasts ¾ of an hour?'

Visual spatial awareness

- Difficulty in recognizing maths symbols
- Difficulty in placing numbers on a number line
- Difficulty in interpreting graphs and tables
- Difficulty in visualizing maths; for example, the net of a 3D shape

Ways to help recognize maths symbols

Colour-coding can help, particularly with the + sign and the × sign. Pick one colour for the + sign and a different colour for the × sign, and then be consistent in your use of those colours. It will also help to physically create the maths symbols with your arms and to say out loud the symbol that you are making.

Placing numbers on a number line

Number lines can be hard to work with because different number lines have different scales. You can have a line that is the same length showing the numbers 1–10 or 1–1000, so a good deal of estimation and visual perception is needed here.

Make sure that you look at the two end points first and then work out what the number line is representing. If it is a blank number line, except for the end numbers, then make a mark in the centre and find the value of that number. The more reference points you have, the easier it will be to work with the number line.

Interpreting graphs and tables

The difficulty here can be that there is too much information being shown in one place.

Aperture cards and L-shaped cards can be useful when interpreting tables. An aperture card is a piece of card with a window cut out in the middle. You can easily make aperture cards in different sizes, depending on the tables that you are looking at. Just place a card over the table, in the section that you are looking at, and it will help you to focus on that information only. You could also use an L-shaped card for reading information from tables as this will help to focus on the column and row that you are looking at.

Visualization

The best way to develop your ability to visualize is to use actual manipulatives, such as base-10 equipment, 3D shapes, counters and cubes. These materials are just as relevant in secondary school as they are in primary school, and using them regularly will help you to 'see' the maths in your head.

This book has many ideas for materials that you can use and diagrams that you can draw to help you develop your visualization skills.

Dyspraxia

The term dyspraxia originates from Greek and means 'difficulty in carrying out an action'. Dyspraxia is a developmental disorder of the brain, causing difficulty in activities requiring coordination and movement. It can be described by a lack of development in a person's ability to 'get our bodies to do what we want and when we want them to do it'. It can cause difficulty with both spatial and perceptual skills, such as:

- speech and language
- handwriting and drawing (dysgraphia)
- whole-body movements and coordination
- physical play/activity.

Dyspraxia is characterized by disorganized wiring of the brain, leading to inconsistent interaction with the environment. There are many different ways in which dyspraxia can manifest itself. The way that it affects maths most are difficulties with visual perception, spatial awareness and visual sequential memory.

VISUAL PERCEPTION

This refers to how the brain interprets information that is received through the eyes. Problems can arise from having difficulties in coordinating eye movement, tracking from left to right, hand–eye coordination, processing visual information at speed and receiving correct visual information. These difficulties can have a huge impact on learning, as the vast majority of information in school lessons is presented visually.

Visual perception difficulties will impact on maths development because you may find it hard to discriminate between different shapes and symbols, for example 'x' and ' + '. You may have difficulty in interpreting diagrams, tables and graphs. Frequently, learners with visual perception problems will set out their maths problems in a messy, unaligned way, leading to errors in calculations.

SPATIAL AWARENESS

This refers to how well we perceive our body position in relation to other objects in the environment. Learners with dyspraxia often have difficulty with spatial awareness as the brain is not giving them the correct messages regarding relative positions and the proximity of objects around them. This can lead to frequently bumping into things or falling over, as well as being unaware of personal space.

In terms of maths development, you may find it difficult to interpret geometric figures. You may have trouble placing numbers on a number line and in drawing and interpreting graphs.

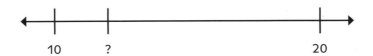

10   ?   20

VISUAL SEQUENTIAL MEMORY

This refers to our ability to store information received through the eyes in the correct sequence. The area of the brain that is affected is the visual spatial working memory. This is important in terms of maths development as we depend on our visual spatial memory in many areas of maths.

For example, to solve a problem like 9 + 6 = 15, you need to perceive how the numbers and symbols are placed in relation to each other on a page and how that placement affects how you approach the problem. You also need to be able to align numbers vertically for column methods of calculations.

IDENTIFICATION: DYSPRAXIA

It is not easy to diagnose dyspraxia as it can manifest itself in so many different ways. For people under the age of 16, the diagnosis will need to be made by medical professionals.

Some of the more common traits of dyspraxia are:

- difficulty with eye–hand and eye–foot coordination (i.e. ball skills), running or using equipment easily
- poor visual spatial awareness; for example, finding it hard to imagine the nets of 3D shapes
- poor posture, poor body awareness and awkward movements
- cross laterality, interchanging between left and right hand for different tasks
- poor short-term visual and verbal memory – difficulty copying from the board or following instructions

- poor organizational skills and difficulty with planning essays
- tiring easily and needing longer periods of rest and sleep
- sensitivity to external stimulation; for example, different levels of light, sound and heat intensity.

STRATEGIES TO IMPROVE VISUAL–SPATIAL AWARENESS

Verbalization

Dyspraxic learners will often become confused when given information visually and verbally at the same time. They tend to completely ignore the visual information. If this applies to you, then ask your teachers to give you the visual information separately from the verbal information and to make sure that the verbal information is very clear. Concrete materials will be useful here, by providing a visual element to support the verbal information.

Seating

Make sure that you are seated with clear line of sight of the teacher. If you are easily distracted by noise, then try to make sure that you are seated somewhere quiet (i.e. not by the classroom door). If you are sensitive to light, then make sure that you are not sat directly under strip lighting.

Presentation of information

Ask your teachers to provide handouts in advance that are clear and uncluttered. It is useful if calculations are set out on graph paper, with one digit per square. Ask your teachers to avoid the need for you to copy information from the board or to give you extra time for copying if it is unavoidable.

Resources

Aperture cards can be very helpful when you are faced with a whole page of calculations. These can easily be made by cutting a small window out of a piece of card. The card can then be placed over the page of calculations so that only one calculation is visible. Reading rules can also be used, as well as coloured overlays.

L-shaped card can help you to read information from a graph or table. Writing slopes can be useful and you may also benefit from

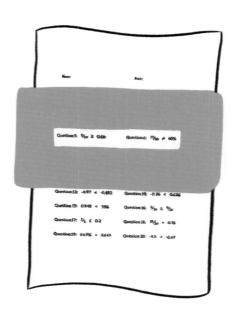

specialized pens and rulers to help you when you are drawing graphs or constructing geometric figures.

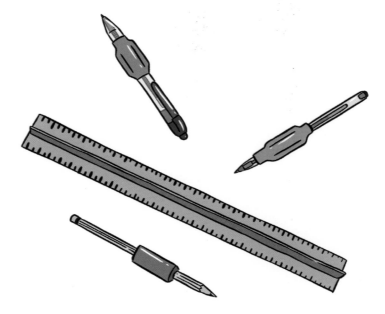

ADHD

Attention deficit hyperactivity disorder (ADHD) is a specific learning difference that can cause impulsive behaviour and difficulty in concentrating for extended periods of time. People with ADHD may also find it hard to sit still and may be very fidgety.

If you have ADHD, then you may have memory difficulties, and this can make it hard for you to recall maths facts and methods. You may also have difficulty in organizing your work or keeping track of the steps in a calculation.

You may get easily frustrated, particularly if you are making lots of mistakes.

WAYS TO HELP

- Make sure that you have sufficient breaks when you are working.
- Break down your work into smaller chunks.
- Use games to help you keep focused on maths tasks.
- Make sure that your teachers are aware of your ADHD and that they understand the effect that it has on you.

Maths Anxiety

Your difficulties with maths may be largely due to maths anxiety. Most of us have felt anxious about maths at some stage, but for some people this can develop into a real fear of maths. You may become so anxious when faced with maths that you find it hard to think clearly, and this sense of panic can have a very severe effect on your learning.

There are lots of techniques that you can use to help to relieve your anxiety. But first, let's have a look at some of the symptoms of maths anxiety, which may help you to identify whether this is contributing to your difficulties with maths.

IDENTIFYING MATHS ANXIETY

Maths anxiety has been defined as a feeling of tension, apprehension or fear that interferes with **maths** performance. There are many definitions, but they all focus on the level of anxiety affecting your ability to carry out mathematical calculations.

You may have physical and/or psychological symptoms. The physical symptoms include:

- nail and lip biting
- stomach aches
- clammy hands
- tension headaches
- clenched fists
- increase in heartbeat
- shortness of breath
- dry mouth.

Psychological symptoms include:

- low self-esteem
- extreme nervousness and anxiety
- confusion and disorganized thought
- inability to retain or recall information.

These symptoms are worse when you are under time pressure or when you are 'put on the spot' to answer a question in front of others.

The Growth Zone Model (shown overleaf) can be helpful in identifying how anxious you are and will alert your teachers to your anxiety so that they can support you.

The Growth Zone Model

Adapted from Lugalia *et al.* (2013) with permission from the authors.[6] For more information, see https://nrich.maths.org/13491

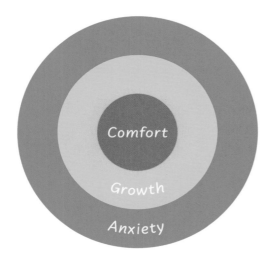

Anxiety zone
- *The work is beyond your reach. You see it as a threat rather than a challenge.*
- *Your stress increases and you are unable to learn.*

Growth zone
- *This is where new learning happens.*
- *You feel safe in making mistakes.*
- *You sometimes get stuck but can ask for help.*
- *The work may be tiring and challenging but you feel it is achievable.*

Comfort zone
- *You can do familiar tasks on your own.*
- *Your confidence is increasing.*
- *You are beginning to do things automatically because you have practised so much.*

STRATEGIES TO REDUCE MATHS ANXIETY

Use concrete materials

Concrete materials are the maths manipulatives that you would have been familiar with in primary school. They tend to be used less in secondary school, which is a great shame as we know that they can really help us to understand maths. Using equipment doesn't mean that you are bad at maths; it is simply a really effective way to help you to learn better and to understand more. Part 2 of this book will give you many examples of the materials that can help and the pictures that you can use to help you understand the maths that you are working on.

If you can 'see' the maths and if you have the apparatus to model the maths, then you will have a much better chance of understanding what you are doing. A great deal of anxiety is caused by maths being too abstract too soon. Resources such as Cuisenaire rods, Numicon, base-10 equipment (Dienes), counters and cubes can all help with understanding mathematical concepts.

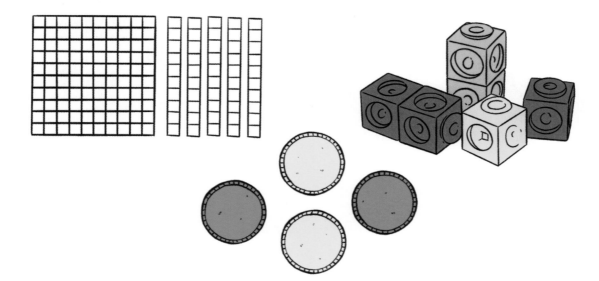

Generate pictorial representation

Representing maths concepts in pictures, for example through diagrams, drawings and models, will help you to understand abstract symbolic maths. Many people find this very hard to do but it is worth the effort as it helps you to visualize the maths and to retain an image of the mathematical concept.

Look for connections and patterns

Maths becomes much easier if you can spot the patterns and connections. For example, if you know that 3 + 4 = 7, then you will also be able to calculate 30 + 40 and 300 + 400 and so on, if you can see the pattern. Part 2 of this book will help you to find these connections and patterns, and this will help you to understand the maths and to reduce the amount of information that you have to remember.

OTHER TECHNIQUES TO REDUCE MATHS ANXIETY

There are many ways that you can try to reduce your maths anxiety and to relax more when you are doing maths.

Deep breathing

This is a very simple and effective way to relax, as it naturally slows down the body's response to stress.

A variation on this is to try to slow down your breathing, to a rate of about 10 breaths per minute.

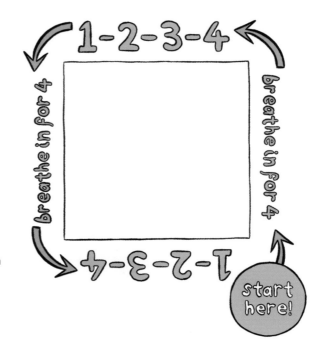

Stretching

Stretching can help to release tension in the muscles. One technique is to isolate different muscle groups and then stretch and relax them in turn.

You could try this routine.

1. Stand with your knees slightly bent or sit up straight.
2. Clasp your hands in front of you, arms parallel to the floor.
3. Keep your head relaxed.
4. Round your upper back. Push hands forward, palms away from your body.
5. Hold for 20–30 seconds, breathing steadily.

Repeat 2–5 times.

Visualization

This is a surprisingly effective technique that is easy to achieve. All you need to do is to imagine a place, feeling or event which is safe, relaxing or enjoyable. Visualization is especially useful if you do this just before a maths test or other stressful maths activity.

Writing down your anxieties

Writing down your worries associated with maths can be effective and can help you to 'let go' of your anxieties, particularly if you do this prior to a stressful maths situation, such as a test or exam.

Music

Playing soothing music in the background while you revise or do your homework can help to create a calm and relaxing environment.

Laughter

Laughter is a good way of relieving tension, so having a bank of funny cartoons and maths jokes can be a useful and light-hearted strategy.

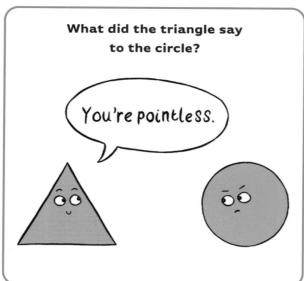

What did the triangle say to the circle?

You're pointless.

Growth Mindset

Have a look at the following statements. What mindset do you have?

Growth mindset	Fixed mindset
Belief that intelligence is not fixed – my intelligence can be improved through learning	Belief that talent is static and that you will only be successful if you are naturally talented
Seeing mistakes as a positive – something to learn from	Preferring to stay in your comfort zone, avoiding challenging situations
Thriving on challenge and being self-confident	Avoiding challenge
Not giving up easily – having resilience in your approach to maths	Anxiety about making mistakes – belief that maths is all about getting the answer right. Giving up easily
Belief that hard work pays off – effort will bring success	Being self-conscious in front of your peers – you won't offer a solution in public for fear of looking 'stupid'
Reflecting on strategies that work for you – developing metacognitive awareness	Not reflecting on what strategies have helped you to learn or to move on
Having learning goals and using feedback to improve	Staying with easy performance goals and enjoying being praised for doing well

If you feel that you have a fixed mindset, then try swapping some of your beliefs using the Swap table below.

SWAP I am stupid	FOR	I can't do this yet
SWAP This is too hard	FOR	This may take a little while
SWAP I wish I was as clever as my classmate	FOR	I am going to work out how my classmate got the answer
SWAP I have never done this before; I have not been shown how to do it	FOR	What has worked in the past that may help me here? Have I done anything similar?
SWAP I have got an answer, so I have finished	FOR	Am I sure this is correct? Can I check it using a different method?
SWAP I will never need to know this area of maths when I leave school	FOR	Working this out will help me to become better at solving problems

Learning Styles

Different people have different ways of approaching maths problems. Some people are very logical and structured in their approach and others are more intuitive and flexible. We call these learning styles the 'Inchworm' and the 'Grasshopper'.

Let's have a look at the stages of solving a problem and at the approaches typically taken by a learner with the traits of the Inchworm and a learner with the traits of the Grasshopper.

Cognitive styles of the Inchworm and the Grasshopper

	Inchworm	**Grasshopper**
Analyzing and identifying the problem	Focuses on parts; attends to detail and separates	Holistic; forms concepts and puts them together
	Sets the objective of looking at facts to determine useful formulae	Sets the objective of looking at facts to determine an estimate of the answer or the range of restrictions
Methods of solving the problem	Formula; recipe-orientated	Controlled exploration
	Constrained focusing, using a single method or serially ordered steps along one route, generally in one direction, which is forward	Flexible focusing, using multi-methods or paths, frequently occurring simultaneously, generally reversing or working back from an answer and trying new routes
	Uses numbers exactly as given	Adjusts, breaks down/builds up numbers to make an easier calculation
	Tending to add and multiply; resists subtraction and division	Tending to subtraction
	Tending to use paper and pencil to compute	Tending to perform all calculations mentally
	Verification unlikely; if done, uses same procedure or method	Likely to verify; probably uses alternative procedure or method

Reproduced from Bath *et al.* (1986) with permission from Steve Chinn.[7]

Is one style better than the other? Well, it depends on what you are doing. Learners who are feeling insecure about an aspect of maths will tend towards an Inchworm approach. Even learners who are naturally Grasshoppers will become Inchworms if they are too far out of their comfort zone.

It will be important for you as you go through this book to think about whether you are a Grasshopper or an Inchworm. Perhaps you are sometimes one and sometimes the other, depending on what you are working on.

There will be lots of strategies offered in Part 2 of this book and you may not understand all of them. That's fine – you don't need to. But hopefully you will find a new strategy that makes sense to you, and you will be able to move forward in your understanding with that new way of thinking.

Metacognition

Many people refer to metacognition as 'thinking about your thinking'. Developing metacognitive skills gives you some control over your learning and helps you to understand what strategies work for you. It encourages you to think more deeply about your learning and this in turn will help to develop your cognitive abilities.

> **Metacognition** *is thinking about one's thinking.*

Metacognition is a process that has three distinct phases.

1. **Plan:** Before starting to solve a maths problem, plan a course of action.
2. **Monitor:** During the problem solving, monitor your progress. Is your plan working? Have you selected the best strategy?
3. **Evaluate:** On completion of the task, evaluate the effectiveness of your chosen approach. Was it successful?

You can develop your metacognitive skills by asking yourself the following types of question at each phase.

Planning stage	• What is the question asking me to do? What should I do first? • Have I seen a problem like this before? What strategies worked for that problem? Can I apply them here?
Monitoring stage	• How am I getting on? • Is this strategy working? • What other methods could I use? • Am I getting nearer to the answer?
Evaluation stage	• Did I solve the problem? • Did I use the most efficient strategy? • Could I have done anything better? • Was there something that I did not understand? • Could I apply what I have done here to other problems in the future?

HOW TO THINK ABOUT YOUR THINKING

Ask questions of yourself at each of the three stages. Discuss strategies with other people and write down your ideas or approaches. Assess your chosen approach once the problem has been solved and evaluate how effective it was. Work on tasks that have more than one solution and more than one method of solving them.

The following questions will help to develop an awareness of how you learn.

- What did you learn?
- How did you learn it?
- Did you find anything very difficult?
- Did you find anything very easy?
- How did you do this task?

The following questions will develop an awareness of attitudes and feelings.

- What did you like about the task?
- What was good about the task?
- What was not so good about the task?

The following questions will help to develop an awareness of setting goals.

- Could you have done anything better?
- What is your next target?
- What will help you to achieve your next target?

Next Steps

Hopefully you now have a better understanding of how you learn and what specific difficulties you face. You may want to discuss what you have discovered with your family, your teachers or the school SENCo. They may be able to offer additional ways of supporting your learning.

As you move on to Part 2 of this book, try and reflect on what strategies are helping you to learn best and make sure that you use these strategies when you are in school as well as at home.

You may find some activities challenging, but don't be disheartened. Sometimes maths is hard, but the main thing is for you to improve.

At the end of each chapter in Part 2, we ask you to think back over the content to see if you feel more confident now. If you do, then that is fantastic; if you don't, then you may need to go back and look over the chapter again. But remember, you don't have to understand and use every method that we have shown you.

It may be that you have not covered all the maths in the chapters in school yet. If so, that is fine, you can just work on the parts that you have covered and come back to other parts later once you have done them in school. The important thing is for you to find the strategies that work best for you.

Endnotes

1   AchieveAbility (2011) The Make-up of Neuro-Diversity. [retrieved from https://www.achieveability.org.uk/files/1275491669/neuro-diversity-diagram.pdf; accessed 20 May 2022]

2   Rose Review (2009) *Identifying and Teaching Children and Young People with Dyslexia and Literary Difficulties*. An independent report from Jim Rose to the Secretary of State for Children, Schools and Families, June 2009, page 9.

3   BDA (2010) What is Dyslexia? [retrieved from www.bdadyslexia.org.uk; accessed 10 January 2022]

4   BDA/SASC (2019) Dyscalculia definition. [retrieved from www.bdadyslexia.org.uk/dyslexia/neurodiversity-and-co-occurring-differences/dyscalculia-and-maths-difficulties; accessed 10 January 2022]

5   Richards, R.G. (2003) *The Source for Learning and Memory Strategies*. LinguiSystems.

6   Lugalia, M. Johnston-Wilder, S. and Goodall, J. (2013) The Role of ICT in Developing Mathematical Resilience in Learners. [retrieved from www.researchgate.net/publication/262950745_ Lugalia_M_ Johnston-Wilder_S_and_Goodall_J_2013_The_Role_of_ICT_in_developing_mathematical_resilience_in_students_INTED_2013; accessed 10 January 2022]

7   Bath, J.B., Chinn, S.J. and Knox, D.E. (1986) *The Test of Cognitive Style in Mathematics*. East Aurora, NY: Slosson.

Part 2

1. Multiplication and Division

AIMS

- To write multiplication tables and use Napier's bones
- To multiply numbers with more than one digit
- To divide a multi-digit number by another number

RESOURCES

- Napier's bones (page 279)

PREVIOUS KNOWLEDGE

- Understand that multiplication is repeated addition and division is repeated subtraction
- Know how to write a multiplication table

USING NAPIER'S BONES FOR MULTIPLICATION

0	1	2	3	4	5	6	7	8	9	10
0/0	0/1	0/2	0/3	0/4	0/5	0/6	0/7	0/8	0/9	1/0
0/0	0/2	0/4	0/6	0/8	1/0	1/2	1/4	1/6	1/8	2/0
0/0	0/3	0/6	0/9	1/2	1/5	1/8	2/1	2/4	2/7	3/0
0/0	0/4	0/8	1/2	1/6	2/0	2/4	2/8	3/2	3/6	4/0
0/0	0/5	1/0	1/5	2/0	2/5	3/0	3/5	4/0	4/5	5/0
0/0	0/6	1/2	1/8	2/4	3/0	3/6	4/2	4/8	5/4	6/0
0/0	0/7	1/4	2/1	2/8	3/5	4/2	4/9	5/6	6/3	7/0
0/0	0/8	1/6	2/4	3/2	4/0	4/8	5/6	6/4	7/2	8/0
0/0	0/9	1/8	2/7	3/6	4/5	5/4	6/3	7/2	8/1	9/0
0/0	1/0	2/0	3/0	4/0	5/0	6/0	7/0	8/0	9/0	10/0

Napier's bones are a tool for multiplying. They are made from a multiplication square cut into vertical strips; each vertical strip is a 'bone'.

Napier's bones are a multiplication square cut into vertical strips. Each 'bone' has 10 squares. The first square indicates the multiplication table (for example, × 5). Each remaining square is divided in half, with the tens written above the diagonal line and the ones below.

To work out 5 × 7, find the 5-bone and count down seven rows. Read the number displayed.

You could also use the 7-bone and count down five rows because 5 × 7 = 7 × 5. We say that multiplication is commutative.

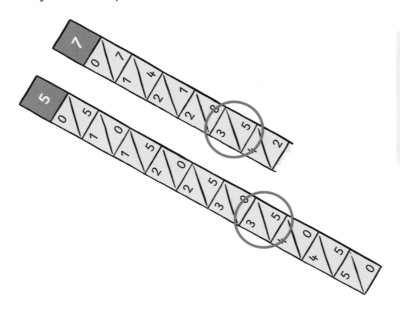

> **Commutative** means the answer is the same regardless of the order in which you multiply the numbers. Multiplication and addition are commutative, but division and subtraction are not.

Using two bones for multiplication

Work out 85 × 9

Find the 8-bone and the 5-bone, then put them side by side to make 85.

Look at the numbers in row 9. Put them in a grid with diagonal lines to separate the tens and ones.

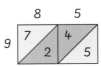

Write '8' above '72', to show that '72' is from the 8-bone.

Write '5' above '45', to show that '45' is from the 5-bone. To the left of the grid, write '9', because you are multiplying by 9.

Starting on the right side of the grid, add the columns along the diagonals.

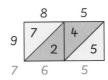

5 will be the ones digit in your answer.

Next column: 2 + 4 = 6

6 will be the tens digit in your answer.

Final column: 7

7 will be the hundreds digit in your answer.

Answer: 85 × 9 = 765

> *Use a calculator to check.*

Use Napier's bones for as long as you need them to help you work out multiplication problems. Eventually you will be able to use your times table knowledge to complete the grids and then use the grid method of multiplication in your GCSE Maths exam.

Why does this method of finding 85 × 9 work?
In the 5-bone, the '4' is in the tens column and the '5' is in the ones column. Putting the 8-bone next to the 5-bone pushes the '2' into the tens column with the '4'. The '7' is in the hundreds column.

You may find it easier to put the bones diagonally at first.

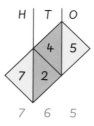

Look at this example for 30 × 4. Notice the 1 is in the hundreds column and the 2 is in the tens column.

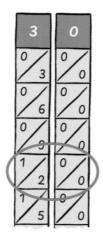
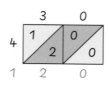

How does this method relate to long multiplication?

Let's look at finding 85 × 9 using long multiplication.

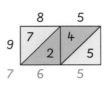

$$
\begin{array}{r}
8\ 5 \\
\times \quad\ 9 \\
\hline
4\ 5 \quad (9 \times 5)\\
7\ 2\ 0 \quad (9 \times 80)\\
\hline
7\ 6\ 5
\end{array}
$$

Can you see the 45 in the grid?

Can you see the 720 in the grid?

Working with bigger numbers

Work out 907 × 7

Find the bones for 9, 0 and 7 and put them side by side to make 907.

Look at the numbers in the seventh row and write them in a grid.

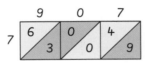

Starting on the right side of the grid, add the columns along the diagonals.

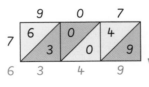

9 will be the ones digit in your answer.

Next column: 0 + 4 = 4

4 will be the tens digit in your answer.

Next column: 3 + 0 = 3

3 will be the hundreds digit in your answer.

Final column: 6

6 will be the thousands digit in your answer.

Answer: 907 × 7 = 6349

> Notice this grid also tells you that 6349 ÷ 7 = 907 and 6349 ÷ 907 = 7

ACTIVITY 1.1

1. Use Napier's bones and grids to work out these multiplications.

a) 456 × 3

b) 239 × 4

c) 713 × 6

d) 837 × 7

e) 942 × 9

2. Write down the related division facts for each multiplication.

INVESTIGATE

Choose two bones and put them side by side. Are there any rows where the two numbers in the tens column add up to a number less than 10? Write down the calculation and the answer that the row gives you.

What if an addition gives a total of 10 or more?

If the numbers in a single column add up to 10 or more, write down the ones digit, carry the 'ten' into the next column and include it in the next addition.

Look at this example, which shows the method for working out 371 × 3.

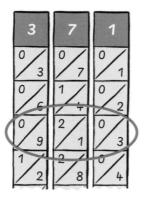 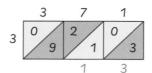 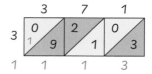

Answer: 371 × 3 = 1113

Let's look at another example and this time break down the individual steps.

Work out 876 × 7

Begin by putting the bones for 8, 7 and 6 side by side.

Copy the values in the seventh row into a grid.

Starting on the right side of the grid, add the columns along the diagonals.

> *Notice you do not have to remember your 7 times table when you do this calculation.*

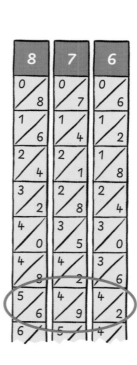

2 will be the ones digit in your answer.

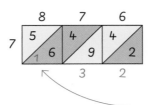

> Remember, when an addition gives a total of 10 or more, write down the ones digit and carry the ten into the next column. Include it in the next addition.

Next column: 9 + 4 = 13

Write the 3 ones below the 9 and 4. Carry the 1 ten to the next column on the left.

Next column: 1 + 6 + 4 = 11

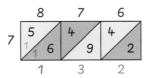

Write the 1 one below the 1, 6 and 4. Carry the 1 ten to the next column on the left.

Final column: 1 + 5 = 6

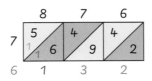

Write 6 below the 1 and 5.

Answer: 876 × 7 = 6132

The grid also shows that 6132 ÷ 7 = 876 and 6132 ÷ 876 = 7

ACTIVITY 1.2

1. Use Napier's bones and grids to work out these multiplications.

   a) 278 × 4   b) 854 × 6   c) 291 × 8   d) 739 × 9   e) 456 × 7

2. Write down the related division facts for each multiplication.

Multiplying by two-digit numbers

You can multiply by a two-digit number in the same way. You just need a bigger grid!

Work out 24 × 56

Place the 2-bone and the 4-bone side by side to make 24.

Circle the numbers in the fifth and sixth rows because you are multiplying by 56.

Draw a 2 × 2 grid.

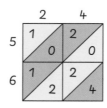

In the grid, write the circled numbers.

Label the columns of the grid ('2' and '4') to show you are using the 2-bone and the 4-bone.

Label the rows of the grid ('5' and '6') to show you are using the fifth and sixth rows of both bones.

Starting on the right side of the grid, add the columns along the diagonals.

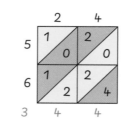

Answer: 24 × 56 = 1344

ACTIVITY 1.3

1. Use Napier's bones and 2 × 2 grids to work out these multiplications.

a) 81 × 34   b) 71 × 23   c) 43 × 45   d) 57 × 34   e) 63 × 45

2. Write down the related division facts for each multiplication in Question 1.

3. Now answer these. Remember to carry at the addition stage.

a) 73 × 67 b) 83 × 56 c) 58 × 78 d) 57 × 45 e) 24 × 89

4. Write down the related division facts for each multiplication in Question 3.

5. What do you notice about all the multipliers in this activity?

What if the rows are not next to each other?

In Activity 1.3, you will have used rows 3 and 4 of the Napier's bones to answer question 1a; you will have used rows 2 and 3 to answer question 1b.

But what if the rows are not next to each other? It doesn't matter; simply copy into your grid the numbers from the relevant rows.

Look at this example.

Work out 74 × 39

Place the 7-bone and the 4-bone side by side to make 74.

Circle the numbers in the third and ninth rows because you are multiplying by 39.

Draw a 2 × 2 grid.

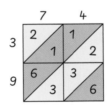

In the grid, write the circled numbers.

Label the columns and rows of the grid.

Starting on the right side of the grid, add the columns along the diagonals.

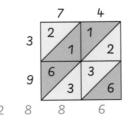

Answer: 74 × 39 = 2886

Here is another example.

Work out 58 × 87

Place the 5-bone and the 8-bone side by side to make 58.

Circle the numbers in the eighth and seventh rows because you are multiplying by 87.

Draw a 2 × 2 grid.

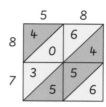

In the grid, write the circled numbers.

Label the columns and rows of the grid.

Starting on the right side of the grid, add the columns along the diagonals.

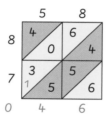 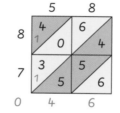

> In this calculation, you have to carry twice; once into the hundreds column and once into the thousands column.

Answer: 58 × 87 = 5046

ACTIVITY 1.4

1. Use Napier's bones and 2 × 2 grids to work out these multiplications. Write the related division facts too.

a) 74 × 39   c) 57 × 24   e) 38 × 47   g) 17 × 52   i) 85 × 94
b) 41 × 35   d) 43 × 58   f) 39 × 41   h) 62 × 72   j) 87 × 54

2. Here's some more practice. Remember to carry!

a) 62 × 26   b) 81 × 36   c) 59 × 59   d) 74 × 48   e) 93 × 24

INVESTIGATE

You can use two sets of bones to make numbers with repeated digits, such as 33.

A 2 × 2 grid to solve 33 × 55 has been started for you.

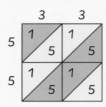

Use a calculator to divide the answer to 33 × 55 by 121.

Repeat for other double-digit numbers like this.

What do you notice?

Can you explain why?

There's no limit to the size of the numbers

Complete the working for 708 × 74

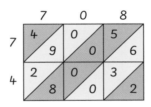

Did you get the answer 52,392?

ACTIVITY 1.5

1. Use Napier's bones and grids to work out these multiplications.

   a) 413 × 45   b) 427 × 12   c) 863 × 67   d) 509 × 83   e) 853 × 812

2. Work out some multiplications of your own. Use a calculator to check your answers. Go as big as you dare! If your answer has more than 10 digits, it will be more accurate than the answer given by your calculator!

USING NAPIER'S BONES FOR DIVISION

Remember, a multiplication grid shows the answer to division calculations, too. The grid below shows four calculations.

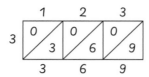

3 × 123 = 369, 123 × 3 = 369, 369 ÷ 3 = 123 and 369 ÷ 123 = 3

When using Napier's bones to divide:

- Below the grid, write the number to be divided. Write one digit below each square.
- On the left of the grid, write the number you are dividing by.
- The answer to the division calculation will appear above the grid.

Work out 567 ÷ 3

Draw a 3 × 1 grid, including the diagonal lines that divide each square in half.

Find the Napier's bone for 3. It includes all the numbers in the three times table.

Write '3' on the left of the grid (to show that you are dividing by 3).

Below the grid, write '567' (this is the number that is being divided). Write one digit below each square.

Look down the 3-bone to find the largest multiple of 3 that is less than 5 (the answer is 3, because 1 × 3 = 3).

Write the row number (1) above the first square.

Write the number from the row itself (3) inside the bottom triangle of the first square. In the top triangle, write '0'.

Work out how many more you need in the top triangle of the second square to make 5. The answer is 2. Write '2' as shown in the diagram.

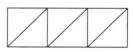

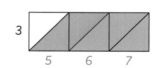

Remember that when the grid is complete, the numbers at the bottom are the total of the numbers in the diagonal columns. You can colour code the numbers and the columns if it helps you.

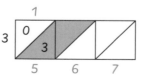

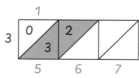

Now look for the row on the 3-bone that has the number nearest to 26 without going over.

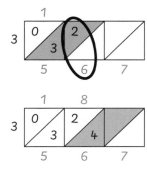

8 × 3 = 24 is nearest to 26, so write '8' above the grid as the next number in the answer.

Write '4' in the lower triangle of the second square, making the number in the second square 24.

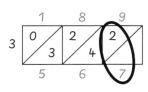

Work out how many more you need in the top triangle of the third square to make 26. The answer is 2. Write '2' in the top triangle of the third square.

Now, consider the number 27.

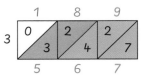

The final step gives an exact match because 9 × 3 = 27. Write '9' above the grid.

The entire number above the grid reveals the answer to the division problem.

Answer: 567 ÷ 3 = 189

Notice our working also shows that 3 × 189 = 567

> Check your answer by adding along the columns diagonally.

Work out 5546 ÷ 5

Draw a 4 × 1 grid.

Have the 5-bone ready.

Write '5' on the left of the grid.

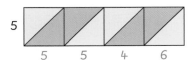

Below the grid, write '5546' – one digit below each square.

For the first square, 1 × 5 = 5 with no remainder. Write '1' above the first square. Write '05' inside the first square.

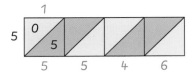

Because 1 × 5 = 5 works exactly, there is no remainder. Nothing extra is needed in the top triangle of the second square, so write '0'.

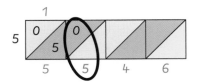

Moving on to the second square, the number to be considered is 05. This is the same number as in the first square.

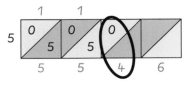

You are now looking at 04 in the third square.

04 is less than any row on the 5-bone, so write '0' above the third square. Also write '0' in the bottom triangle of the third square.

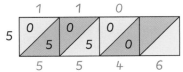

You need an extra 4 in the top triangle of the fourth square, so the next number to be considered is 46.

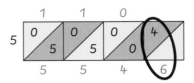

Look at 46. This is not in the five times table so there is a remainder. Draw an extra triangle to put the remainder in. Write '9' above the fourth square and '5' in the bottom triangle of the fourth square, to make 45. The remainder 1 goes in the extra triangle.

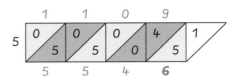

Be careful to write the answer clearly.

Answer: 5546 ÷ 5 = 1109 remainder 1

ACTIVITY 1.6

Use Napier's bones and grids to do these division calculations. Give the remainder if there is one.

a) 96 ÷ 3   e) 6496 ÷ 8   i) 9257 ÷ 6
b) 824 ÷ 2   f) 557 ÷ 5   j) 25,972 ÷ 3
c) 192 ÷ 6   g) 989 ÷ 4
d) 378 ÷ 7   h) 9757 ÷ 2

Check your answers using a calculator.

> *If an answer has a remainder, your calculator will probably state the answer as a fraction or a decimal.*
>
> - *Can you change your answer on the calculator to a mixed number?*
> - *Can you adapt the method to work out decimal answers of your own?*

Find 1439 ÷ 6

Draw a 4 × 1 grid.

Have the 6-bone ready.

Write '6' on the left of the grid.

Below the grid, write '1439' – one digit below each square.

1 is less than any number on the 6-bone, so write '0' above the first square. Write '00' in the first square. Write the extra 1 you need in the top triangle of the second square.

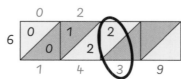

Look for the row on the 6-bone that has the number nearest to 14 without going over. 2 × 6 = 12 is nearest to 14, so write '2' above the grid as the next number in the answer. Write '2' in the lower triangle of the second square, making the number in the second square 12.

Next, look at 23.

3 × 6 = 18 is nearest to 23 without going over.

Split 23 into 18 and 5. Write '3' above the third square, '8' in the bottom triangle of the third square, and carry the extra 5 over to the top triangle of the fourth square.

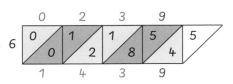

Now, look at 59.

59 is not in the six times table so there is a remainder. Draw an extra triangle to put the remainder in. 9 × 6 = 54. Write '9' above the fourth square. Write the remainder '5' in the extra triangle.

Answer: 1439 ÷ 6 = 239 remainder 5

ACTIVITY 1.7

1. Use Napier's bones and grids to do these division calculations. Give the remainder if there is one.

a) 4956 ÷ 7   c) 7295 ÷ 5   e) 1125 ÷ 9   g) 5156 ÷ 7   i) 3153 ÷ 4

b) 1756 ÷ 4   d) 807 ÷ 3   f) 241 ÷ 7   h) 2063 ÷ 3   j) 22,317 ÷ 8

2. Make up some divisions of your own to do. Solve them using Napier's bones and grids. Use a calculator to check your answers.

Dividing by a two-digit number

Find 3297 ÷ 15

Begin by creating the 15 times table.

Put the 1-bone and the 5-bone side by side and write down the 15 times table as a list.

Draw a 4 × 1 grid.

Write '15' on the left of the grid.

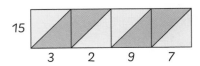

Below the grid, write '3297' – one digit below each square.

Look at the first square – you need 00 here and 3 in the top triangle of the second square.

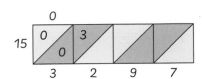

77

Look at the 15 times table to find the largest multiple of 15 that is less than 32. You can see that 2 × 15 = 30 is nearest to 32. Complete the second square and write the extra 2 needed to make 32 in the top triangle of the third square.

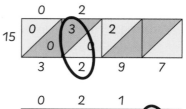

Look at the 15 times table to find the largest multiple of 15 that is less than 29. Notice 1 × 15 = 15 is nearest to 29.

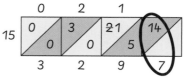

Complete the third square and write the extra 14 needed to make 29 in the top triangle of the fourth square.

For the last square you need to find a number in the 15 times table as near to 147 as you can.

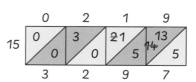

9 × 15 = 135 so the final step gives 9 in the answer, with an extra 12 needed to make 147.

Draw an extra triangle for the remainder.

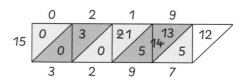

Answer: 3297 ÷ 15 = 219 remainder 12

Check this answer using a calculator. Explain what the calculator does with the remainder.

CHAPTER SUM-UP

Practice

Make up some long division calculations and use Napier's bones and the grid method to find the answers. Check your answers using a calculator.

Write some word problems for a friend that need long division to solve them. Can your friend answer them?

Reflection

Having worked through this chapter, how do you feel about these skills?

Skill	I have tried this	I need more practice	I am confident with this
Writing multiplication tables and using Napier's bones			
Multiplying numbers with more than one digit			
Dividing a multi-digit number by another number			

Quiz

Which of these questions gives the largest answer?

a) 197 × 8

b) 37 × 42

c) 6312 ÷ 4

d) 26,367 ÷ 17

2. Place Value and Decimals

AIMS
- To understand the place value of whole numbers
- To round numbers to the nearest ten, hundred, and so on
- To multiply and divide by powers of ten
- To compare and order decimal numbers
- To round decimal numbers
- To add and subtract decimal numbers
- To multiply decimal numbers
- To divide a decimal number by a whole number
- To divide by a decimal number

RESOURCES
- Base-10 tiles (see page 281). Print and stick the tiles onto card and cut them out
- Rounding viewer (see page 282)

PREVIOUS KNOWLEDGE
- Multiplication and division

◄◄ **Rewind** – look at page 65 for the grid method of multiplication
►► **Fast forward** – look at page 125 for percentages, decimals and fractions

THE PLACE VALUE OF WHOLE NUMBERS

You have been using the idea of place value since you first learned to work in tens and ones.

You represent the number 145 using one large square for the hundred, four strips for the tens and five small squares for the ones.

H	T	O
1	4	5

In the number 145, it is the hundreds that make the biggest contribution, so the number in the hundreds column is the first significant figure. The number that makes the next biggest contribution is in the tens column, so it is the second significant figure. The number in the ones column makes the least contribution and is the third significant figure.

> The first **significant figure** is the first non-zero digit needed to write the number. Zeros that are only included as place-fillers are not significant (e.g. 0.05), but trapped zeros are significant (e.g. 205).

INVESTIGATE

Use the digits 2, 7 and 5 to write as many whole numbers as you can.

How many different numbers can you make? Write them down from largest to smallest.

Include two-digit and one-digit numbers.

How many of your numbers are in the five times table?

ROUNDING NUMBERS

Rounding to the nearest hundred

Use the base-10 tiles to make any number between 100 and 200.

You will have one large square, and the tens and ones will start to fill a second large square.

If less than half the second large square is filled, then your number is nearer to 100 than 200.

If more than half the second large square is filled, then your number is nearer to 200 than 100.

When you round a number, you are trying to get to the nearest chosen multiple of ten. Here, you are trying to get to the nearest multiple of 100.

You can see from the diagram below that the number 163 is nearer to 200 than 100. 163 rounds up to 200 when rounded to the nearest hundred.

> The zeros do not count as significant here. They are only there to keep the digit 2 in the hundreds column.

200 is the result when 163 is rounded to one significant figure.

Now make 145 from base-10 tiles. Can you see that 145 is nearer to 100 than 200?

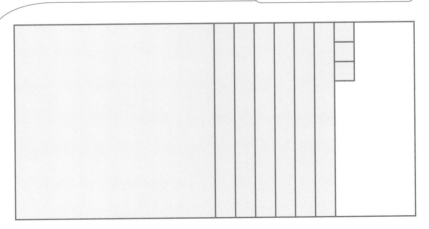

145 rounds down to 100 when rounded to the nearest hundred. 100 is the result when 145 is rounded to one significant figure.

ACTIVITY 2.1

Make two lists of whole numbers between 100 and 200. In the first list, write numbers that round up to 200 to the nearest hundred. In the second list, write numbers that round down to 100 to the nearest hundred.

How can you tell from the numbers whether to round up or down?

How much do the ones digits influence your decision?

Would you round 150 up or down to the nearest hundred?

Rounding to the nearest ten

The number 163 must round to either 160 or 170 to the nearest ten. It is nearer to 160, so we round down. You can see this on the number line below or by using base-10 tiles.

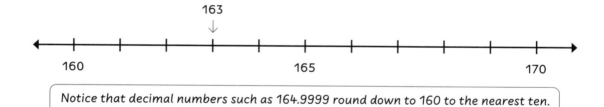

Notice that decimal numbers such as 164.9999 round down to 160 to the nearest ten.

Any number that is greater than 160 but less than 165 rounds down to 160 to the nearest ten.

Any number that is greater than or equal to 165 but less than 170 rounds up to 170 to the nearest ten.

Three-digit numbers rounded to the nearest ten are rounded to two significant figures. Both the hundreds digit and the tens digit are significant.

ACTIVITY 2.2

Round these numbers to the nearest ten.

Use the base-10 tiles if they help you.
Draw a number line if that is better for you.

Which method do you prefer when rounding numbers to the nearest ten? Base-10 tiles or number lines?

a) 168   c) 217   e) 65
b) 143   d) 1.7   f) 1249

Rounding using a viewer

You may prefer to use a viewer when rounding numbers; there is a template for one on page 282.

Place the viewer over the number you want to round. For example, to round 163 to the nearest ten, position the viewer so that the red window is over the ones digit (3) and the green window is over the tens digit (6, representing 60), as shown in the image to the right.

Look at the number in the red window. If it is five or more, then round the 60 up to 70. If it is four or less, then round down and leave the 60 as it is. Write the answer 160.

To round 163 to the nearest hundred, position the viewer so that the red window is over the tens digit (6, representing 60) and the green window is over the hundreds digit (1, representing 100).

Look at the number in the red window. If it is five or more, then round up. If it is four or less, then round down.

In this example, 163 rounded to the nearest hundred is 200.

A REMINDER OF ADDITION AND SUBTRACTION

To represent the addition 138 + 75, make the numbers 138 and 75 with the base-10 tiles. To find the total, put the small squares together, put the strips together, and put the large square on its own. You will have 13 small squares, ten strips and one large square.

You have enough small squares to exchange ten of them for a strip. You have enough strips to exchange ten of them for a square. You now have two large squares, one strip and three small squares, which represent 213.

You might be used to writing the calculation as a vertical addition. Notice the exchanged tiles are the numbers that are carried into the next column.

```
    1 3 8
+     7 5
  ─────────
    2 1 3
    1 1
```

To represent 145 - 58, make the number 145 using base-10 tiles. See what is left when you take away 58.

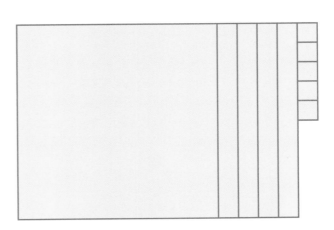

You do not have enough small squares to take away eight, so exchange one of the strips for ten small squares, giving you 15 small squares all together. Now you can take away eight of the squares, leaving you with seven squares. To take away five strips, you need to exchange the large square for ten strips, giving you 13 strips all together. When you take away five strips from the 13 strips, there are eight strips remaining.

You can write the calculation as a vertical subtraction, like this:

$$4 \ \ ^{1}\cancel{4}^{3} \ ^{1}5$$
$$- \ \ \ \ 5 \ \ 8$$
$$\overline{\ \ \ \ \ 8 \ \ 7}$$

> Make up subtraction (and addition) calculations of your own to represent with base-10 tiles. Make sure you understand the link between the written calculation and the tiles.

Representing bigger numbers

If you have 10 large squares, then they can be put together to make a large strip representing a thousand. Ten of these larger strips go together to make a bigger square (ten thousand) and 10 of these go together to make an even bigger strip...and so on. Starting with a 1 cm small square, a million of these would be a square 10 m wide and 10 m long! A billion 1 cm small squares would be 100 m wide and 1 km long – that's a very big base-10 tile!

Representing numbers less than one

You can use a square of any size to represent a whole. Use a large square from a set of base-10 equipment to represent 1 instead of 100. Now, each column represents one tenth of the whole, which is written as the decimal 0.1 or the fraction $\frac{1}{10}$. Break up each row and you will get the small squares that each represent one hundredth, which is written as 0.01 or $\frac{1}{100}$.

Break up one small square into 10 tiny strips that are 1 mm wide to make thousandths. Break up each tiny strip into small squares to make ten-thousandths.

> If you start with a giant square for a whole, the tiny strips and small squares may be easier to see!

MULTIPLYING AND DIVIDING BY POWERS OF TEN

People say 'add a nought' to multiply by 10. It depends on what they mean whether they are right or not!

'Adding a nought' like this 5 × 10 = 5 + 0 = 5 is wrong.

'Adding a nought' like this £1.25 × 10 = £1.250 is wrong too.

'Adding a nought' like this 5 × 10 = 50 is right, but why? The zero has pushed the 5 into the tens column, because each of the ones becomes a ten. If there were tens and hundreds, then each ten would become a hundred and each hundred would become a thousand. What matters is that the numbers move into the next column.

5 × 10 = 50
50 × 10 = 500
500 × 10 = 5000

For decimals, multiplying a tenth by 10 gives a whole, multiplying a hundredth by 10 gives a tenth and so on, so the numbers move into the next column in the same way as whole numbers.

$0.1 \times 10 = 1$
$0.01 \times 10 = 0.1$
$0.001 \times 10 = 0.01$

Multiplying by 100 moves the digits two columns; multiplying by a thousand moves the digits three columns, and so on.

So $2.35 \times 10 = 23.5$ and $2.35 \times 100 = 235$ and $2.35 \times 1000 = 2350$

You may find it helpful to use a place-value slider; there is a template for one on page 282.

Write the number you are multiplying on a strip of paper. Thread this number into the slider.

In this example, the number being multiplied is 265. Notice how the digits are lined up under the correct place-value headings.

HTh	TTh	Th	H	T	O	.	$\frac{1}{10}$
			2	6	5	.	

To multiply by 10, move the paper strip one place to the left.

HTh	TTh	Th	H	T	O	.	$\frac{1}{10}$
		2	6	5	0	.	

Now you can see that $265 \times 10 = 2650$

To divide by 10, move the paper strip one place to the right.

How many places would you move the paper strip if you were dividing by 100? By 1000?

Dividing by 10 makes the number 10 times smaller, as each ten becomes one, each one becomes a tenth, each tenth becomes a hundredth, and so on.

So $2.35 \div 10 = 0.235$ and $2.35 \div 100 = 0.0235$ and $2.35 \div 1000 = 0.00235$

ACTIVITY 2.3

Multiply and divide each number in the middle column by 10 and 100.
Do not use your answer for one calculation for the start of the next.

÷ 100	÷ 10	Number	× 10	× 100
		16		
		1.52		
		46.43		
		0.605 ←		
		0.0087		

Check your answers using a calculator.

> 0.605 has a 'trapped' zero. Treat numbers with one or more trapped zeros like any other number when multiplying and dividing by 10 and 100.

COMPARING AND ORDERING DECIMAL NUMBERS

When comparing two or more decimal numbers that are less than one, it is important to remember that the first decimal place represents tenths, which are 10 times bigger than hundredths. Begin by comparing the digits in the tenths place. If there are two numbers with the same tenths digit, compare the digits in the hundredths place, and so on.

Put 0.203, 0.2, 0.023, 0.23 and 0.25 in order from smallest to largest
Represent each number with base-10 tiles. Here is a sketch of the strips, small squares and tiny strips needed.

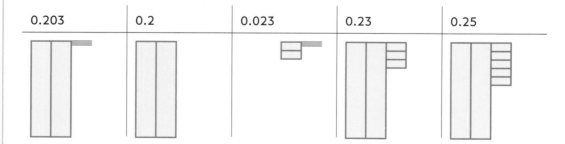

The numbers, arranged from smallest to largest, are 0.023; 0.2; 0.203; 0.23; 0.25

> Read the values (from left to right) as:
>
> nought point nought two three, nought point two, nought point two nought three, nought point two three, nought point two five

Money can be a false friend!

A false friend is something that can cause you to make a mistake.

In money calculations, you always give the answer as a whole number of pounds or as pounds and pence.

'Two pounds twenty-three pence' is written as £2.23; never £2.23p or 2.23p.

'Two pounds and two pence' is written as £2.02; never £2.20 because that would be 'two pounds twenty pence'.

When writing money, you have to make sure that the digits are put in the correct place-value columns.

You might find it helpful to think of the columns in money calculations like this.

hundreds	tens	ones	tenths	hundredths	thousandths
£100 notes (there aren't any of these in the real world!)	£10 notes	£1 coins	10p coins	1p coins	fractions (tenths) of a penny

Fractions of a penny are best rounded to the nearest penny at the end of a calculation.

ACTIVITY 2.4

1. Write each list of numbers in order, starting with the smallest.

a) 5.5; 0.55; 0.505; 0.50   c) 0.1; 0.99; 0.099; 0.0999

b) 0.705; 0.075; 0.570; 0.75

2. Insert the sign = (equals), < (less than) or > (more than) between these pairs of numbers to make a true statement.

a) 007 ☐ 7   c) 0.45 ☐ 0.045   e) 001.1000 ☐ 1.1

b) 0.750 ☐ 0.75   d) 00.02 ☐ 0.2   f) 0.03 ☐ 0.000 300

ROUNDING DECIMAL NUMBERS

Sometimes a calculator gives an answer to a lot of decimal places. The answer might be more useful if it were given to the nearest tenth (1 decimal place) or hundredth (2 decimal places).

Round 1.248 to 1 decimal place
Use base-10 tiles to represent the number.

You can see that 1.248 is more than one whole and two strips but less than one whole and three strips. The tiny strips make no difference to the way the number is rounded.

Less than half of the last strip is used, so round down.

Answer: 1.248 is 1.2 (to 1 dp) ⟵————————————— | dp stands for decimal place.

You might prefer to use a number line to round decimal numbers. Each of the divisions on this number line is for the digit in the second decimal place. 1.248 is less than the halfway number (1.25) so it rounds down to 1.2 (1 dp).

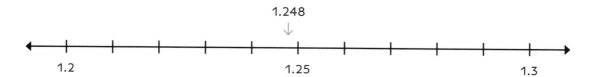

How would you use a place-value slider for rounding 1.248 to 1 decimal place? Which numbers would you be looking at through the windows of the slider?
  You can round 8.52094 to 2 decimal places in the same way. You might find it helps to cover up the end of the number so that only 2 decimal places are visible, which gives 8.52. The only other possibility is to round to 8.53. However, the rest of the decimal is very small, not enough to get to 8.521, so 8.52094 rounds down to 8.52 (to 2 dp).

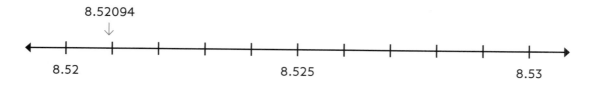

When rounding 0.499785 to 2 decimal places, one option is 0.49 and the other option is 0.50. Round 0.499785 up to 0.50 (to 2 dp) and for once the zero on the end, in the hundredths place, is important. The zero does not change the position of the other digits in the number but it shows that the number is accurate to 2 decimal places and not 1 decimal place.

ACTIVITY 2.5

1. Round these numbers to the given number of decimal places. Use base-10 tiles, a number line or a viewer to help you. Which method do you prefer?

a) 0.267 (1 dp)   c) 2.6109 (2 dp)   e) 0.1499 (3 dp)

b) 0.564 (2 dp)   d) 6.05191 (3 dp)

2. Round 0.149 to 2 decimal places. Round the answer to 1 decimal place. Compare the answer with the result of rounding 0.149 to 1 decimal place. What do you notice?

ADDING AND SUBTRACTING DECIMAL NUMBERS

Earlier in this chapter (see the section 'A reminder of addition and subtraction', page 83) you saw how to make representations of the calculations 138 + 75 and 145 - 58 using base-10 tiles. If the large square were a whole instead, the same representations would represent 1.38 + 0.75 and 1.45 - 0.58.

You also looked at 138 + 75 presented as a vertical addition and 145 - 58 presented as a vertical subtraction. The same idea of lining up the digits in the correct columns works for 1.38 + 0.75 and 1.45 - 0.58 too.

The digits in these   are aligned just like the digits in these

```
    1  3  8        4  ¹4̸³ ¹5            1 . 3  8         4 . ¹4̸³ ¹5
 +     7  5      -    5  8           + 0 . 7  5        - 0 . 5  8
    2  1  3           8  7             2 . 1  3          0 . 8  7
    1  1                               1     1
```

Work out 5 + 2.7 + 0.375
You could represent each number with base-10 tiles, using the large squares for the whole numbers. You would need seven large squares (5 + 2), and then some strips and small squares to represent the decimal parts. The decimal parts are shown in the diagram on the right.

There are five tiny strips, seven small squares and enough strips to make a large square with no additional strips.
All together that is 7 + 1.075 = 8.075

Written as a vertical addition, 5 + 2.7 + 0.375 would look like this, with the whole numbers aligned in the first column.

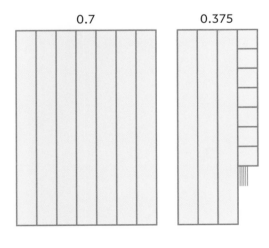

```
      5
      2 . 7
 +    0 . 3 7 5
   _____
```

Some people like to make all the columns the same width because it looks neater. They insert a decimal point and three zeros at the end of the top line. They insert two zeros at the end of the middle line and insert a decimal point in the answer space, aligned with the existing decimal points. They then add the numbers like whole numbers.

```
      5 . 0 0 0              5 . 0 0 0
      2 . 7 0 0              2 . 7 0 0
  +   0 . 3 7 5          +   0 . 3 7 5
  _____              8 . 0 7 5
          .                    1
```

MULTIPLYING DECIMAL NUMBERS

Look at this grid of calculations. Look for a pattern in the arrangement. What do you notice?

300 × 5 = 1500	300 × 50 = 15 000	300 × 500 = 150 000
30 × 5 = 150	30 × 50 = 1500	30 × 500 = 15 000
3 × 5 = 15	3 × 50 = 150	3 × 500 = 1500

> You can check these calculations are correct by thinking about repeated addition.

For any of the whole-number calculations in the grid, you can work out 3 × 5 and multiply the answer by the right number of tens. For example, to work out 30 × 500, think of 3 × 10 × 5 × 100, then shuffle the order to get 3 × 5 × 10 × 100, to give 15 × 1000 = 15,000.

> You can multiply the numbers in a multiplication in any order — the answer will always be the same. This is called the commutative property of multiplication.

The grid below extends the pattern to include decimal numbers. Think of each calculation as 3 × 5 after the digits have been multiplied or divided by 10 or 100.

300 × 0.05 = 15	300 × 0.5 = 150	300 × 5 = 1500	300 × 50 = 15 000	300 × 500 = 150 000
30 × 0.05 = 1.5	30 × 0.5 = 15	30 × 5 = 150	30 × 50 = 1500	30 × 500 = 15 000
3 × 0.05 = 0.15	3 × 0.5 = 1.5	3 × 5 = 15	3 × 50 = 150	3 × 500 = 1500
0.3 × 0.05 = 0.015	0.3 × 0.5 = 0.15	0.3 × 5 = 1.5	0.3 × 50 = 15	0.3 × 500 = 150
0.03 × 0.05 = 0.0015	0.03 × 0.5 = 0.015	0.03 × 5 = 0.15	0.03 × 50 = 1.5	0.03 × 500 = 15

For example, 0.3 × 0.05 = (3 ÷ 10) × (5 ÷ 100). This gives the same answer as 3 × 5 ÷ 1000 = 0.015

> You could compare the calculation with 3 × 5 = 15 and say 'but I must make the digit 3 smaller by one place and make the digit 5 smaller by two places. Therefore, I must make 15 smaller by a total of three places.'

ACTIVITY 2.6

1. Work out these multiplications without a calculator.

a) 2 × 80   c) 0.02 × 3   e) 0.002 × 5   g) 0.6 × 0.7   i) 60 × 0.7

b) 5 × 0.5   d) 3 × 0.007   f) 0.4 × 0.2   h) 0.7 × 0.09   j) 0.09 × 8000

2. Rewrite all the multiplications in Question 1 as division statements. For example, part a) gives 160 ÷ 2 = 80 and 160 ÷ 80 = 2.

Using the grid method for multiplying decimal numbers

 Rewind – look at page 64 for Napier's bones and the grid method for multiplication

The grid method automatically keeps the digits in the correct place-value columns when multiplying numbers. A decimal point can be inserted into a grid so that you can see which columns the digits of a decimal calculation go in.

Work out 3 × 0.5

Draw a multiplication grid like this. Notice that the decimal point is inserted after the ones column and all the decimal points are aligned.

Watch out that you do not make a mistake in the nought times table!

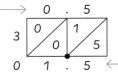

Notice that multiplying by 0.5 makes 3 smaller. You have found half of three.

Work out 1.7 × 0.23

Put the numbers on the outside of a grid and insert a decimal point in line with the decimal points in the numbers being multiplied. Numbers above and to the left of the diagonal line with the point are whole numbers and those below and right of the diagonal line are decimals.

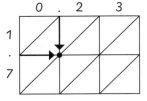

Complete the grid and make sure the columns that are after the decimal point in the grid are after the decimal point in the answer.

To check your work, you could round 1.7 to 2 and round 0.23 to 0.2. The easier calculation 2 × 0.2 = 0.4 is close to 0.391, so the answer is likely to be correct. A check like this will show if you have made a mistake with the postion of the decimal point in the grid.

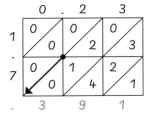

ACTIVITY 2.7

1. Use the grid method to work out these calculations.
Use a calculator to check your answers.

a) 0.27 × 9

b) 0.5 × 3.8

c) 0.7 × 38

d) 2.6 × 6.5

e) 0.87 × 7.3

> If you have the correct digits but the wrong size of number, look again at where the decimal point is on your grid.

2. Make up some similar calculations of your own and check the answers using a calculator.

DIVIDING NUMBERS

Dividing whole numbers

A division such as 150 ÷ 4 can be done using the grid method.

Notice there is a remainder of 2 in the answer. Instead of leaving a remainder, the 2 whole ones can be exchanged for 20 tenths, which can be divided by 4 to give 5 tenths. You can write these 5 tenths above the grid after the whole-number answer. The completed grid is shown on the right.

Some division calculations might need more squares in the grid, and some divisions could keep going for ever. (These are called recurring decimals.)

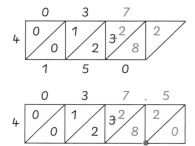

> Notice you can think of the number to be divided as 150.0 and the decimal point in the top row lines up with the decimal point in the bottom row.

Dividing a decimal number by a whole number

Sometimes the number to be divided is already a decimal. Put the decimal points you know already into the grid and use the method exactly as before.

Here is the starting grid and the final grid for 6.52 ÷ 5

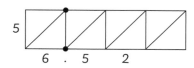

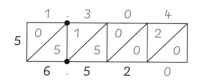

ACTIVITY 2.8

Work out these divisions. Two of them give recurring decimals – which two?

a) 64 ÷ 5   c) 2 ÷ 3   e) 2.73 ÷ 3   g) 0.75 ÷ 6   i) 0.419 ÷ 2

b) 20 ÷ 8   d) 18.2 ÷ 7   f) 14.9 ÷ 7   h) 0.385 ÷ 7   j) 1.81818 ÷ 9

Dividing by a decimal number

Dividing by a decimal is hard! It is easier to change the division to another calculation which gives the same answer and then divide by a whole number instead.

The calculation 0.6 ÷ 0.3 asks the question 'How many lots of 0.3 are there in 0.6?' 0.6 can be represented by six strips and you can make two groups of 0.3 with them. So, 0.6 ÷ 0.3 = 2. A similar calculation that gives the same answer is 6 ÷ 3. Both the 6 and 3 are 10 times bigger than the original numbers, so the answer is the same because there are two lots of three in six.

You can use this method for any division by a decimal. Notice how you make a whole number from the decimal and make the same change to the number you want to divide. Then, use the grid method to find the answer.

Work out 0.64 ÷ 0.4

Multiply both numbers by 10 so that 0.4 becomes a whole number. This gives 6.4 ÷ 4 as a calculation with the same answer as 0.64 ÷ 0.4. The grid looks like this.

So, 0.64 ÷ 0.4 = 1.6. Notice this says you need one 0.4 and part of another 0.4, which seems right.

> Dividing by a number less than one gives an answer which is bigger than the number being divided.

> It doesn't matter that 6.4 is not a whole number. You have a method to deal with that!

Work out 2.4 ÷ 0.02

Multiply both numbers by 100 to make two whole numbers. This gives 240 ÷ 2 as a calculation with the same answer as 2.4 ÷ 0.02. So, 2.4 ÷ 0.02 = 120.

Is the answer reasonable? 0.02 is represented by a pair of small squares and 100 of these would be enough to make two large squares (which is 2). Another 20 pairs of small squares is 40 small squares (enough squares to make four strips, which is 0.4). Therefore, 120 is the correct answer to the division.

ACTIVITY 2.9

Work out these calculations. Use base-10 tiles if you would find these helpful.

a) 0.8 ÷ 0.4

c) 10.4 ÷ 0.8

e) 22.5 ÷ 0.09

b) 15.5 ÷ 0.5

d) 1.848 ÷ 0.07

CHAPTER SUM-UP

Reflection

Having worked through this chapter, how do you feel about these skills?

Skill	I have tried this	I need more practice	I am confident with this
Understanding the place value of whole numbers			
Rounding numbers to the nearest ten, hundred, and so on			
Multiplying and dividing by powers of ten			
Comparing and ordering decimal numbers			
Rounding decimal numbers			
Adding and subtracting decimal numbers			
Multiplying decimal numbers			
Dividing a decimal number by a whole number			
Dividing by a decimal number			

Quiz

Put these calculations in order of size of the answer – the one with the smallest answer first.

a) 0.0025 × 10

e) 0.4 × 0.49

b) 24 ÷ 100

f) 0.057 ÷ 0.03

c) 0.0526 + 0.147

d) 0.124 + 0.09

3. Multiples, Factors and Primes

 Rewind – look at page 64 for using Napier's bones for multiplication
look at page 92 for division

MULTIPLES

The multiples of 7 are 7, 14, 21, 28, 35 ...
The list could go on for ever.

> Notice the list starts with the number itself.

> The **multiples** of a number are all the numbers that are products of the number and any other integer.

ACTIVITY 3.1

Write down the first five multiples of these numbers. Use Napier's bones to help if you wish.

a) 3   b) 8   c) 12   d) 20   e) 21   f) 240

Lowest common multiple

Find the lowest common multiple (LCM) of 20 and 12

Write the first few multiples for each number. Look for the first number that is in both lists.

The multiples of 20 are 20, 40, 60, 80, 100 …

The multiples of 12 are 12, 24, 36, 48, 60 …

Answer: The LCM of 20 and 12 is 60

The **lowest common multiple (LCM)** of two numbers is the smallest multiple that is common to both.

You don't know how far to go. You may have to go back and put in more multiples.

You can stop once you get to 60 because it is also in the list of multiples of 20.

The LCM is often a big number!

ACTIVITY 3.2

Find the LCM for these pairs of numbers.

a) 4 and 6

b) 24 and 32

c) 75 and 100

d) 20 and 100

e) 21 and 28

f) 17 and 10

FACTORS

Find the factors of 15

To explore the factors of 15, put 15 counters in a row. This arrangement shows that 15 = 1 × 15, so 1 and 15 are factors of 15.

Factors are numbers you multiply together to make another number. For example, 3 and 5 are factors of 15.

Try to put the counters into two equal rows. You can't make equal rows, so 2 is not a factor of 15.

Try to put the counters into three equal rows. Each row has five counters. This shows that 15 = 3 × 5, so 3 and 5 are factors of 15.

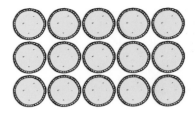

Try to put the counters into four equal rows. You will have counters left over, so 4 is not a factor of 15.

The next number to try is 5, but you already know that 5 is a factor of 15, so you do not have to go any further.

Answer: The set of factors of 15 is {1, 3, 5, 15}

You can keep track of the factors on a diagram (a sunshine diagram)
Write 15 in a circle and put 1 and 15 opposite each other to show they are a factor pair.

Put in another two lines for 3 and 5.

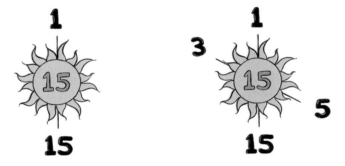

Some numbers, such as 72, have a lot of factors. Find all the factors of 72.

Start the sunshine diagram with 1 and 72 opposite each other.

Check if 2 is a factor of 72. It is, so put 2 on your sunshine diagram with its partner opposite.

Check if 3 and 4 are factors of 72. They are, so add them and their partners to your sunshine diagram.

5 leaves a remainder, so is not a factor of 72.

6 is a factor of 72 and its partner is 12.

7 is not a factor of 72.

8 is a factor of 72 and its partner is 9.

You do not need to check 9 as it is already on your sunshine diagram.

Your sunshine diagram is now complete, with all the factors of 72 shown.

The set of factors of 72 is {1, 2, 3, 4, 6, 8, 9, 12, 18, 24, 36, 72}

People often miss the bigger factors. Putting them in pairs makes it easier to get a complete list.

ACTIVITY 3.3

1. Draw diagrams and write the set of factors for these numbers.

a) 24   c) 64   e) 77

b) 42   d) 84   f) 45

2. Write lists of factors for some more odd numbers.

What do you notice?

How can this help you to learn your times tables?

CLASS GAME

Version 1

- Each player chooses a number between 10 and 100 and writes a list of its factors.
- All players stand up.
- One player rolls a six-sided dice. Sit down if the number rolled is a factor of your number.
- Repeat until there is only one player left standing. This player is the winner.

What happens if 1 is rolled?

Play several games. Are there tactics you can use to win?

Version 2

Change the rules so that rolling a 1 means you must sit down if your number is a prime number.

Are you going to change your tactics?

Square numbers

Arrange 16 counters to make as many rectangles as you can. What do you notice? Repeat with 36 counters.

    Most numbers have an even number of factors. Why?

    Square numbers have an odd number of factors. This is because in one pair of factors, the number is the same.

> **Square numbers** are made by multiplying a number by itself. A square number of counters can be arranged in a square.

ACTIVITY 3.4

Colour all the square numbers on a multiplication square. What do you notice?

Highest common factor

Find the highest common factor (HCF) of 15 and 72
Draw a factor diagram or list the factors of each number.
Underline the numbers which appear in both diagrams.
The HCF will be the largest number you have underlined.

> The **highest common factor (HCF)** of two numbers is the largest number which is a factor of both numbers.

Answer: The HCF of 15 and 72 is 3

> Notice the HCF might not be a high number!

ACTIVITY 3.5

Find the HCF for these pairs of numbers.

a) 4 and 6

b) 24 and 32

c) 75 and 100

d) 20 and 100

e) 21 and 28

f) 17 and 10

INVESTIGATE

The numbers in Activity 3.2 and Activity 3.5 are the same. Put your answers in a table like this.

Start numbers	Lowest common multiple (LCM)	Highest common factor (HCF)	Product
4 and 6			
24 and 32			
75 and 100			
20 and 100			
21 and 28			
17 and 10			

Use a calculator to work out the product of the two numbers. Can you see a connection?

> Multiply numbers to work out the **product**.

> Work out the product by multiplying together each pair of start numbers.

PRIME NUMBERS

If a number is in another times table, it is not a prime number.

> A **prime number** has only two factors, 1 and itself.

ACTIVITY 3.6

Print a copy of the grid of numbers 1 to 100 (page 280).

Put a square round number 1 – it is a square number.

Put a circle round 2 – it is a prime number. Shade all the multiples of 2 in the square.

1	2	3	4	5	6	7	8	9	10
11	12	13	14	15	16	17	18	19	20
21	22	23	24	25	26	27	28	29	30
31	32	33	34	35	36	37	38	39	40
41	42	43	44	45	46	47	48	49	50
51	52	53	54	55	56	57	58	59	60
61	62	63	64	65	66	67	68	69	70
71	72	73	74	75	76	77	78	79	80
81	82	83	84	85	86	87	88	89	90
91	92	93	94	95	96	97	98	99	100

The smallest number not shaded is 3. 3 is a prime number. Shade all the multiples of 3.

1	2	3	4	5	6	7	8	9	10
11	12	13	14	15	16	17	18	19	20
21	22	23	24	25	26	27	28	29	30
31	32	33	34	35	36	37	38	39	40
41	42	43	44	45	46	47	48	49	50
51	52	53	54	55	56	57	58	59	60
61	62	63	64	65	66	67	68	69	70
71	72	73	74	75	76	77	78	79	80
81	82	83	84	85	86	87	88	89	90
91	92	93	94	95	96	97	98	99	100

Some of them are shaded already but that does not matter.

Repeat with the next smallest number that is not shaded (5), and the next, and the next and so on until there are no more numbers to shade.

The unshaded numbers are all prime numbers. List them. Notice they do not follow a pattern.

PRIME FACTORIZATION

If a number is not a prime number, it is the answer to two or more prime numbers multiplied together. Finding the set of numbers is called prime factorization. Choose which of these two methods you prefer.

Method 1: Factor trees

Write 120 as the product of prime factors
Write 120 at the top of your page. Now, think of a pair of numbers that multiply together to make 120. Draw two branches from 120 and write the numbers you thought of, one number under each branch.

Split these numbers into factors until each branch ends in a prime number.

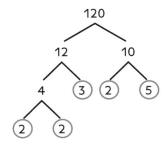

Circle all the prime numbers.

Answer: The prime factorization of 120 is 2 × 2 × 2 × 3 × 5

You can use powers to write the answer 2 × 2 × 2 × 3 × 5 more neatly

$120 = 2^3 × 3 × 5$

> Remember $2^3 = 2 × 2 × 2$

ACTIVITY 3.7

Draw another factor tree for 120, starting with 120 = 3 × 40 as the first step. How many different versions of this factor tree can you draw? What do you notice about the answer?

Method 2: Factor ladders
Some people prefer to find the factors in the right order.

Decide whether 2 is a factor of 120. If it is, then complete the division.

2	1	2	0
	6	0	

Continue dividing until the answer is an odd number.

2	1	2	0
2	6	0	
	3	0	

2	1	2	0
2	6	0	
2	3	0	
	1	5	

Then, divide the odd prime numbers in order until you get to 1 at the bottom of the ladder.

> *Only use numbers that divide exactly.*

2	1	2	0
	2	6	0
	2	3	0
	3	1	5
			5

2	1	2	0
	2	6	0
	2	3	0
	3	1	5
	5	5	
		1	

> *Some people draw these ladders going up instead of down.*

The numbers on the outside of the ladder are the prime factors and you write
$120 = 2^3 \times 3 \times 5$

ACTIVITY 3.8

Write these numbers as the product of prime factors. Use factor trees or factor ladders. Which method do you prefer?

a) 70   b) 72   c) 80   d) 88   e) 375

CHAPTER SUM-UP

Reflection

Having worked through this chapter, how do you feel about these skills?

Skill	I have tried this	I need more practice	I am confident with this
Finding multiples of a number			
Finding the lowest common multiple of two numbers			
Knowing what the factors of a number are and how to find them			
Knowing what a square number is			
Finding the highest common factor of two numbers			
Knowing what a prime number is			
Writing a number as the product of prime factors			

Quiz

Which is the biggest answer?

a) The prime number that is between 90 and 100
b) The HCF of 270 and 630
c) The LCM of 32 and 48

4. Fractions

◀◀ **Rewind** – look at page 89 for the addition, subtraction, multiplication and division of decimals

▶▶ **Fast forward** – look at page 125 for converting between fractions, decimals and percentages

FRACTIONS ARE PARTS OF A WHOLE

Like decimals, fractions are used to describe amounts between one whole number and the next.

A fraction consists of two numbers: one above and one below a horizontal line.

*The **numerator** of a fraction tells you how many of the parts indicated by the denominator you have. It is written above the horizontal line.*

$$\frac{1}{2}$$

*The **denominator** of a fraction tells you into how many equal parts a whole has been divided. The number is written below the horizontal line.*

EQUIVALENT FRACTIONS

This square represents one whole. It is split into three equal parts and $\frac{1}{3}$ of the square is shaded.

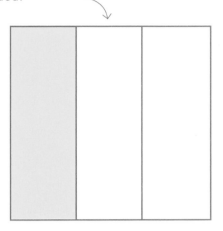 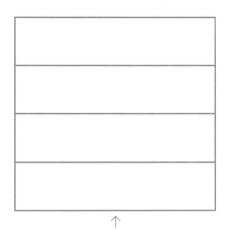

This is the fraction grid for quarters.

This diagram shows the effect when the two fraction grids are printed onto acetate and placed on top of each other. The shaded area seems to be made up of more, smaller parts. These parts can be described using other fractions.

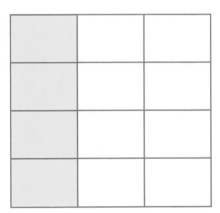

You can see that the same amount of shaded area can be described as $\frac{1}{3}$ or $\frac{4}{12}$

$\frac{1}{3}$ and $\frac{4}{12}$ are equivalent fractions.

> **Equivalent fractions** may look different but they represent the same value.

ACTIVITY 4.1

1. Use a set of fraction grids (see page 283) to find as many ways of describing $\frac{1}{3}$ as you can.

Write your answer in this format $\frac{1}{3} = \frac{4}{12} = \frac{\square}{\square} =$

2. Make a chain of fractions that are equivalent to $\frac{2}{3}$

Write your answer in this format $\frac{2}{3} = \frac{\Box}{\Box} = \frac{\Box}{\Box}$

3. Draw a 7 cm square, which is the same size as your fraction grids. Divide the square into equal parts.

Shade some of the parts. Write down the fraction of the square you have shaded.

INVESTIGATE

Use any of your other fraction grids to find as many equivalent fractions as you can.

Describe any patterns you can see in the numbers.

Using a multiplication square or Napier's bones to find equivalent fractions

It is important you understand that equivalent fractions are fractions with different numbers representing the same size part.

You can see the numbers for equivalent fractions on a multiplication square. For example, look at the numbers 3 and 4. Imagine these numbers as the fraction $\frac{3}{4}$. The other numbers in the same rows give the fractions equivalent to $\frac{3}{4}$

$$\frac{3}{4} = \frac{6}{8} = \frac{9}{12} = \frac{12}{16} = \frac{15}{20} = \frac{18}{24} =$$

Here you can see the numbers for the equivalent fractions.

Use the fraction grids to check whether this idea works for all the fractions you can see or imagine.

The numbers do not have to be next to each other on the multiplication square.

A similar method using Napier's bones works in the same way. Put the 1-bone next to another bone. Find both numbers in the fraction on the 1-bone. The numbers in the same rows on the other bone give an equivalent fraction.

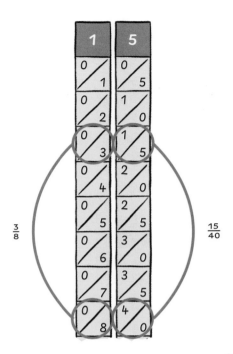

$\frac{3}{8}$ $\frac{15}{40}$

Using movement

If you like to use movement to learn, then imagine a fraction on your body – the numerator on your left shoulder and the denominator on your left hip. Point to this shoulder and hip. As you move your hands across to your other shoulder and hip, think of each part being cut into the same number of pieces, so the numerator and denominator are multiplied by the same number.

The diagram on the right represents the movement and the end result.

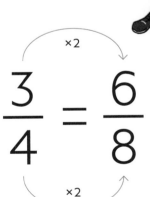

> When you place the $\frac{1}{2}$ fraction grid over the $\frac{3}{4}$ diagram, you get twice as many pieces.

$$\frac{3}{4} = \frac{6}{8}$$

×2

×2

> And twice as many in the whole as well.

FRACTIONS AS DIVISIONS

If Chloe, Jasprit, Maddie and Oli share three varieties of pizza equally, each person gets a quarter of each variety.

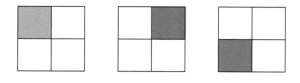

Mushroom   Cheese and tomato   Vegetarian

Chloe puts all her pieces of pizza on one plate. Can you see that Chloe has $\frac{3}{4}$ of a whole pizza?

A division sign ÷ even looks like a fraction, with dots where the numbers go!

Divide this number...

...by this number.

Remember that the denominator is the number to **divide** by.

SIMPLIFYING FRACTIONS

You have seen that there are lots of ways of writing fractions for the same amount. When you have found the equivalent fraction using the smallest possible numbers, you have simplified the fraction.

$\frac{6}{8}$ of this square is shaded.

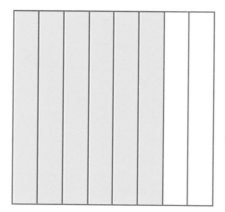

Lay other fraction grids on top of this square, with the lines running in the same direction. For most grids, the shaded area covers some of the strips and a part of the next strip. The fraction grid for $\frac{1}{4}$ fits exactly over the lines and the shaded area is exactly three of the strips. So, you can simplify $\frac{6}{8} = \frac{3}{4}$

Notice how exactly seven and a half of the tenths strips fit the shaded area and we know that $\frac{3}{4} = 0.75$.

Using Napier's bones or a multiplication square to simplify fractions

Napier's bones or a multiplication square can help you to simplify fractions. 6 and 8 (the digits from $\frac{6}{8}$) are both in the two times table, so place the 2-bone on the left and the 1-bone on the right. The numbers in the same rows as 6 and 8 are 3 and 4, so $\frac{6}{8} = \frac{3}{4}$

Using a multiplication square, look for a column with both 6 and 8 in it, then note down the numbers that are in the same rows of the one times table.

$\frac{6}{8} = \frac{3}{4}$

Using movement

As you move your hands from one side of your body to the other, imagine the numerator and the denominator being divided by the same number.

The diagram represents the movement and the end result.

When you lift the $\frac{1}{2}$ fraction grid off the $\frac{3}{4}$ diagram, you have half as many pieces.

And half as many in the whole as well.

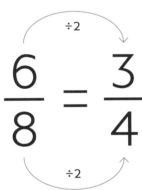

$$\frac{6}{8} = \frac{3}{4}$$

÷2

÷2

ACTIVITY 4.2

Lowest terms means the fraction will not simplify any more.

Simplify these fractions to their lowest terms.

a) $\frac{2}{4}$

b) $\frac{7}{14}$

c) $\frac{5}{15}$

d) $\frac{12}{18}$

e) $\frac{40}{90}$

f) $\frac{9}{21}$

g) $\frac{12}{60}$

h) $\frac{49}{56}$

i) $\frac{55}{88}$

j) $\frac{0.5}{1.5}$

Hint: Try multiplying to get whole numbers first.

INVESTIGATE

You have seen that if you multiply or divide the numerator and the denominator of a fraction by the same number you get an equivalent fraction.

Can you produce equivalent fractions by adding the same number to the numerator and the denominator of a fraction?

Use the fraction grids to see if $\frac{3}{5}$ and $\frac{4}{6}$ are equivalent. Try adding other numbers and other fractions.

What about subtraction?

USING A CALCULATOR FOR FRACTIONS

Find the fraction key on your calculator. It is easiest to work with a calculator that displays fractions that look like fractions (some older calculators do not). Find out how to key fractions into your calculator.

ACTIVITY 4.3

Repeat Activity 4.2 using your calculator. Just key in the fraction and press the equals key.

TOP-HEAVY FRACTIONS AND MIXED NUMBERS

If four people share five pizzas equally, then each person has more than a whole pizza.

> A **top-heavy fraction** is a fraction where the numerator is bigger than the denominator. There are more parts than you need to make a whole.

You might decide to divide the pizzas into quarters, so that each person gets five quarters ($\frac{5}{4}$) of a pizza.

$\frac{5}{4}$ is a top-heavy fraction. Top-heavy fractions are also called improper fractions.

Or, you might decide to give each person a whole pizza and just cut the last pizza into quarters to share it equally among four people. In this case, each person gets one and a quarter ($1\frac{1}{4}$) pizzas.

> A **mixed number** is a whole number and a fraction. The whole number and the fraction are added together. A mixed number is a top-heavy fraction that has been split into whole numbers and fractions.

$1\frac{1}{4}$ is a mixed number.

Changing a top-heavy fraction to a mixed number
Using fraction grids, you can represent $\frac{7}{2}$ as seven halves.

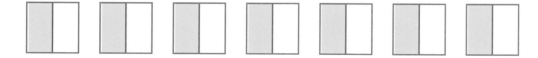

Two halves put together make a whole. So, there are enough halves to make three wholes, with one half left over.

So $\frac{7}{2} = 3\frac{1}{2}$

Notice this process is the same as division.

$\frac{7}{2} = 7 \div 2$, which has the answer 3 remainder 1. The 'remainder 1' is one half left over.

In the same way, in $\frac{18}{4}$ there are enough quarters to make four wholes, with two quarters left over.

> *Always draw or think about the parts of a whole. Don't just do tricks with numbers!*

You can also combine the two quarters left over to make a half, so $\frac{18}{4} = 4\frac{2}{4} = 4\frac{1}{2}$

Changing a mixed number to a top-heavy fraction

Change $4\frac{2}{3}$ to a top-heavy fraction

Draw a diagram to represent $4\frac{2}{3}$

The fraction part is in thirds, so divide each whole number into thirds to match. Count the thirds.

There are three thirds in each whole and an extra two thirds.

Answer: $4\frac{2}{3} = \frac{14}{3}$

ACTIVITY 4.4

1. Draw diagrams to change these top-heavy fractions to mixed numbers.

> *Use the fraction grids to help if you want to be exact. Or make sketches if you prefer.*

    a) $\frac{3}{2}$ c) $\frac{12}{5}$ e) $\frac{40}{9}$

    b) $\frac{7}{4}$ d) $\frac{17}{10}$

2. Draw diagrams to change these mixed numbers to top-heavy fractions.

    a) $3\frac{1}{2}$ b) $2\frac{1}{3}$ c) $5\frac{3}{4}$ d) $2\frac{7}{10}$ e) $5\frac{7}{8}$

Using your calculator

There will probably be a mixed number template on your calculator. It often shares a key with the fraction template. If you enter $1\frac{1}{2}$ without the template, the calculator will think you want to multiply 1 by $\frac{1}{2}$, and pressing the equals key will give the answer $\frac{1}{2}$. If you use the mixed number template for $1\frac{1}{2}$ and press the equals key, then the calculator will display $\frac{3}{2}$

Find the key on your calculator that turns $\frac{3}{2}$ back to $1\frac{1}{2}$ (you might have to use the Shift key).

Your calculator will also have a key that changes fraction answers into decimal answers. Make sure you know where this key is on your calculator. Pressing it twice should get you back to where you started.

FINDING A FRACTION OF A WHOLE NUMBER

Find $\frac{1}{4}$ of 20

You could begin with a fraction grid for quarters and shade $\frac{1}{4}$ of the square. Draw a total of 20 dots, sharing the dots equally between each quarter.

$\frac{1}{4}$ of 20 is the number of dots in the shaded section, which is 5.

Answer: $\frac{1}{4}$ of 20 = 5

From the fraction grid, you can work out $\frac{3}{4}$ of 20.

$\frac{3}{4}$ of 20 is the total number of dots in the unshaded sections, which is 15 dots.

Answer: $\frac{3}{4}$ of 20 = 15

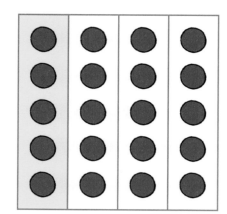

An alternative method is to draw a bar model instead.

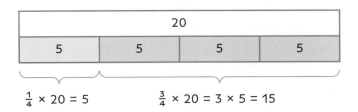

$\frac{1}{4} \times 20 = 5$ $\quad\quad$ $\frac{3}{4} \times 20 = 3 \times 5 = 15$

> You could call this a division bar model.

You can use a division bar model like this for any fraction calculation. Remember, the top bar represents the whole amount. The bottom bar represents the parts.

Find $\frac{5}{8}$ of 56

Draw a division bar model with eight parts.

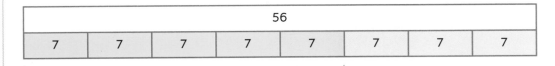

Put five parts together to give $\frac{5}{8}$ of 56

Answer: $\frac{5}{8}$ of 56 = 35

ACTIVITY 4.5

Work out these amounts.

a) $\frac{1}{2}$ of 18   c) $\frac{1}{3}$ of 36   e) $\frac{3}{8}$ of 64   g) $\frac{7}{10}$ of 90   i) $\frac{7}{6}$ of 12

b) $\frac{1}{4}$ of 24   d) $\frac{2}{5}$ of 45   f) $\frac{7}{12}$ of 48   h) $\frac{4}{7}$ of 14   j) $\frac{3}{4}$ of 10

MULTIPLYING FRACTIONS

You can multiply fractions together by using the word 'of' in place of the multiplication. Use fraction grids to work out your answers.

> When the word 'of' is used, the calculation is a multiplication.

Work out $\frac{1}{2} \times \frac{1}{4}$

Change the question to 'Work out $\frac{1}{2}$ of $\frac{1}{4}$'.

Use the fraction grid for quarters. Shade $\frac{1}{4}$ yellow.

Place the fraction grid for halves, with the lines running the other way round, on top of your fraction grid for quarters. Notice how half of the yellow part is now shaded blue.

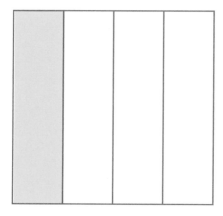 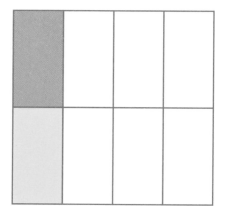

The blue section is one of eight equal parts in the whole square, so it is $\frac{1}{8}$

Answer: $\frac{1}{2} \times \frac{1}{4} = \frac{1}{8}$

INVESTIGATE

Find one quarter of one half. Copy the method used for working out $\frac{1}{2} \times \frac{1}{4}$

Is the answer the same?

Work out $\frac{1}{3} \times \frac{4}{5}$

Change the question to 'Work out $\frac{1}{3}$ of $\frac{4}{5}$'.

Shade $\frac{4}{5}$ of a square. Use the fraction grid for thirds the other way round.

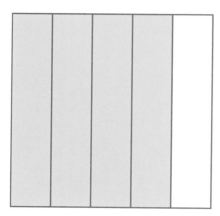 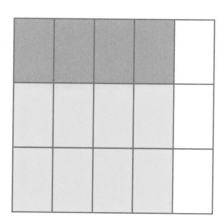

The blue section is 4 parts of the 15 parts in the whole square.

Answer: $\frac{1}{3} \times \frac{4}{5} = \frac{4}{15}$

Find $\frac{2}{5} \times \frac{3}{4}$

Shade $\frac{3}{4}$ of a square.

Use the fraction grid for fifths the other way round.

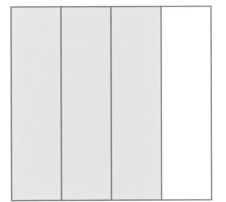 

The blue section is 6 parts out of the 20 parts in the whole square.

Answer: $\frac{2}{5} \times \frac{3}{4} = \frac{6}{20}$

You could rearrange the blue section and merge the parts together so that there are only 10 parts in the whole, of which 3 are shaded blue. Therefore, the answer simplifies to $\frac{3}{10}$

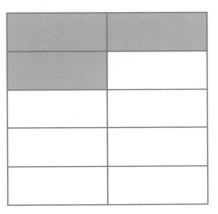

ACTIVITY 4.6

1. Use fraction grids to solve these fraction multiplications. Write down your answers and simplify them where possible.

a) $\frac{1}{2} \times \frac{1}{3}$ c) $\frac{1}{2} \times \frac{3}{5}$ e) $\frac{1}{10} \times \frac{7}{9}$ g) $\frac{3}{4} \times \frac{7}{8}$ i) $\frac{4}{5} \times \frac{3}{8}$

b) $\frac{1}{4} \times \frac{1}{4}$ d) $\frac{1}{5} \times \frac{3}{4}$ f) $\frac{2}{3} \times \frac{2}{5}$ h) $\frac{1}{2} \times \frac{4}{5}$ j) $\frac{3}{10} \times \frac{5}{12}$

2. Can you see a pattern in the unsimplified answers? Is there a pattern to which answers will simplify?

Keep using the diagrams until you are sure why the pattern works.

> *Some people look for tricks with the numbers. Some of these people get all the tricks mixed up, so keep drawing as long as you need to!*

DIVIDING BY A FRACTION

The division 6 ÷ 2 can be thought of as 'How many lots of two are there in six?'

To solve it, you could draw an addition bar model and see how many lots of two fit against the six.

6		
2	2	2

$6 \div 2 = 3$

Similarly, the division $6 \div \frac{1}{2}$ can be thought of as 'How many halves are there in six?'

Here is the addition bar model that will help you to find the answer.

6											
1		1		1		1		1		1	
$\frac{1}{2}$	$\frac{1}{2}$	$\frac{1}{2}$	$\frac{1}{2}$	$\frac{1}{2}$	$\frac{1}{2}$	$\frac{1}{2}$	$\frac{1}{2}$	$\frac{1}{2}$	$\frac{1}{2}$	$\frac{1}{2}$	$\frac{1}{2}$

The answer to $6 \div \frac{1}{2}$ is 12 and you could get the same answer by working out 6×2.

> If you watch episodes of a TV show that are half an hour long, you could watch 12 of them in six hours.

The division $\frac{1}{2} \div \frac{1}{10}$ is asking you: 'How many tenths are there in a half?'

If you put the tenths grid over the half grid, you can see there are five tenths, so $\frac{1}{2} \div \frac{1}{10} = 5$.

> Notice this is the same answer as $\frac{1}{2} \times 10$

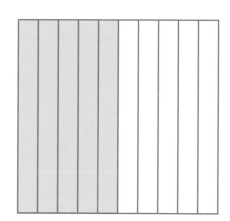

You could also have a bar model for one whole to represent this.

1									
$\frac{1}{2}$					$\frac{1}{2}$				
$\frac{1}{10}$	$\frac{1}{10}$	$\frac{1}{10}$	$\frac{1}{10}$	$\frac{1}{10}$	$\frac{1}{10}$	$\frac{1}{10}$	$\frac{1}{10}$	$\frac{1}{10}$	$\frac{1}{10}$

Here are the five tenths that make up one half, so $\frac{1}{2} \div \frac{1}{10} = 5$.

There are ten tenths in a whole, and half as many in a half. So $\frac{1}{2} \div \frac{1}{10} = 5$ gives the same answer.

The division $\frac{1}{2} \div \frac{1}{3}$ is asking you: 'How many thirds are there in a half?'

The answer is not a whole number. In the diagram below, half of the square is shaded and the thirds grid is put on top of it.

There are one and a half thirds in a half.
So $\frac{1}{2} \div \frac{1}{3} = 1\frac{1}{2}$, which is the same answer as $\frac{1}{2} \times 3$.

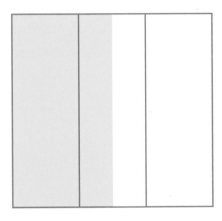

ACTIVITY 4.7

1. Rewrite these questions using the format 'how many lots of ___ are there in ___?' Use the fraction grids to help you work them out.

a) $1 \div \frac{1}{2}$

b) $1 \div \frac{1}{5}$

c) $4 \div \frac{1}{3}$

d) $\frac{1}{2} \div \frac{1}{8}$

e) $\frac{2}{3} \div \frac{1}{9}$

f) $\frac{3}{4} \div \frac{1}{6}$

2. Write down the multiplication you could do to get the same answers.

Another division example

When you think about the division $3 \div \frac{3}{4}$, you could ask yourself: 'How many lots of three quarters are there in three?'

The bar model to represent the problem looks like this. You can see from the third row that there are 12 quarters in 3.

3												
1				1				1				
$\frac{1}{4}$	$\frac{1}{4}$	$\frac{1}{4}$	$\frac{1}{4}$	$\frac{1}{4}$	$\frac{1}{4}$	$\frac{1}{4}$	$\frac{1}{4}$	$\frac{1}{4}$	$\frac{1}{4}$	$\frac{1}{4}$	$\frac{1}{4}$	
$\frac{3}{4}$			$\frac{3}{4}$			$\frac{3}{4}$			$\frac{3}{4}$			

You can see from the bottom row that there are four lots of three quarters in three.

Answer: $3 \div \frac{3}{4} = 4$

Another division example

When you think about the division $\frac{1}{2} \div \frac{3}{4}$, you could ask yourself: 'How many lots of three quarters are there in one half?' The answer will be less than one because three quarters is bigger than one half.

The bar model to represent the problem looks like this.

1			
$\frac{1}{2}$		$\frac{1}{2}$	
$\frac{1}{4}$	$\frac{1}{4}$	$\frac{1}{4}$	$\frac{1}{4}$
$\frac{3}{4}$			$\frac{1}{4}$

Looking at the dark blue part of the bar model, you can see that you need two thirds of three quarters to make a half.

Answer: $\frac{1}{2} \div \frac{3}{4} = \frac{2}{3}$

ACTIVITY 4.8

Draw bar models to work out these fraction divisions.

a) $6 \div \frac{3}{4}$ b) $4 \div \frac{2}{3}$ c) $\frac{3}{4} \div \frac{3}{8}$ d) $\frac{1}{10} \div \frac{2}{5}$ e) $1 \div \frac{7}{8}$

Check you can use your calculator to multiply and divide fractions. Does your calculator display the answers in a way you can understand?

ADDING AND SUBTRACTING FRACTIONS

Adding and subtracting fractions with the same denominators

Adding and subtracting fractions is easier when you say the calculations in words.

For example, 'two quarters plus one quarter is three quarters'. The equivalent subtraction fact in words is 'three quarters take away one quarter is two quarters'.

When written as $\frac{2}{4} + \frac{1}{4} = \frac{3}{4}$ and $\frac{3}{4} - \frac{1}{4} = \frac{2}{4}$ the calculations look much more difficult!

1			
$\frac{1}{4}$	$\frac{1}{4}$	$\frac{1}{4}$	$\frac{1}{4}$

When you add fractions with the same denominator, you are just adding more parts of the same fraction.

For example, $\frac{1}{8} + \frac{5}{8} = \frac{6}{8}$ can be shown as a bar model. There are six shaded pieces out of eight in a whole. The fraction is $\frac{6}{8}$, which is $\frac{3}{4}$ when simplified.

1							
$\frac{1}{8}$	$\frac{1}{8}$	$\frac{1}{8}$	$\frac{1}{8}$	$\frac{1}{8}$	$\frac{1}{8}$	$\frac{1}{8}$	$\frac{1}{8}$

When you subtract fractions with the same denominator, you are just taking away parts of the original fraction.

This bar model shows that $\frac{7}{10} - \frac{3}{10} = \frac{4}{10}$

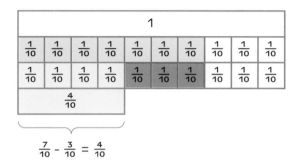

$$\frac{7}{10} - \frac{3}{10} = \frac{4}{10}$$

ACTIVITY 4.9

Draw bar models for these calculations.

> *Some calculations involve addition, some involve subtraction.*

a) $\frac{1}{4} + \frac{1}{4}$ b) $\frac{1}{5} + \frac{3}{5}$ c) $\frac{5}{7} - \frac{2}{7}$ d) $\frac{3}{8} + \frac{5}{8}$ e) $\frac{5}{6} - \frac{2}{6}$

Look at your answers. Will any of them simplify?

Use your calculator to check your answers – notice the answer in its simplest form is displayed.

Adding and subtracting fractions with different denominators

If you watch a 30-minute TV show followed by a 15-minute TV show, you have spent half an hour and a quarter of an hour watching TV. That's 45 minutes, which is three quarters of an hour. Notice the answer is given in quarters not halves.

1			
$\frac{1}{2}$		$\frac{1}{4}$	$\frac{1}{4}$
$\frac{1}{4}$	$\frac{1}{4}$	$\frac{1}{4}$	$\frac{1}{4}$

To add fractions that have different denominators, you have to use equivalent fractions so that both fractions have the same denominator, then add those instead. Use the fraction grids for this work.

Work out $\frac{1}{4}$ + $\frac{1}{8}$

Have the quarters and eighths fraction grids ready. Put them on top of each other, with the lines running in the same direction and lined up exactly. You can see that $\frac{1}{4}$ is equivalent to $\frac{2}{8}$

The bar model shows $\frac{1}{4}$ + $\frac{1}{8}$ but it looks like $\frac{2}{8}$ + $\frac{1}{8}$. You can see that the answer is $\frac{3}{8}$

1			
$\frac{1}{4}$	$\frac{1}{4}$	$\frac{1}{4}$	$\frac{1}{4}$
$\frac{1}{8}$ $\frac{1}{8}$ $\frac{1}{8}$	$\frac{1}{8}$	$\frac{1}{8}$ $\frac{1}{8}$	$\frac{1}{8}$ $\frac{1}{8}$

Answer: $\frac{1}{4}$ + $\frac{1}{8}$ = $\frac{2}{8}$ + $\frac{1}{8}$ = $\frac{3}{8}$

Work out $\frac{2}{3}$ + $\frac{1}{5}$

Put the thirds fraction grid and the fifths fraction grid on top of each other. You can see that the lines do not line up as they did in the previous example. So, turn one of the grids round so you can see the square in 15 parts. You will be working in fifteenths here.

> *You know it's 15 parts because there are 3 columns with 5 rows, so 3 × 5 = 15 parts in a whole.*

The squares below show the two fractions to be added.

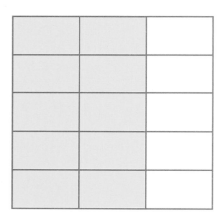 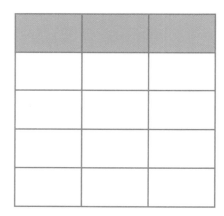

Instead of adding two thirds and one fifth, you add ten fifteenths and three fifteenths.

You write $\frac{2}{3}$ + $\frac{1}{5}$ = $\frac{10}{15}$ + $\frac{3}{15}$ = $\frac{13}{15}$

Work out $\frac{7}{8}$ - $\frac{5}{6}$

To do this subtraction, check whether the fraction grids line up. They don't, so turn one grid the other way and work with 8 × 6 = 48 parts in a whole.

> *There are other ways of doing this calculation, but this is the easiest when you use the fraction grids.*

Find the equivalent fractions for $\frac{7}{8}$ and $\frac{5}{6}$ in forty-eighths.

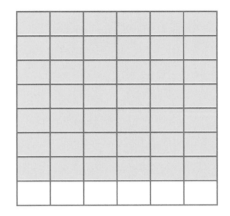 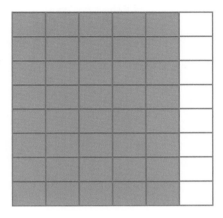

So, the calculation $\frac{7}{8} - \frac{5}{6}$ becomes $\frac{42}{48} - \frac{40}{48} = \frac{2}{48}$

This answer will simplify to $\frac{1}{24}$

ACTIVITY 4.10

Use fraction grids to answer these calculations. Remember to show the equivalent fractions that you add or subtract, as well as the answer. Simplify the answers where possible.

a) $\frac{1}{2} + \frac{1}{8}$ c) $\frac{5}{6} - \frac{1}{3}$ e) $\frac{7}{9} + \frac{1}{3}$ g) $\frac{1}{3} + \frac{1}{2}$ i) $\frac{5}{8} - \frac{1}{3}$

b) $\frac{5}{8} - \frac{1}{4}$ d) $\frac{7}{10} - \frac{2}{5}$ f) $\frac{1}{2} + \frac{1}{5}$ h) $\frac{3}{10} + \frac{2}{7}$ j) $\frac{7}{10} + \frac{3}{4}$

Check your answers using your calculator.

INVESTIGATE
Investigate what these calculations have in common. Can you describe the pattern in words?

$\frac{1}{2} - \frac{1}{3}$, $\frac{1}{3} - \frac{1}{4}$, $\frac{1}{4} - \frac{1}{5}$, $\frac{1}{5} - \frac{1}{6}$...

What about $\frac{1}{2} - \frac{1}{4}$, $\frac{1}{3} - \frac{1}{5}$, $\frac{1}{4} - \frac{1}{6}$, $\frac{1}{5} - \frac{1}{7}$...?

> *Leave the answer unsimplified to see the pattern.*

CHAPTER SUM-UP

Reflection

Having worked through this chapter, how do you feel about these skills?

Skill	I have tried this	I need more practice	I am confident with this
Knowing that fractions describe parts of a whole			
Understanding and identifying equivalent fractions			
Simplifying a fraction			
Finding a fraction of a whole number			
Multiplying fractions			
Dividing fractions			
Adding fractions			
Subtracting fractions			

Quiz

Which calculation gives the biggest answer?

a) $\frac{3}{4} \times \frac{2}{3}$ b) $\frac{3}{4} \div \frac{2}{3}$ c) $\frac{3}{4} + \frac{2}{3}$ d) $\frac{3}{4} - \frac{2}{3}$

Are you surprised by what you discovered?

Try it for another pair of fractions. Is it the same operation that gets the bigger answer?

5. Percentages, Decimals and Fractions

AIMS
- To know that percentages, decimals and fractions describe parts of a whole
- To write parts of a whole in different ways:
  - a percentage as a fraction or a decimal
  - a decimal as a fraction or a percentage
  - a fraction as a decimal or a percentage
- To write one number as a percentage of another number
- To find a percentage of an amount
- To increase or decrease an amount by a given percentage
- To understand repeated percentage change
- To understand reverse percentages

RESOURCES
- A set of fraction grids (see page 283). Print the grids on acetate (or trace them onto tracing paper) and cut them out
- A scientific calculator

PREVIOUS KNOWLEDGE
- Place value and calculations for whole numbers and decimals
- Fractions
- Grid method for division

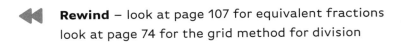 **Rewind** – look at page 107 for equivalent fractions
look at page 74 for the grid method for division

PERCENTAGES

1% is the same as the fraction $\frac{1}{100}$
and the decimal 0.01.

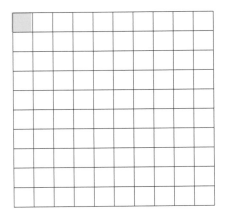

> **Percentages** *are equivalent to fractions where the denominator is 100.*
> *1% means 1 part in every 100.*

The percentage key on your calculator

Investigate whether your calculator has a percent (%) key. If it does, try typing 10% and then press = . You should get 0.1 or $\frac{1}{10}$ as the answer. Many calculators have a key which will switch the answer between a fraction and a decimal and back again. Make sure you know where this key is if you have it on your calculator.

> Many calculators use S↔D for this.

WRITING PARTS OF A WHOLE IN DIFFERENT WAYS

The fraction grids with 10 strips and with 10 rows of 10 squares are useful for decimals and percentages. Each strip represents 10% or 0.1 or $\frac{1}{10}$ of the whole. Each small square represents 1% or 0.01 or $\frac{1}{100}$ of the whole.

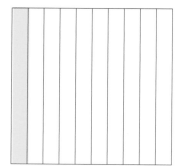 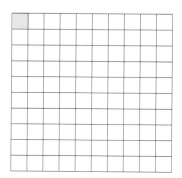

You can also have 0.1%, which is one strip of 10 equal-sized strips inside a small square. 0.1% = 0.001 = $\frac{1}{1000}$

You can go smaller still, with numbers that have more decimal places and fractions that have bigger denominators.

> Notice in each case, the decimal is the percentage when divided by 100.

Write 20% as a fraction and a decimal

Use a fraction grid to represent 20%. You can use any 20 squares in the grid, but keeping the squares in strips of 10 really helps to change a percentage to a fraction and a decimal.

20 squares out of 100 is the fraction $\frac{20}{100}$. You can simplify this fraction to $\frac{2}{10}$ and to $\frac{1}{5}$

You can see that 20 squares is two strips, so the decimal is 0.2.

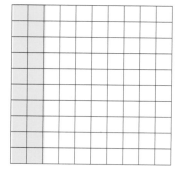 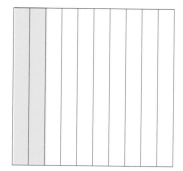

> You can redraw this grid with every alternate vertical line removed to see the fifths better.

Answer: 20% as a fraction is $\frac{1}{5}$; 20% as a decimal is 0.2

Write 0.45 as a fraction and a percentage
Use a fraction grid to represent 0.45.

You can see that 0.45 is 45 squares, so 0.45 can be written as $\frac{45}{100}$ or as 45%.

> Notice you can change a decimal to a percentage by multiplying by 100 and putting the % sign at the end.

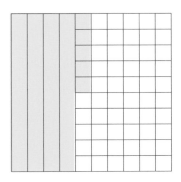 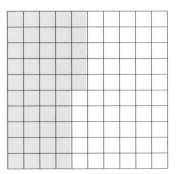

The fraction $\frac{45}{100}$ will simplify because both numbers are in the five times table.

Combine squares together in groups of five. You can see that $\frac{45}{100} = \frac{9}{20}$

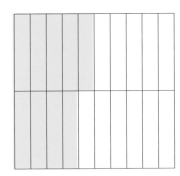

$$\frac{45}{100} \overset{\div 5}{\underset{\div 5}{=}} \frac{9}{20}$$

Answer: 0.45 as a fraction is $\frac{9}{20}$; 0.45 as a percentage is 45%

 Rewind – Look back at page 110 to revise simplifying fractions.

Change $\frac{3}{4}$ to a decimal and a percentage
You can use the hundredths square and shade three quarters of the squares, which is 75 squares.

So $\frac{3}{4}$ = 75% = 0.75

Another method is to remember that a fraction is a way of writing a division calculation: $\frac{3}{4}$ = 3 ÷ 4

Use the grid method for division to complete the calculation.

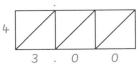

Below the grid, write the number to be divided. In this example, the number to be divided is 3. Write it as 3.00. You can put more zeros in the decimal part if you need them. Insert a decimal point in the answer space, ready.

Write the number you are dividing by on the left of the grid. In this example, the number is 4.

The answer to the division will appear across the top of the grid.

Complete the division. You can see the answer is 0.75

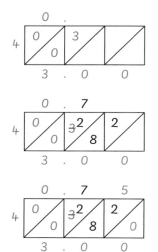

 Rewind – Look back to page 92 to revise the grid method for division with decimals.

Write $\frac{3}{8}$ as a decimal and a percentage

You can use treat $\frac{3}{8}$ as a division calculation to change the fraction to a decimal. Then, use the decimal to find the percentage.

$\frac{3}{8} = 3 \div 8$

Set out the division calculation in a grid.

Work from left to right, dividing the numbers by 8.

The division is not complete after calculating two decimal places. Add an extra square to the grid and write an extra zero below it.

Answer: $\frac{3}{8} = 3 \div 8 = 0.375$

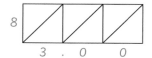

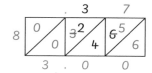

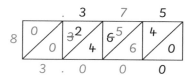

To write 0.375 as a percentage, use a fraction grid for hundredths.

You can see that $\frac{3}{8} = 0.375 = 37.5\%$

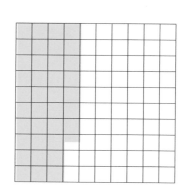

> *Notice you can change this decimal to the percentage by multiplying by 100 and putting in the % sign. The answer needs a decimal point as well as the % sign.*

ACTIVITY 5.1

1. Complete the table by converting each number to the other forms. Use the fraction grids to help you if you want to.

	Fraction	Decimal	Percentage
a)	$\frac{1}{2}$		
b)			25%
c)		0.7	
d)			30%
e)		0.15	
f)	$\frac{9}{10}$		
g)	$\frac{4}{5}$		
h)		0.73	
i)			12.5%
j)	$\frac{11}{20}$		

2. Put these numbers in order of size, smallest first.

0.4, $\frac{1}{4}$, $\frac{4}{5}$, 44%

> Hint: Convert them all to decimals or all to percentages first.

INVESTIGATE

What happens when you try to convert $\frac{1}{3}$ to a decimal? Try $\frac{2}{3}$ as well.

What happens for $\frac{1}{7}$ or $\frac{2}{7}$ or any other number of sevenths?

These are examples of recurring decimals. They can be written with a dot, or two dots, to show the number or groups of numbers which repeat.

> Check your calculator. Some calculators have a setting where they show recurring decimals. Use S↔D to see the first 10 decimal places of the answer.

$\frac{1}{9} = 0.1111111111... = 0.\dot{1}$

$\frac{2}{11} = 0.1818181818... = 0.\dot{1}\dot{8}$

$\frac{3}{7} = 0.4285714285... = 0.\dot{4}2857\dot{1}$

Investigate which denominators give recurring decimals.

WRITING ONE NUMBER AS A PERCENTAGE OF ANOTHER NUMBER

Sometimes it is useful to think of one number as a percentage of another number.

For example, if 17 out of 25 members of a choir are girls, what percentage is this?

First, write the numbers as a fraction: $\frac{17}{25}$

Then, change the fraction to a percentage.

$$\frac{17}{25} \overset{\times 4}{\underset{\times 4}{=}} \frac{68}{100} = 68\%$$

> You could also use a calculator to change the fraction to a decimal. Multiply the result by 100 to give the percentage.

ACTIVITY 5.2

In which subject did Antonio do best? Here are his test marks.
Write them all as a percentage.

a) Maths 46 out of 50

b) English 18 out of 25

c) German 14 out of 20

d) History 8 out of 10

FINDING A PERCENTAGE OF AN AMOUNT

You can find a percentage of an amount using a division bar model.

You might find it helpful to think about 50% and 25% or maybe 10% and 1%. You can then stack parts together to make the percentage you need.

100%			
50%		50%	
25%	25%	25%	25%

100%									
10%	10%	10%	10%	10%	10%	10%	10%	10%	10%

5% 5% 5% 5% 5% 5% 5% 5% 5% 5% 5% 5% 5% 5% 5% 5% 5% 5% 5% 5%

1%

Find 40% of £80

Make a division bar model with 10% divisions.

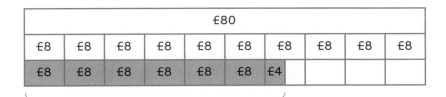

£8 × 4 = £32

Answer: 40% of £80 is £32

Find 65% of £80

£80									
£8	£8	£8	£8	£8	£8	£8	£8	£8	£8
£8	£8	£8	£8	£8	£8	£4			

(£8 × 6) + £4 = £52

> Some people prefer to work out 50%, 10% and 5% and then add the answers together.

Answer: 65% of £80 is £52

Find 23% of 300 m

300 m									
30 m	30 m	30 m	30 m	30 m	30 m	30 m	30 m	30 m	30 m

1% is 3 m

Therefore, 23% of 300 m is 30 + 30 + 3 + 3 + 3 = 69 m

INVESTIGATE

Four people explain how to work out 12.5% of £120 in different ways.

Follow their instructions to see if they are correct.

Anna says: Find 50%, 25% and 12.5% by halving each time.

Billy says: Find 10% then halve to find 5% and halve again to find 2.5%. Add the answers for 10% and 2.5%.

Celmira says: Find 10%, 1% and 0.1% by dividing by 10 each time. Add one of the first answer, two of the second answer and five of the third answer.

Daoud recognizes that 12.5% is the fraction $\frac{1}{8}$. He says: Divide £120 by 8.

How would you find 12.5% of £120?

ACTIVITY 5.3

Work out these amounts. Do not use your calculator. Draw the bar model or write down the calculations you did to get your answers.

a) 10% of £50

b) 20% of £90

c) 40% of £20

d) 50% of £70

e) 1% of £500

f) 5% of £40

g) 6% of £50

h) 8% of £20

Finding a percentage of an amount using a calculator

The bar method described above works well, especially if you don't have a calculator to use.

When you have a calculator, you can find a percentage of an amount using the % key and the multiplication sign for 'of'.

If your calculator does not have this key, you should multiply the amount by the decimal equivalent of the percentage stated. For example, to find 28% of 76, enter into your calculator 76 × 0.28

Find 28% of 76

Enter into your calculator 76 × 28% or 28% × 76

Answer: 21.28

ACTIVITY 5.4

1. Return to Activity 5.3 and check your answers using a calculator.

2. Now use your calculator to answer these questions. They are no harder when you have a calculator!

a) 23% of £8

b) 42% of £65

c) 85% of £40

d) 93% of £23

PERCENTAGE INCREASE AND DECREASE

Sometimes you will be asked to increase or decrease an amount by a given percentage. You can work out the value of the percentage and then add or take it away from the original amount.

You can also draw a bar model with the percentage increase or decrease shown.

Increase £50 by 10%

Begin with the usual bar model.

£50									
£5	£5	£5	£5	£5	£5	£5	£5	£5	£5

Draw an extra 10% box at the end of the second row.

£50										
£5	£5	£5	£5	£5	£5	£5	£5	£5	£5	£5

You can see that the amount increases to £55.

Another way to do this is to think of the final amount as 110% of the original. Use the × key and the % key on your calculator.

Answer: £50 increased by 10% is £55

Decrease £50 by 10%

The same bar model as above can be used. This time, you do not include the last 10%.

So, the final amount is £5 × 9 = £45

In the end, you have 90% of the amount you started with. The multiplier method looks like this.

Answer: £50 decreased by 10% is £45

Increase £40 by 15%

Draw the bar model for £40 and put an additional 10% and 5% on the end.

You can see that the final amount is £46.

In the end, you have 115% of £40. The multiplier method looks like this.

ACTIVITY 5.5

Work out these amounts. Try the bar model method and the multiplier method as a way of checking your work.

a) Increase £800 by 10%

b) Decrease £800 by 10%

c) Increase £70 by 20%

d) Decrease £70 by 20%

e) Increase £60 by 25%

f) Decrease £60 by 25%

g) Increase £140 by 5%

h) Decrease £140 by 5%

i) Increase £7.50 by 30%

j) Decrease £7.50 by 30%

REPEATED PERCENTAGE CHANGE

Sometimes an amount changes several times.

A car loses 20% of its value for three years in a row. It is worth £17,000 at the start. What is the value of the car after three years?

One way to solve the problem is shown below.

Year 1   Value £17,000   10% is £1700   20% is £3400
             subtract to give the new value: £13,600

Year 2   Value £13,600   10% is £1360   20% is £2720
             subtract to give the new value: £10,880

Year 3   Value £10,880   10% is £1088   20% is £2176
             subtract to give the new value: £8704

This is quite complicated. The multiplier method is simpler.

A 20% drop in value leaves 80%. So, use the multiplier of 80% three times over.

£17,000   £13,600   £10,880   £8704

On your calculator:

- Enter 17000 =
- Ans
- × 80%

This will give you the answer for the value of the car after one year. Press = again for the value after two years. Press = again for the value after three years.

You can usually scroll up through a list of answers if you press = too many times!

If money is invested in a bank, it might earn interest which is paid into the account at the end of a year. The next year, interest is paid not only on the original amount but also on the interest earned in the first year.

> **Interest** is money that the bank adds to your account at the end of a year.

If £500 is in a bank account for 3 years at 2% compound interest, the amounts at the end of each year can be calculated in separate stages.

For £500   1% is £5 so   2% is £10   There is £510 after 1 year.

For £510   1% is £5.10   2% is £10.20   There is £520.20 after 2 years.

For £520.20   1% is £5.202   2% is £10.404   There is £530.604 after 2 years.

You would have to round off the answer to make an exact amount of money.

£530.604 rounded to the nearest penny is £530.60

The multiplier method is simpler here, too.

A 2% increase in value gives 102%. So, use the multiplier of 102% three times over.

> On your calculator:
> - Press 500 =
> - × 102% =
> - =
> - =

£500   £510   £520.20 £530.604

The number of members in a society goes up by 10%. The following year it goes down by 10%. What is the percentage change in two years?

In a question like this, there is no amount given at the start. Try using 100 members as the starting amount. The bar model looks like this for the first year.

100										
10	10	10	10	10	10	10	10	10	10	10

So, at the end of the first year there is 110% of the original amount.

In the following year, the amount goes down by 10% of the new value. You need another bar model to show this.

110										
11	11	11	11	11	11	11	11	11	11	11

So, there are 99 members after two years. This is 99% of the original value, so there has been a 1% decrease in the number of members over two years.

> You might have expected no change. But the decrease was 10% of a bigger amount than 10% of the original amount.

135

The multipliers give this.

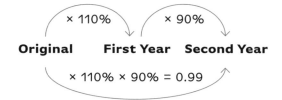

Multiply the multipliers to get 0.99, which is the decimal for 99%

So, you do not need to know the original amount to see that there is a 1% decrease to 99% all together.

ACTIVITY 5.6

1. Work out the final amounts.

a) Start value = £500. Increase by 50% four times.

b) Start value = £200. Increase by 15% three times.

c) Start value = 120. Decrease by 10% twice.

d) Start value = 90. Decrease by 5% and then decrease by 30%. What percentage change is this?

e) Start value = 300. Increase by 10% and then decrease by 20%. What percentage change is this?

2. Work out the amount in the bank after 3 years of compound interest.

a) £1000 at 5% compound interest

b) £200 at 4% compound interest

c) £950 at 2.5% compound interest

3. Work out the size of the population after 4 years.

a) The original population of 700 decreases by 10% each year

b) The original population of 5 million decreases by 30% each year

REVERSE PERCENTAGES

Sometimes you know the value of something after a percentage change has happened and you want to know what the amount was before the change. In the previous section you saw that a 10% increase followed by a 10% decrease does not get you back to the original amount.

Find the original amount when the value after a 10% increase is £220

The bar model to solve the problem looks like this.

100%										
10%	10%	10%	10%	10%	10%	10%	10%	10%	10%	10%
£220										
£20	£20	£20	£20	£20	£20	£20	£20	£20	£20	£20

> *Divide the amount (£220) into 11 boxes.*

You can see from the bar model that the original amount is £200.

If you have a calculator, you might find the multiplier method easier.

The original amount is multiplied by 110% for this percentage change. The diagram for working out the increase looks like this. You can undo the change by starting with the answer and dividing by 110%. Draw this as a reverse arrow underneath.

So, the original amount is 220 ÷ 110%

×110%

Original amount   £220

÷110%

Answer: The original amount is £200

Find the original cost when a coat in a sale is £72 after a 20% discount is applied

The bar model to solve the problem looks like this.

> *Discount is an amount that is taken off a price when an item is in a sale.*

100%									
80%								20%	
£72									
£9	£9	£9	£9	£9	£9	£9	£9	£9	£9

> *This part is the discount.*

> *Divide £72 into 8 boxes.*

From the bar model, you can see that the original cost is £90.

Here is the multiplier method for the same question. The 20% decrease gives a multiplier of 80%. You can undo the change by starting with the answer and dividing by 80%. Draw this as a reverse arrow underneath.

The original amount is 72 ÷ 80%

×80%

Original amount   £72

÷80%

Answer: The original amount is £90

> *Notice dividing by 80% makes the amount larger.*

ACTIVITY 5.7

Each question tells you the final amount and the percentage change. Work out the original amount.

> You can use a calculator. Draw the bar model or write down the calculation you would do to get each answer.

a) £120 after a 50% increase

b) £45 after a 10% decrease

c) £70 after a 30% decrease

d) £10.50 after a 5% increase

e) £50.40 after a 20% increase

f) £55.25 after a 15% decrease

CHAPTER SUM-UP

Reflection

Having worked through this chapter, how do you feel about these skills?

Skill	I have tried this	I need more practice	I am confident with this
Knowing that percentages, decimals and fractions describe parts of a whole			
Writing parts of a whole in different ways: • a percentage as a fraction or a decimal • a decimal as a fraction or a percentage • a fraction as a decimal or a percentage			
Writing one number as a percentage of another number			
Finding a percentage of an amount			
Increasing or decreasing an amount by a given percentage			
Understanding repeated percentage change			
Understanding reverse percentages			

Quiz

Which of these questions gives the smallest amount?

a) 5% of £3500

b) £200 when decreased by 20%

c) The original price of an item that costs £108 after a 40% discount

d) £150 when increased by 18%

6. Directed Number

THE NUMBER (-1)

You can think of the number 1 as the answer to the calculation 0 + 1

If you want to do the calculation 0 - 1 you need a new number (-1).

Hello, new number! Shall I call you minus 1 or negative 1?

Negative 1 is better, please!

REPRESENTING POSITIVE AND NEGATIVE NUMBERS ON A NUMBER LINE

In this chapter, positive whole numbers are represented by yellow counters and negative whole numbers are represented by red counters.
   Look at these number lines.

Horizontal number line

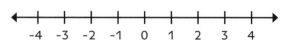

On a horizontal number line, negative numbers are to the left of zero. Positive numbers are to the right of zero.

On a vertical number line, negative numbers are below zero. Positive numbers are above zero.

Vertical number line

ACTIVITY 6.1

Draw the counters you need to represent each number on the horizontal number line. Hint: Think about the colours!

A ZERO PAIR

When you have one yellow counter and one red counter, they add up to make zero.

> Adding 1 and (-1) gives zero. They are called a **zero pair**. Other zero pairs include x and $-x$.

> You might say they cancel out.

   $1 + (-1) = 0$

You can have as many pairs of red and yellow counters as you like; the total will still be zero.

This means there are lots of ways of representing the number 1.

You need one yellow counter and as many zero pairs as you like.

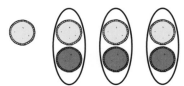 This example is 1 + 0 + 0 + 0

ACTIVITY 6.2

1. Find different ways of representing the number 1 with your counters.
Draw the different arrangements of counters you make.

2. Make each of these numbers with your counters. Put counters together to make as many zero pairs as you can. Count the counters. Write the number represented.

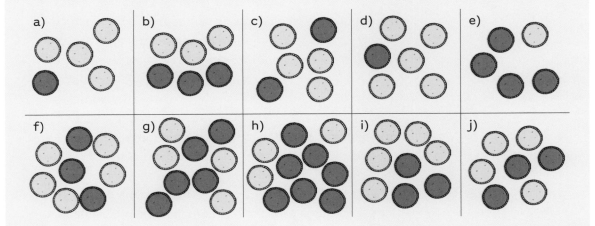

a) b) c) d) e)

f) g) h) i) j)

3. Find at least three ways of representing each of the numbers -3 to 4.
Draw the arrangements of counters you make.

GAME

Play in a group. Pick up a handful of double-sided counters and let them fall onto the table. Work out the number represented by your counters. Play eight rounds. Use the same handful of counters for each round. Record your score each round.

Round 1	1 point	your number is positive
Round 2	1 point	your number is negative
Round 3	3 points	your number is the biggest of all the numbers in your group
Round 4	3 points	your number is the smallest of all the numbers in your group (most negative)

→

Round 5	2 points	your number is odd (include (-1), (-3), etc.)
Round 6	2 points	your number is even (include 0, (-2), etc.)
Round 7	5 points	your number is 0
Round 8	5 points	your number is (-1)

Work out your total points scored. The winner is the player with the biggest score. Did anyone get all 22 points?

INVESTIGATE

Choose another handful of counters and let them fall onto the table. Record the number represented by your counters. Repeat 20 times. Write down what you notice. Did you ever get zero? Is it possible?

Give yourself an extra counter and repeat the experiment. Did you ever get zero now or is it impossible?

ADDING POSITIVE AND NEGATIVE NUMBERS

To add a positive number and a negative number, make each number with your counters. Push the two sets together to add them.

Work out 6 + (-2)
You will need these counters. Regroup them with as many zero pairs as you can.

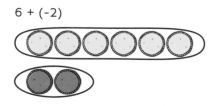

6 + (-2)   = 4

Answer: 6 + (-2) = 4

ACTIVITY 6.3

> Remember zero pairs – one red counter and one yellow counter together make zero.

Make these numbers using counters. Then, put the two sets of counters together and write down the number represented.

a) 2 + (-1)
b) 5 + 4

c) (-1) + 6
d) (-4) + 3

e) 5 + (-7)
f) (-5) + (-7)

SUBTRACTING POSITIVE AND NEGATIVE NUMBERS

Make the first number with your counters and use lots of zero pairs.
Take the right number of yellow or red counters and write down the answer.

4 – 5

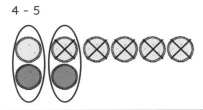

= (–1)

4 – (–2)

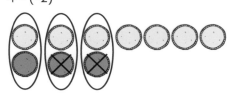

= 6

ACTIVITY 6.4

1. Answer these subtractions.

   a) 5 – 7   b) (–2) – 3   c) 5 – (–1)   d) 2 – (–8)   e) (–2) – (–5)

2. Make up some questions of your own. Type your subtraction into your calculator. Use the brackets keys. Use the minus key for the instruction 'take away' and the key with the minus sign in brackets for all negative numbers.

MULTIPLICATION

Multiplying a positive number by a negative number

Recall how you can represent 3 × 4 with counters. Starting with zero, put four yellow counters onto the table and then another four and then another four – that's three lots of four.

So 3 × (–4) can be made by putting three lots of four red counters onto the table.

3 × 4 = 12

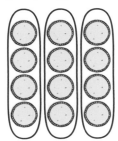

3 × (–4) = (–12)

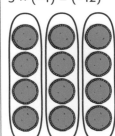

ACTIVITY 6.5

1. Represent the following multiplications with your counters. Write down the answers.

> *Remember the first number tells you how many 'lots of ...' you have.*

   a) 2 × 5   b) 4 × (-2)   c) 2 × (-4)   d) 3 × (-5)   e) 5 × (-3)

2. Choose two numbers of your own to multiply. The first number should be positive, and the second can be either positive or negative. Represent the multiplication of your numbers with counters. What do you notice?

Multiplying a negative number by a positive or a negative number

(-3) × 4 can be read as take three lots of four from zero.

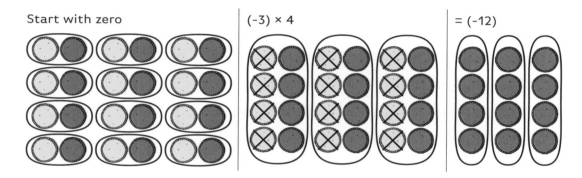

Notice this is the same answer as (-4) × 3, 3 × (-4) and 4 × (-3)

   (-3) × (-4) can be read as take three lots of (-4) from zero.

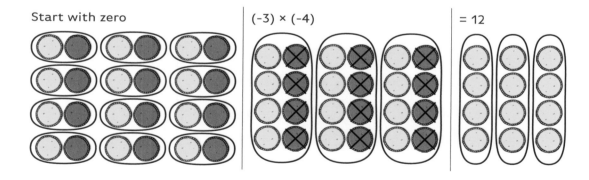

ACTIVITY 6.6

> *Remember, the first number tells you how many 'lots of ...' you must take from your zero-pair collection.*

1. Represent these multiplications with your counters. Start with as many zeros as you need.

   a) (-2) × 5   c) (-4) × (-2)   e) (-3) × (-5)
   b) (-5) × 2   d) (-2) × (-4)   f) (-5) × (-3)

2. Choose two numbers of your own to multiply. The first number should be negative, and the second number can be either positive or negative. Represent the multiplication of your numbers with counters.

What do you notice?

3. How could you use the patterns you have noticed to answer multiplications without the counters?

4. What happens if you multiply three negative numbers together? What about four negative numbers?

Write a list of answers for $(-1)^2$, $(-1)^3$, $(-1)^4$, $(-1)^5$, $(-1)^6$ etc. What do you notice?

What do you think the answer to $(-1)^{99}$ would be?

5. What does your calculator give for $(-1)^2$ and what does it give for -1^2?

Explain the difference.

DIVISION

How would you explain to a young child what the division $12 \div 4$ means?

Using the patterns in multiplication for division

One way to understand the division $12 \div 4$ is to ask the question 'What do I multiply 4 by to get the answer 12?'

Can you think of another way of understanding $12 \div 4$?

This is because multiplication and division are inverse operations, just like addition and subtraction.

Maybe 'how many groups of 4 are there in 12?'

$12 \div 4 = \boxed{}$ means $4 \times \boxed{} = 12$ so $\boxed{} = 3$. You can just write $12 \div 4 = 3$

Other divisions follow the pattern.

$(-12) \div 4 = \boxed{}$ means $4 \times \boxed{} = (-12)$ so $\boxed{} = (-3)$. You write $(-12) \div 4 = (-3)$

$12 \div (-4) = \boxed{}$ means $(-4) \times \boxed{} = 12$ so $\boxed{} = (-3)$. You write $12 \div (-4) = (-3)$

$(-12) \div (-4) = \boxed{}$ means $(-4) \times \boxed{} = (-12)$ so $\boxed{} = 3$. You write $(-12) \div (-4) = 3$

ACTIVITY 6.7

Use the missing number approach to solve these divisions.

Write: 'I know (–6) × ☐ = 12 so 12 ÷ (–6) = ☐' putting your answer instead of the box.

a) 12 ÷ (–6)　　c) 12 ÷ (–4)　　e) 36 ÷ 9　　g) (–36) ÷ (–12)　　i) (–45) ÷ 3
b) (–12) ÷ (–4)　　d) (–36) ÷ 9　　f) (–36) ÷ (–6)　　h) 45 ÷ (–9)　　j) (–45) ÷ (–3)

POSITIVE AND NEGATIVE NUMBERS – THE HUMAN NUMBER LINE

Imagine a big thermometer stuck to your T-shirt so that zero is in line with your middle. Warmer temperatures (positive numbers) are above zero. Colder temperatures (negative numbers) are below zero.

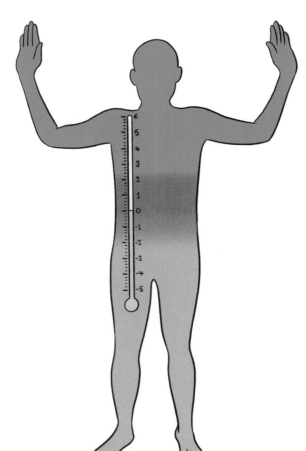

ACTIVITY 6.8

Put these numbers in order of size, smallest first.

a) 5, (–2), 9, (–5), 0
b) 15, (–23), (–9), 32, (–45)
c) 2.5, (–12), 1.5, (–7.5), (–8)

Moving up the number line

To do a calculation, point to the start number with both hands. Then, move one hand to the finish number. Which way should you move your hand? Up or down?

2 + 3 = 5

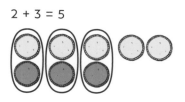

2 – (–3) = 5

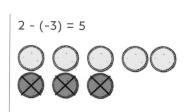

In both calculations the start number is 2 and the finish number is 5.

In 2 + 3 = 5, the addition of a positive number means you move your hand up the number line from the start number to the finish number.

In 2 − (−3) = 5, the subtraction of a negative number also moves your hand up the number line from the start number to the finish number.

Try some pairs of calculations of your own. Point to different start numbers.

Add a positive number in one calculation. Subtract the corresponding negative number in the other calculation.

Moving down the number line

5 − 4 = 1

5 + (−4) = 1

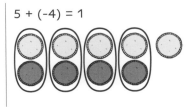

In both calculations the start number is 5 and the finish number is 1.

In 5 − 4 = 1, the subtraction of a positive number means you move your hand down the number line from the start number to the finish number.

In 5 + (−4) = 1, the addition of a negative number also moves your hand down the number line from the start number to the finish number.

POSITIVE AND NEGATIVE NUMBERS
– NUMBER LINES USED IN MATHS

You can add and subtract positive and negative numbers using a number line.

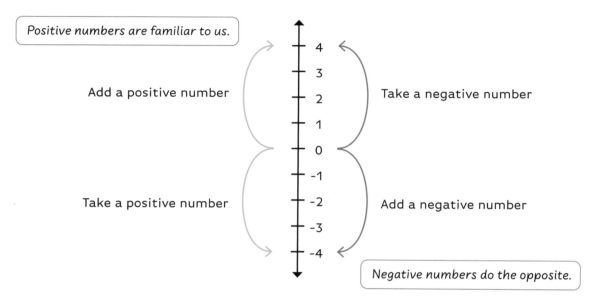

You can draw the movement that occurs on a number line as a result of adding and subtracting positive and negative numbers. Draw an arrow from the start number that leads to the finish number.

Work out 3 – 5
Start at 3 and
move down five

3 – 5 = (–2)

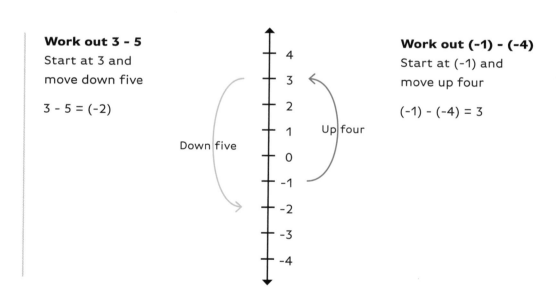

Work out (–1) – (–4)
Start at (–1) and
move up four

(–1) – (–4) = 3

ACTIVITY 6.9

1. Use number lines to answer these calculations.

a) 1 – 6   c) (–4) + 8   e) (–3) + 6   g) (–1) – (–2)   i) 4 + (–7)
b) (–2) + 6   d) (–3) – 1   f) 8 + (–9)   h) (–9) – (–4)   j) 2 – (–1)

2. Write more addition and subtraction calculations that give the answer 3.

Check your answers on your calculator.

> This could keep you busy for ever!

> Remember to use the bracket keys and the key with a minus symbol in brackets for the negative numbers.

Number lines for bigger numbers

You can draw a number line with just a few numbers on it and then move up or down the number line in several smaller jumps.

Work out (-8) + 25

Start at (-8)

Add 8 to get up to zero

Add another 2 (that's 10 added so far)

Add another 10 (that's 20)

Add the last 5

That's up 17 from zero.

Answer: (-8) + 25 = 17

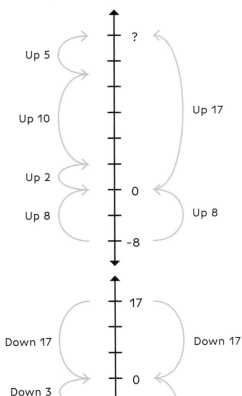

Work out 17 - 43

Start at 17

Take 17 to get to zero

Take another 3 (that's 20 taken so far)

Take another 20 (that's 40)

Take another 3

Answer: 17 - 43 = -26

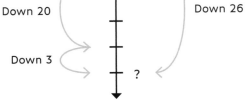

ACTIVITY 6.10

1. Draw number lines with just a few numbers marked to answer these calculations.

a) 21 - 36

b) (-12) + 26

c) (-24) + 18

d) (-33) - 12

e) 46 + (-33)

f) 84 + (-99)

g) (-21) - (-32)

h) (-19) - (-34)

i) 41 + (-57)

j) (-32) - (-17) + 15

2. Did you get the answer 0 for part j? Write some more calculations with three numbers that give the answer zero.

Use your calculator to check your work.

USING NUMBER PATTERNS FOR MULTIPLICATION AND DIVISION

A tables square can help you with multiplication and division. Here we show you how to extend your tables square to include zero and negative numbers as well.

In the first grid, the numbers from a vertical −4 to 4 number line and a horizontal −4 to 4 number line are in the blue shaded squares.

The numbers in white squares show the result of multiplying a positive number by another positive number.

The second grid records the fact that every number multiplied by zero is zero.

First grid:

-4	-3	-2	-1	0	1	2	3	4
				4	4	8	12	16
				3	3	6	9	12
				2	2	4	6	8
				1	1	2	3	4
-4	-3	-2	-1	0	1	2	3	4
				-1				
				-2				
				-3				
				-4				

Second grid (shaded cells show the product 0 above the axis value):

-4	-3	-2	-1	0	1	2	3	4
				0/4	4	8	12	16
				0/3	3	6	9	12
				0/2	2	4	6	8
				0/1	1	2	3	4
0/-4	0/-3	0/-2	0/-1	0	0/1	0/2	0/3	0/4
				0/-1				
				0/-2				
				0/-3				
				0/-4				

Working down the columns on the right side of the grid, continue the number pattern into the empty squares.

Working from right to left, along the top part of the grid, continue the number pattern into the empty squares.

Third grid:

-4	-3	-2	-1	0	1	2	3	4
				0/4	4	8	12	16
				0/3	3	6	9	12
				0/2	2	4	6	8
-4	-3	-2	-1	0/1	1	2	3	4
0/-4	0/-3	0/-2	0/-1	0	0/1	0/2	0/3	0/4
				0/-1	-1	-2	-3	-4
				0/-2				
				0/-3				
				0/-4				

Repeat for the other columns and rows. All of these numbers are negative.

-16	-12	-8	-4	0 / 4	4	8	12	16
-12	-9	-6	-3	0 / 3	3	6	9	12
-8	-6	-4	-2	0 / 2	2	4	6	8
-4	-3	-2	-1	0 / 1	1	2	3	4
0 / -4	0 / -3	0 / -2	0 / -1	0	0 / 1	0 / 2	0 / 3	0 / 4
				0 / -1	-1	-2	-3	-4
				0 / -2	-2	-4	-6	-8
				0 / -3	-3	-6	-9	-12
				0 / -4	-4	-8	-12	-16

Work across or down the grid to finish the tables square, using the number patterns. Check you get the same values going the other way.

Can you see from the completed tables square that two negative numbers multiplied together must give a positive answer?

-16	-12	-8	-4	0 / 4	4	8	12	16
-12	-9	-6	-3	0 / 3	3	6	9	12
-8	-6	-4	-2	0 / 2	2	4	6	8
-4	-3	-2	-1	0 / 1	1	2	3	4
0 / -4	0 / -3	0 / -2	0 / -1	0	0 / 1	0 / 2	0 / 3	0 / 4
4	3	2	1	0 / -1	-1	-2	-3	-4
8	6	4	2	0 / -2	-2	-4	-6	-8
12	9	6	3	0 / -3	-3	-6	-9	-12
16	12	8	4	0 / -4	-4	-8	-12	-16

The tables square with negative numbers gives you another way of solving multiplications and divisions. Use your ordinary tables square or Napier's bones and decide whether the answer should be a positive or negative number. Two numbers with the same sign (+) or (-) give a positive answer.

One positive and one negative number multiply or divide to give a negative answer.

Don't say two minuses 'make' a plus. You will get addition and subtraction wrong if you do!

CHAPTER SUM-UP

Reflection

Having worked through this chapter, how do you feel about these skills?

Skill	I have tried this	I need more practice	I am confident with this
Understanding the concept of (-1)			
Representing positive and negative numbers on a number line			
Understanding the idea of a zero pair			
Adding with positive and negative numbers			
Subtracting with positive and negative numbers			
Multiplying with negative numbers			
Dividing with negative numbers			

Quiz

Write the answers to these calculations in order of size; largest first.

a) 15 - (-36)

b) (-18) × 5

c) (-16) + (-41)

d) (-42) ÷ (-2)

7. Using Indices

AIMS

- To understand powers of a number
- To know about the laws of indices
- To understand standard form for large and small numbers
- To understand rounding to a given number of significant figures
- To understand the order of operations (BIDMAS)

RESOURCES

- Scientific calculator
- Base-10 tiles (see page 281). Print and stick the tiles onto card and cut them out

PREVIOUS KNOWLEDGE

- Multiplying and dividing by ten, a hundred, a thousand, etc.
- Rounding to the nearest ten, hundred, thousand, etc.
- Rounding to a given number of decimal places

⏪ **Rewind** – look at page 82 for rounding to the nearest ten
look at page 88 for rounding to 1 decimal place

POWERS OF A NUMBER

Powers of ten

This table shows the first four powers of ten.

10	10^1
100	10^2
1000	10^3
10,000	10^4

Each number in the left-hand column can be made by repeatedly multiplying a number of tens. For example, $10,000 = 10 \times 10 \times 10 \times 10$.

Mathematicians write 10,000 as 10^4 because it is quicker to write and easier to read. They say: 'ten thousand is ten to the power of four'.

A **power** is used to write a multiplication where a number is multiplied by itself many times.

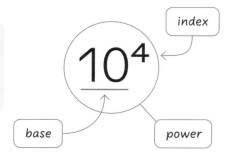

index

An **index** (plural: indices) is positioned above and to the right of the base number. It indicates how many times the base number is multiplied by itself when the index is a positive number.

base

power

Mathematicians have used the patterns in the table to write other numbers, including decimals, in index form as well. Can you spot the patterns?

Some powers of ten have names, such as a hundred, a thousand, and so on. A million is 10^6 and a billion is 10^9

Multiplying 10 strips by ten creates a bigger square. There are 100 small squares in this bigger square.

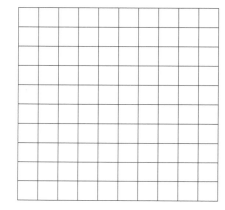

Whatever size of square you choose for a whole, multiplying one square by ten creates 10 squares (which are put together to make a strip).

Powers of other numbers

Multiplications can be written using an index when the same number is multiplied by itself at least once. For example: $4 \times 4 \times 4 \times 4 \times 4 = 4^5$ and $5 \times 5 \times 5 \times 5 = 5^4$

Does $4^5 = 5^4$? If not, why not?

Notice neither of these gives the answer 20.

ACTIVITY 7.1

1. Write each of these as a repeated multiplication. Use a calculator, if you need it, to work out the answers.

a) 3^2 b) 2^3 c) 7^3 d) 6^3 e) 5^5

2. Find the power key on your calculator and check that you can use it to answer all the parts in Question 1.

Many calculators have $x^\blacksquare$

INVESTIGATE

Look at the table below. The first four rows should be familiar to you; notice how they follow a pattern. Notice how the pattern continues for the negative powers of ten.

10,000	10^4
1000	10^3
100	10^2
10	10^1
1	10^0
0.1	10^{-1}
0.01	10^{-2}
0.001	10^{-3}
0.0001	10^{-4}

$\div 10$

Take one from the power

Notice negative powers of ten give small numbers but not negative numbers.

Notice 10^0 is not what you might have expected!

INVESTIGATE

Use your calculator to work out the answers to these powers of other numbers.

$2^3 =$	$3^3 =$	$4^3 =$	$5^3 =$
$2^2 =$	$3^2 =$	$4^2 =$	$5^2 =$
$2^1 =$	$3^1 =$	$4^1 =$	$5^1 =$
$2^0 =$	$3^0 =$	$4^0 =$	$5^0 =$
$2^{-1} =$	$3^{-1} =$	$4^{-1} =$	$5^{-1} =$
$2^{-2} =$	$3^{-2} =$	$4^{-2} =$	$5^{-2} =$
$2^{-3} =$	$3^{-3} =$	$4^{-3} =$	$5^{-3} =$

What do you notice about the power of 0?

Notice that a negative power of a number gives a fraction, with 1 as the numerator and the positive power of the number as the denominator. So $9^{-1} = \frac{1}{9^1} = \frac{1}{9}$ and $11^{-2} = \frac{1}{11^2} = \frac{1}{121}$

ACTIVITY 7.2

Write these numbers as fractions without indices.

a) 6^{-2} b) 10^{-4} c) 7^{-1} d) 8^{-2} e) 15^0

INVESTIGATING THE LAWS OF INDICES

Law 1
You know that any positive number raised to the power of 0 is 1.

For example: $5^0 = 1$; $127^0 = 1$

Law 2
You know that a number raised to a negative power is a fraction, with 1 as the numerator and the positive power of the number as the denominator.

For example: $8^{-2} = \frac{1}{8^2}$

Law 3
$10^2 \times 10^3$ means $(10 \times 10) \times (10 \times 10 \times 10) = 10^5$

INVESTIGATE

Investigate the answers to these calculations. Use your calculator but write your answers as a power.

> You can use the list of the powers of ten above, too.

a) $10^1 \times 10^4$ b) $10^2 \times 10^2$ c) $10^4 \times 10^2$ d) $10^3 \times 10^{-1}$ e) $10^{-2} \times 10^{-3}$

What do you notice?

Law 4

INVESTIGATE

Investigate the answers to these calculations.

a) $10^4 \div 10^2$ b) $10^3 \div 10^2$ c) $10^2 \div 10^3$ d) $10^{-1} \div 10^3$ e) $10^{-3} \div 10^{-2}$

What do you notice?

Law 5
Think about the calculation $(10^3)^2$. It means multiply the number 10^3 by itself.

So $(10^3)^2 = 10^3 \times 10^3 = 10^6$

INVESTIGATE

Investigate the answers to these calculations.

a) $(10^2)^2$ b) $(10^4)^2$ c) $(10^2)^3$ d) $(10^3)^3$ e) $(10^3)^{-1}$

What do you notice?

Check that these patterns work for powers of other numbers, not just 10.

ACTIVITY 7.3

Here are the laws of indices, including the ones you have discovered.

- Law 1: Any positive number raised to the power of 0 is 1.
- Law 2: A number raised to a negative power is a fraction, with 1 as the numerator and the positive power of the number as the denominator.
- Law 3: When multiplying indices with the same base, add the powers.
- Law 4: When dividing indices with the same base, subtract the powers.
- Law 5: When there is a power outside the bracket, multiply the powers.

Use the laws of indices to work out the calculations below. Give each answer as a power.

a) $4^2 \times 4^1$

b) $8^3 \div 8^2$

c) $(3^2)^3$

d) $3^5 \div 3^2$

e) $5^4 \times 5^{-2}$

f) $(5^2)^2$

g) $6^2 \times 6^{-2}$

h) $2^3 \div 2^{-2}$

i) $(3^3)^3$

j) $1^2 \times 1^2$

STANDARD FORM FOR LARGE AND SMALL NUMBERS

Large numbers can be quite difficult to read and write accurately. It is easy to miss a digit out, which can change the size of the number considerably. Scientists often use numbers in standard form to make writing large numbers easier.

> A number is in **standard form** when it is written as a number between one and ten multiplied by a power of ten.

Use base-10 tiles to make the number 124. You will need one large square, two strips and four small squares. Your tiles should resemble something like the one shown. In this arrangement, the small square represents one whole.

In Chapter 2 (Place Value and Decimals) you used the large square to represent one whole. That being the case here, your arrangement of tiles would represent 1.24.

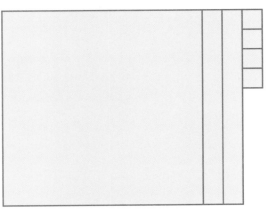

If you used the 1 mm squares to represent one whole, then the small square would be 100 and the large square would be 10,000. Your arrangement of tiles would now represent 12,400.

If you used a 1 m square to represent one whole, then the large square would represent one hundredth. Your arrangement of tiles would represent 0.0124.

You use 1.24 multiplied by a power of ten for all these numbers.
To get the value 124, you multiply 1.24 by 100, so $124 = 1.24 \times 10^2$
In the same way, $12{,}400 = 1.24 \times 10^4$ and $1240 = 1.24 \times 10^3$
For decimals, you need to use negative powers of ten, so
$0.124 = 1.24 \times 10^{-1}$ and $0.0124 = 1.24 \times 10^{-2}$
You could even use 1.024×10^0 for 1.024.

These numbers are all given in standard form (sometimes called scientific notation).

> Think of this as a bit more than 1 multiplied by 100.

Write 612,873 in standard form

Write the number that is between 1 and 10 and has the same digits by putting a decimal point between the 6 and the 1. Beside it, write × 10

$$6.12873 \times 10^{\square}$$

Now, count how many times you need to multiply 6.12873 by $10^{\square}$ to get the original number (612,873). The number of times is the power of ten that you need in your answer.

The digit 6 needs to move five places, so you need 10^5 in your answer.

HTh	TTh	Th	H	T	O	t	h	th	tth	hth
6	1	2	8	7	3					
					6.	1	2	8	7	3

Some people like to imagine that the decimal point is moving five places.

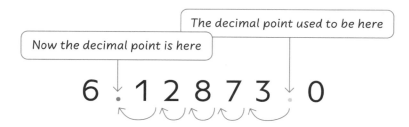

> The decimal point used to be here
> Now the decimal point is here

$$6 . 1 2 8 7 3 . 0$$

Answer: 6.12873×10^5

> Small numbers have negative powers of ten.

Write 0.03057 in standard form

Write the number that is between 1 and 10 and has the same digits by putting a decimal point between the 3 and the 0. Beside it, write × 10

$$3.057 \times 10^{\square}$$

0.03057 is a small number, so the power of ten will be a negative number.

The digit 3 needs to move two places, so you need 10^{-2} in your answer.

O	t	h	th	tth	hth
0.	0	3	0	5	7
3.	0	3	0	5	7

> Remember, the column headings are ones, tenths, hundredths, thousandths, ten-thousandths and hundred-thousandths.

Some people like to imagine that the decimal point is moving two places.

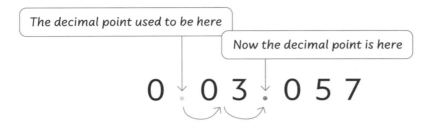

The decimal point used to be here

Now the decimal point is here

0 . 0 3 . 0 5 7

Answer: 3.057×10^{-2}

Write 5.067×10^5 as an ordinary number

The index is 5, so you need to multiply the decimal number by 10, five times.

$$5.067 \times 10 \times 10 \times 10 \times 10 \times 10$$

Each digit moves five places to the left.

Fill the tens and ones columns with a zero (shown in red) to stop the digits sliding back down into a different column.

> If you simplify the first part of the number to 5 and think of the power of ten in words (a hundred thousand) then you can see that the ordinary number will be close to 500,000.

HTh	TTh	Th	H	T	O	t	h	th	tth	hth
					5.	0	6	7		
5	0	6	7	0	0					

Answer: $5.067 \times 10^5 = 506{,}700$

Write 6.47×10^{-3} as an ordinary number

The index is −3, so you need to divide the decimal number by 10, three times.

$$6.47 \div 10 \div 10 \div 10$$

Each digit moves three places to the right.

> You could think of 6 times by a thousandth here. The answer will be a bit more than 6 thousandths.

O	t	h	th	tth	hth
6.	4	7			
0.	0	0	6	4	7

Answer: $6.47 \times 10^{-3} = 0.00647$

ACTIVITY 7.4

1. Write these numbers in standard form.

a) 3472

b) 778,899

c) 368

d) 0.057

e) 0.000 243

f) 0.499

2. Write these numbers as ordinary numbers.

a) 5.9×10^1

b) 3.47×10^4

c) 6.02×10^6

d) 5×10^{-1}

e) 5.1×10^{-3}

f) 2.8×10^0

Standard form on your calculator

You can type numbers in standard form exactly as you see them using the $x^{\blacksquare}$ key on your calculator. Many calculators also have a standard form key with $\times 10^{\blacksquare}$. When you use this key, you do not need to type the multiplication sign or the number 10.

Your calculator may automatically give small answers in standard form. Investigate whether you can change the settings so that small numbers are displayed with all the zeros present rather than in standard form.

ACTIVITY 7.5

Practise typing numbers in standard form into your calculator. Notice how the number appears on your screen – this is not the same on all calculators.

What happens when you press the equals sign? If pressing the equals sign changes the number in standard form back to an ordinary number, think about how you could use this function to check your work in Activity 7.4.

CALCULATIONS IN STANDARD FORM

Multiplying numbers in standard form

Multiply 2.1×10^4 **by** 3×10^2

You can change the order of the numbers to make them easier to multiply.

$$(2.1 \times 3) \times (10^4 \times 10^2)$$

> *Remember, multiplication is commutative, so the order does not matter.*

> *The brackets just show you the two separate calculations. You can do the calculations in brackets first, then multiply the answers.*

Answer: 6.3×10^6

Notice the answer is in standard form.

Multiply 5×10^4 **by** 7×10^{-2}
Change the order of the numbers to make them easier to multiply.

The answer might look like it is in standard form, but it isn't. The number before the multiplication sign is not between 1 and 10. Rewrite your answer.

Use the law of indices to write the final answer.

$$(5 \times 7) \times (10^4 \times 10^{-2})$$
$$= 35 \times 10^2$$
$$= 3.5 \times 10^1 \times 10^2$$

Answer: 3.5×10^3

Dividing numbers in standard form

Divide 8×10^4 **by** 2×10^3
Change the order of the numbers to be divided, just like you did when multiplying.

Work out the two parts separately.

$$8 \div 2 \times 10^4 \div 10^3$$
$$(8 \div 2) \times (10^4 \div 10^3)$$

Answer: 4×10^1

Divide 3×10^4 **by** 6×10^2
Change the order of the numbers to be divided.

The answer might look like it is in standard form, but it isn't. The number before the multiplication sign is not between 1 and 10. Rewrite your answer.

Use the law of indices to write the final answer.

$$3 \div 6 \times 10^4 \div 10^2$$
$$= 0.5 \times 10^2$$
$$= 5 \times 10^{-1} \times 10^2$$

Answer: 5×10^1

Adding and subtracting numbers in standard form
It is quite tricky to add and subtract numbers in standard form, as you can get confused about which column the numbers belong in. Most people find it easiest to change the numbers to ordinary numbers, carry out the addition or subtraction, and then change the answer back into standard form.

Work out $6 \times 10^2 + 4 \times 10^3$
Write your answer in standard form.

Change the numbers in standard form to ordinary numbers, then add them together.

Change the answer back to standard form.

$$600 + 4000 = 4600$$

$$4.6 \times 10^3$$

Answer: $6 \times 10^2 + 4 \times 10^3 = 4.6 \times 10^3$

Make sure you can key all these calculations into your calculator. Your calculator might give the answer as an ordinary number, so check the question to see if you are asked to write the answer in standard form. Check whether your calculator has a setting which means it gives the answers in standard form all the time.

> *It may be the Sci setting. Make sure you know how to change it back!*

ACTIVITY 7.6

Work out these calculations. Give your answers in standard form. Use your calculator to check your work.

a) $(3 \times 10^2) \times (3 \times 10^3)$

b) $(6 \times 10^2) \times (9 \times 10^4)$

c) $(6 \times 10^8) \div (2 \times 10^3)$

d) $(2.5 \times 10^2) \div (5 \times 10^4)$

e) $(3 \times 10^4) + (4 \times 10^4)$

f) $(5 \times 10^4) + (5 \times 10^2)$

g) $(7 \times 10^3) - (2 \times 10^2)$

h) $(4 \times 10^{-1}) - (3 \times 10^{-2})$

SIGNIFICANT FIGURES

Significant means important. Zeros at the start of 007 and at the end of 15,000 or 0.25000 do not usually count as significant figures.

> *The first **significant figure** is the first non-zero digit needed to write the number. Zeros that are only included as place-fillers are not significant (e.g. 0.05), but trapped zeros are significant (e.g. 205).*

The measurements 65 million years, 35 thousand miles, 1.7m, 23cm and 0.0075g are all given to 2 significant figures. This means there would be two digits in the standard form of the number.

Trapped zeros are a bit different. The number 205 is written as 2.05×10^2 so it has three significant figures and so does the number $205,000 = 2.05 \times 10^5$.

Rounding to one significant figure

Look at which column the first significant figure is in, and round to that.

Example 1: to round 3481 to 1 significant figure, notice the first significant figure is in the thousands column, so round to the nearest thousand to get 3000.

Example 2: to round 0.029 to 1 significant figure, notice the first significant figure is in the second decimal place, so round to 2 decimal places to get 0.03.

Rounding to two significant figures

Notice where the second significant figure is.

Example 1: to round 557 to 2 significant figures, you need to round to the nearest ten, which gives 560.

Example 2: to round 0.0798 to 2 significant figures, you need to round to 3 decimal places. The number is between 0.079 and 0.080 and this rounds up to 0.080. Here the zero on the end is significant and you must include it so that you have 3 decimal places.

ACTIVITY 7.7

1. Round these numbers to 1 significant figure.

a) 6448 b) 398 c) 76 d) 0.6757 e) 0.0439

2. Round these numbers to 2 significant figures.

a) 532 b) 6709 c) 0.123 d) 0.486 e) 0.199

3. Do these calculations on your calculator.
Give the answers correct to 3 significant figures.

> You must round the answer to 3 significant figures.

a) 15 ÷ 7 b) 348 + 2.34 c) 500 − 23.74 d) 0.25^4 e) 60.5 × 5.1

ORDER OF OPERATIONS

Indices are sometimes included in a calculation that has other operations. When a calculation has two or more things to do, the order in which you do them can affect the answer. There is a convention used by mathematicians that dictates the order in which operations are carried out.

> Brackets can be used to show the part which is done first.

> A **convention** is an agreed way of doing things that everyone accepts.

After the brackets come the indices. The expression 2×5^2 means you must work out the answer to $5^2 = 25$ and then work out $2 \times 25 = 50$. People who have not understood the convention might want to work out 2×5 first and then work out $10^2 = 100$. That is incorrect. If you intend people to do the multiplication first, you should put that part in a bracket and write the power for the whole bracket: $(2 \times 5)^2$

Multiply and divide come next. The expression $3 + 2 \times 5$ means that you must work out $2 \times 5 = 10$ and then $3 + 10 = 13$. People who do not understand the convention might work from left to right and solve $3 + 2$ to get 5 and

> Type this expression into your calculator. Does your calculator know the rules?

then do 5 × 5 = 25. That is incorrect. If you intend people to do the adding first, you should put that part in a bracket. (3 + 2) × 5 does give 25 for the answer.

Addition and subtraction come last. So, the expression 24 ÷ 3 - 2 × 2 is not done following the instructions from left to right. You must work out the division 24 ÷ 3 = 8, then the multiplication 2 × 2 = 4 and finally subtract one answer from the other, giving 8 - 4 = 4. You can use brackets round any part of the calculation to show that the normal rules do not apply and the part in the bracket must be done first. Otherwise, you do work through a set of calculations from left to right.

When all the operations are of the same type, then the order is not so important. The calculation 2 × 3 × 5 can be done by working out 2 × 3 = 6 and then 6 × 5 = 30. You get the same answer if you do 2 × 5 = 10 and then 10 × 3 = 30. If the answer is the same, the order does not matter.

Some people use the mnemonic **BIDMAS** to help them to remember the order of operations.

B – brackets
I – index
D – division
M – multiplication
A – addition
S – subtraction

What strategies do you use to help remember things like this? Is there a better way for you?

ACTIVITY 7.8

Match each of the calculations with the answers on the right. You can use the answers more than once!

Questions

a) 2×3^2
b) $(2 \times 3)^2$
c) 3×2^3
d) $(3 \times 2)^3$
e) $2 + 4 \times 4$

f) $(2 + 4) \times 4$
g) $(4 \div 8)^2 + 7$
h) $2 \times 5 + 24 \div 8$
i) $2 \times (5 + 24) \div 8$
j) $2 \times 3^2 \times (10 + 2)$

Answers
A) 7.25
B) 13
C) 18
D) 24
E) 36
F) 216

CHAPTER SUM-UP

Reflection

Having worked through this chapter, how do you feel about these skills?

Skill	I have tried this	I need more practice	I am confident with this
Understanding powers of a number			
Knowing the laws of indices			
Understanding standard form for large and small numbers			
Understanding rounding to a given number of significant figures			
Understanding the order of operations (BIDMAS)			

Quiz

Which of these calculations gives the answer 25 when rounded to 2 significant figures?

a) $3 \times 7 + 7 \div 2$

b) 2.43849×10^1

c) $2^{-2} \times 9 \times 11$

d) $(5.439 \times 10^4) \div (2.13 \times 10^3)$

e) $(5 - 3)^8$

f) $7 + \dfrac{15 + 20}{2}$

8. Ratio and Proportion

AIMS
- To understand ratio
- To simplify a ratio
- To find a missing value
- To divide a number in a given ratio
- To solve tricky problems involving ratio

RESOURCES
- Red, yellow and blue counters
- Monopoly money
- Envelopes

PREVIOUS KNOWLEDGE
- Multiplication and division

 Rewind – look at page 65 for the grid method for multiplication

UNDERSTANDING RATIO

Make a pattern using red counters and yellow counters.
Perhaps your pattern looks like one of these.

> Use a colon : for ratio.

Patterns that show the ratio 1:1	Patterns that do not show the ratio 1:1
⚫⚫⚫ ⚪⚪⚪	⚪⚪⚪ ⚫⚫⚫⚫
⚪⚫ ⚪⚫ ⚪⚫	⚪⚫ ⚪⚫ ⚪⚫ ⚫
⚫⚪⚫⚪⚫⚪⚫⚪	⚫⚪⚫⚪⚫⚪⚪

Now, make a pattern using two red counters for every one yellow counter. This pattern will show the ratio of red counters to yellow counters as 2:1

> *The order in the ratio matters. In this example, red counters come first (each group you make must contain two of these); yellow counters come next (there will be one counter in each group you make).*

Here are some possible solutions.

Notice the ratio does not tell you how many counters to use. It does tell you, however, that there are twice as many red counters as yellow counters – or half as many yellow counters as red counters – or that the counters are in groups of three. But when you know how many yellow counters there are, you know how many red counters there are too (and vice versa).

Red and yellow counters in the ratio 1:2 will not make the same pattern as above, where the ratio was 2:1

Here are two possible solutions for red and yellow counters in the ratio 1:2

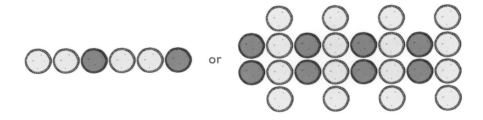

Make a pattern with red and yellow counters in the ratio 2:3. Do you need more red or more yellow counters?

Two possible solutions are:

ACTIVITY 8.1

1. Use counters to make and continue the patterns below.

For each pattern, write down the ratio of red counters to yellow counters.

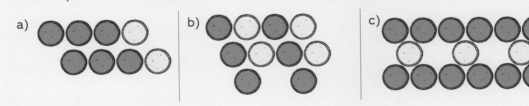

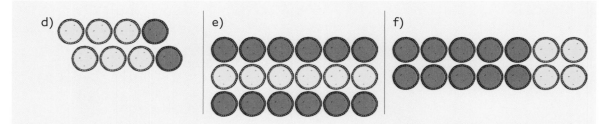

2. Use counters to make some other patterns with ratios that match those in Question 1.

SIMPLIFYING RATIOS

Use nine red counters and three yellow counters to make different patterns.

This pattern clearly shows the nine red counters and the three yellow counters.

You could say the ratio of red to yellow counters is 9:3

This arrangement of counters makes an attractive pattern but it hides the link between the numbers 9 and 3.

Arrange the counters so that each group has the same number of red and yellow counters.

Here, you can clearly see the ratio of red to yellow counters. It is 3:1

3:1 is the simplest way of describing the ratio 9:3

Each group has a ratio of red to yellow counters of 3:1

ACTIVITY 8.2

Make a pattern using the counters stated. Group the counters so you can write the simplest ratio.

a) 9 red and 9 yellow

b) 36 red and 6 yellow

c) 10 red and 30 yellow

d) 4 red and 16 yellow

e) 24 red and 16 yellow

f) 14 red and 6 yellow

FINDING A MISSING VALUE

Knowing the ratio of red counters to yellow counters does not tell you how many counters you need. But if you are told how many counters of one colour to use, then you can work out how many counters of the other colour you need.

The ratio of red counters to yellow counters is 1:3. You have five red counters. How many yellow counters do you need?

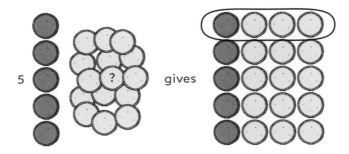

Answer: 15 yellow counters are needed

The ratio of red counters to yellow counters is 2:3. You have 12 yellow counters. How many red counters do you need?

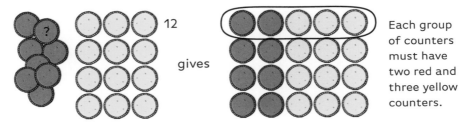

Each group of counters must have two red and three yellow counters.

Answer: 8 red counters are needed

ACTIVITY 8.3

Find the missing value.

a) The ratio of red to yellow counters is 1:3; this is 6 red counters and ☐ yellow counters

b) The ratio of red to yellow counters is 1:3; this is ☐ red counters and 9 yellow counters

c) The ratio of red to yellow counters is 4:1; this is ☐ red counters and 2 yellow counters

d) The ratio of red to yellow counters is 4:1; this is 20 red counters and ☐ yellow counters

e) The ratio of red to yellow counters is 2:5; this is 8 red counters and ☐ yellow counters

f) The ratio of red to yellow counters is 2:5; this is ☐ red counters and 30 yellow counters

g) The ratio of red to yellow counters is 7:3; this is ☐ red counters and 12 yellow counters

h) The ratio of red to yellow counters is 7:3; this is 21 red counters and ☐ yellow counters

DIVIDING A NUMBER IN A GIVEN RATIO

Sometimes you know the ratio of red to yellow counters and the total number of counters. In this case, you can work out how many of each coloured counter there must be.

There are 20 counters, with red to yellow counters in the ratio 2:3. Work out the number of red counters and yellow counters.

Start with a row of two red and three yellow counters; this is five counters all together.

 5

Put more rows of counters underneath, until there are 20 counters all together.

5
10
15
20

> Notice how the pattern is linked to the five times table. (See the 5-bone from Napier's bones.)

Four rows give 20 counters all together, which is 8 red counters and 12 yellow counters.

Answer: 8 red counters and 12 yellow counters

ACTIVITY 8.4

1. Work out how many red counters and how many yellow counters there are for each total and the ratio of red to yellow counters.

a) 10 counters in the ratio 1:4

b) 27 counters in the ratio 2:1

c) 36 counters in the ratio 4:5

d) 24 counters in the ratio 5:3

e) 16 counters in the ratio 1:1

f) 18 counters in the ratio 5:1

g) 28 counters in the ratio 5:2

h) 30 counters in the ratio 3:7

2. Is it possible to divide 10 counters in the ratio 3:1? If not, why not?

Some tricky questions

Ratio is useful because it tells you the relationship between red counters and yellow counters. It is not so easy to answer questions where you are told how many extra counters you have of one colour. You need to think carefully to answer questions like this.

The ratio of red to yellow counters is 3:7. There are 12 more yellow counters than red counters. How many counters are there of each colour? How many counters are there all together?

Make one row of three red and seven yellow counters.

There are four more yellow counters in the row than red counters.

Put more rows of counters underneath until there are 12 extra yellow counters in total.

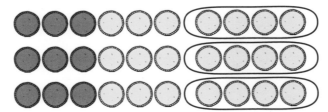

Three rows make 12 extra counters all together.

Answer: There are 9 red counters and 21 yellow counters; that is 30 counters all together

ACTIVITY 8.5

Work out how many red counters and how many yellow counters are needed.
Each ratio states the number of red counters to the number of yellow counters.

a) Ratio 1:2; there are 10 more yellow counters than red counters

b) Ratio 3:1; there and 6 more red counters than yellow counters

c) Ratio 3:5; there are 8 more yellow counters than red counters

d) Ratio 8:7; there are 5 more red counters than yellow counters

WORKING WITH THREE NUMBERS IN A RATIO

**The ratio of red counters to yellow counters to blue counters is 1:2:5
How many counters are there all together if there are six yellow counters?**
Make a pattern that has one red, two yellow and five blue counters in each group.
Continue your pattern until you have six yellow counters.

> *The order matters. For each group, the red counters come first (one counter); then the yellow counters (one, two counters); finally, the blue counters (one, two, three, four, five counters).*

Count all the counters.

3 + 6 + 15 = 24 counters

Answer: There are 24 counters all together

ACTIVITY 8.6

Red, yellow and blue counters are in the ratio 2:3:5.

a) If there are 10 red counters, how many yellow counters and blue counters are there?

b) If there are 15 blue counters, how many counters are there all together?

c) If there are 40 counters all together, how many counters are there of each colour?

d) If there are two more yellow counters than red counters, how many counters are there of each colour?

WORKING WITH BIGGER NUMBERS

Divide £3235 in Monopoly money between Alex and Ben in the ratio 3 : 2

You could start by laying out the notes in the ratio 3 : 2

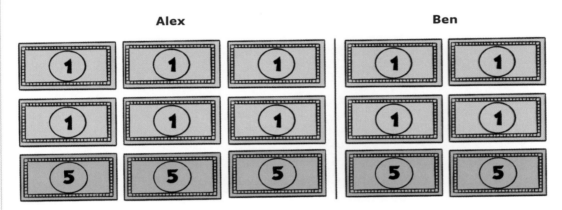

You could use £1 or £5 notes, as long as there are equal amounts of money in each of the five columns.

But it would be easier to use five envelopes and share the money into five equal amounts.

Alex gets three envelopes and Ben gets two.

Count or work out how much money is in each envelope. Then, work out how much each person gets.

Represent each envelope with a bar model like this.

£3235				
£647	£647	£647	£647	£647

Alex gets 3 × 647 = £1941   **Ben** gets 2 × 647 = £1294

ACTIVITY 8.7

1. Use the envelopes method to divide each amount between Alex and Ben in the given ratio. Draw bar models to help you to work out the answers and provide evidence of your method.

a) £30 in the ratio 2:1

b) £450 in the ratio 1:2

c) £600 in the ratio 1:4

d) £550 in the ratio 2:3

e) £750 in the ratio 3:2

f) £3570 in the ratio 4:3

g) £8992 in the ratio 3:5

You can cut corners with these large amounts and go straight to the bar model if you like!

2. Make up some questions of your own by putting money into envelopes. Draw the bar models as well to record your work. Don't forget to show your answers clearly.

USING MONEY AND THE BAR MODEL FOR RATIO QUESTIONS

Simplifying ratios

Alex has £300 and Ben has £200. What ratio is this?

Using £100 notes, this is the ratio 3:2

What about when Alex has £210 and Ben has £280? How much would you put in each envelope?

You could try putting £10 in each envelope, but you would need a lot of envelopes.

The highest common factor of £210 and £280 is £70, so Alex will need three envelopes and Ben will need four envelopes.

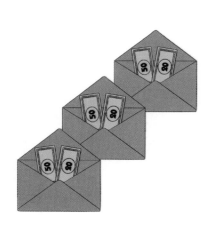 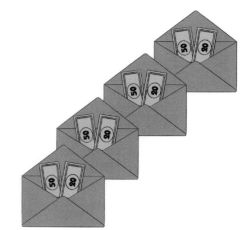

Record your answer using a bar model.

£210			£280			
£70	£70	£70	£70	£70	£70	£70

So, the ratio is 3:4

Finding an unknown amount

Alex and Ben have money in the ratio 1:4. Ben has £720. How much does Alex have? How much do Alex and Ben have all together?

Draw the bar model for the ratio. Write the amount that Ben has underneath.

Work out how much is in each bar using the division 720 ÷ 4. The answer is 180, so write '£180' in each of the small bars.

£180	£180	£180	£180	£180
	£720			

Alex has £180   **Ben** has £720

Answer: Alex and Ben have £180 + £720 = £900 all together

Another way of finding out how much money Alex has is to draw comparative bar models, with a bar for Alex above a bar for Ben. The bar for Ben is four times as long as the bar for Alex.

 **Alex**

Ben

You can work out that 720 ÷ 4 = 180 goes in each section.

£180	£180	£180	£180
	£720		

Alex has £180.

TRICKY CALCULATIONS

Alex and Ben have money in the ratio 2:5 and Alex has £90 less than Ben. How much do Alex and Ben have all together?

Explore with envelopes and Monopoly money. Did you find a strategy?

Draw the bar model for the ratio.

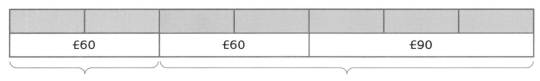

				£90			

Work out how much goes in each bar.

This is the extra that **Ben** has

£30	£30	£30	£30	£30	£30	£30
			£90			

Complete the amounts.

£60		£60		£90		

Alex has £60   **Ben** has £150

Alternatively, you might like to use comparative bar models, with a bar for Alex drawn above a bar for Ben.

Alex has two parts.

Ben has five parts. It is easier to see the £90 that Ben has more than Alex.

		£90		

Each part is worth £30 (£90 ÷ 3 = £30)

Now you can find out how much money Alex and Ben have.

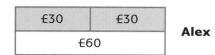

£30	£30
£60	

Alex

Alex has £60

Ben

£30	£30	£30	£30	£30
£90			£60	

Ben has £150

ACTIVITY 8.8

Use bar models for these calculations. Work out how much money Ben and Alex have in each question.

a) Alex and Ben share money in the ratio 1:3. Ben has £20 more than Alex.

b) Alex and Ben share money in the ratio 5:4. Alex has £30 more than Ben.

c) Alex and Ben share money in the ratio 2:7. Alex has £35 less than Ben.

Using movement

Another way to work with ratio is to use the human ratio machine. Imagine the numbers from the ratio sitting on each shoulder. The corresponding amounts sit on each hip.

This set of diagrams shows the same information as the bar model that you used in the previous example, where Ben and Alex had money in the ratio 2:5 and Alex had £90 less than Ben. Here it is again.

£30	£30	£30	£30	£30	£30	£30
				£90		

The amount in each bar of the bar model is a multiplier as you move from shoulder to hip.

Notice there is a multiplier as you go sideways, either at the shoulder or at the hip.

The example below fully explains how to use your body as a human ratio machine.

Divide £32 between Alex and Ben in the ratio 3:5

Imagine the numbers 3 and 5 on your shoulders and the total of 3 and 5 (8) beyond.

Decide where the £32 should go – it is under the 8.

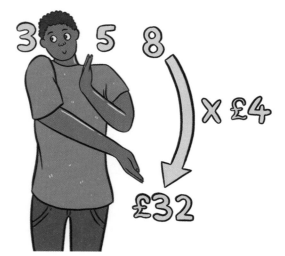

To find the multiplier that turns 8 into £32, do the division 32 ÷ 8. The multiplier is £4.

This gives £12 and £20.

Answer: Alex gets £12 and Ben gets £20

You can record your work as a video, or you can put it in a table.

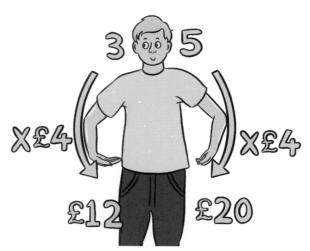

	Alex	Ben	Total
	3	5	8
	£12	£20	£32

×4 ... ×4

Using movement works well for exchange rates and for converting between units of measurement too.

1 inch is 2.54 centimetres. What is 4 inches in centimetres?

Put 1 and 2.54 on your shoulders and into a table.

	inches	centimetres
	1	2.54
	4	

×4 ... ×4

Use your calculator to work out 2.54 × 4

Answer: 4 inches is 2.54 × 4 = 10.16 centimetres

What is 1 m in inches?

×39.37

inches	centimetres
1	2.54
39.37	100

×39.37

First, change 1 m to 100 cm.

Divide 100 by 2.54 to find the multiplier.

Answer: 1 metre is 39.37 inches

ACTIVITY 8.9

1. Change these lengths to centimetres. There are 2.54 cm in 1 inch.

a) 5 inches

b) 1 foot (12 inches)

2. Change these lengths to inches. There are 2.54 cm in 1 inch.

a) 25.4cm

b) 80cm

3. Change these amounts from pounds to dollars. Use £1 for $1.30

a) £50

b) £12.40

4. Change these amounts from dollars to pounds. Use £1 for $1.30

a) $50

b) $1

CHAPTER SUM-UP

Reflection

Having worked through this chapter, how do you feel about these skills?

Skill	I have tried this	I need more practice	I am confident with this
Understanding ratio			
Simplifying a ratio			
Finding a missing value			
Dividing a number in a given ratio			
Solving tricky problems involving ratio			

Quiz

Manjinder and Natalie share £80 in the ratio 3:5.

Xander, Yolande and Zoe share US$100 in the ratio 2:3:5.

Who gets the most money? You will need to find out today's exchange rate to be sure.

9. Introduction to Algebra

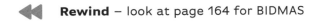

AIMS

- To represent a number with x
- To add and subtract algebraic expressions
- To collect like terms together
- To substitute values into algebraic expressions

RESOURCES

- Two-colour double-sided counters
- A set of card tubes with yellow and red ends (see page 284)
- A set of Napier's bones (see page 279)

PREVIOUS KNOWLEDGE

- Positive and negative numbers using zero pairs

⏪ **Rewind** – look at page 164 for BIDMAS

If you want to tell a person how to work something out, you could give them instructions in words. Of course, the person you are talking to would have to understand the language you are speaking. If you are talking to someone who understands the language of algebra, you can write the instructions in only a few symbols and then use the rules of algebra to work out lots of other useful stuff.

In algebra, you can use a letter to represent a number – think of it as acting!

Algebra can do all the things numbers can do and must follow the same rules.

Don't use 'a is for apple' because a is a number. a could be the number of apples in a bag, or the cost of an apple, or another number entirely!

⏪ **Rewind** – look at page 140 for positive and negative numbers

ACTIVITY 9.1

Use two-colour double-sided counters to model and answer these calculations. Each counter has a value of 1 or –1 depending on which colour is facing upwards.

a) (–1) + (–5)   c) 7 – 9   e) 3 – (–4)
b) 5 + (–3)   d) (–2) – 5   f) (–2) – (–8)

REPRESENTING A NUMBER WITH x

Make up some tubes from the templates on page 284. When the yellow end is at the top of a tube, it represents the number x. When the red end is at the top, it represents the number -x.

Use x to represent the number of counters stacked inside a tube that has the yellow end at the top. In this book, x is drawn as a yellow tube.

> You might not know how many counters that is.

A second, identical tube with the same number of counters stacked inside is another x. But if the second tube has a different number of counters stacked inside than the first tube, the second tube needs to be labelled with a different letter.

If a tube has the red end at the top, use -x to represent the number of counters stacked inside. In this book, -x is drawn as a red tube.

REPRESENTING ALGEBRAIC EXPRESSIONS

You can build expressions by combining counters and stacks of counters.

> An **expression** is a combination of letters and numbers with no equals sign.

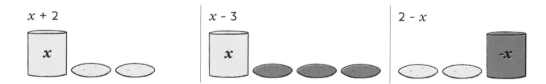

You can work with multiple stacks as well. In the first diagram below, $3x$ is the number of counters in three stacks.

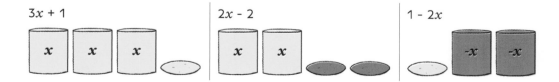

You can use zero pairs to find other ways of representing expressions.

> One yellow stack and one red stack together make $x + (-x) = 0$

These diagrams of stacks show three different ways of representing x. Can you draw other combinations of stacks that represent x?

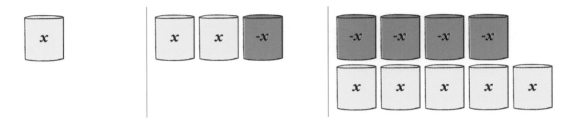

ACTIVITY 9.2

1. Build these representations and write expressions for them.

You will need to show the x's and the ones separately.
This means you will need two terms in each expression.

A **term** is the part of an expression between the + or - signs.

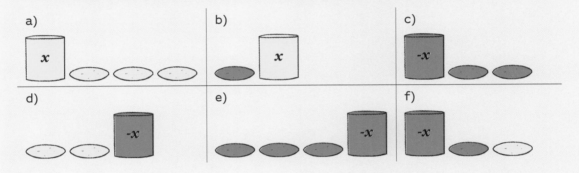

2. Add zero pairs (counters or stacks) to make other ways of representing these expressions.

3. Write some expressions of your own and build them in several ways.

ADDING ALGEBRAIC EXPRESSIONS

To add two expressions together:

- build each expression using counters and stacks
- rearrange the counters and stacks – group the counters together; group the stacks together
- remember to take out any zero pairs.

Find $(x + 2) + (x - 3)$

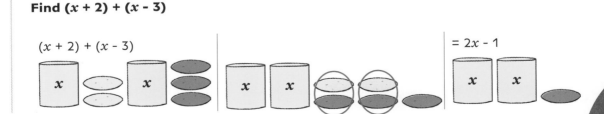

Find (3x - 4) + (2 − x)

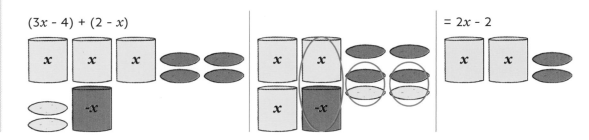

ACTIVITY 9.3

1. Build these additions and write down the algebraic expression as simply as possible.

a) (x - 3) + (3x + 1)   b) (2x - 3) + (6 - 3x)   c) (-x - 4) + (1 - 3x)

2. Write some additions of your own. Build them, collect like terms (i.e. group the stacks together; group the counters together), then simplify by finding zero pairs.

SUBTRACTING ALGEBRAIC EXPRESSIONS

To subtract one expression from another:

- build the first expression
- take away the second expression; remember to add in as many zero pairs as you need
- the answer is what is left behind.

Find (3x + 4) - (x + 8)

> *You need to take a tube of x and eight counters as well.*

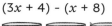
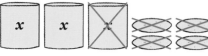
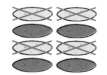
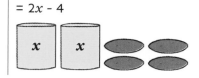

Find (2x + 3) - (-x + 4)

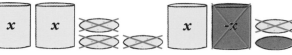
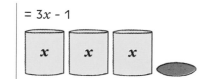

ACTIVITY 9.4

1. Build these subtractions and write down the algebraic expression as simply as possible.

a) $(x - 3) - (3x + 1)$ b) $(2x - 3) - (6 - 3x)$ c) $(-x - 4) - (1 - 3x)$

2. Write some subtractions of your own. Build them and then find the simplified expression.

USING MOVEMENT – THE HUMAN NUMBER LINE FOR ADDING AND SUBTRACTING IN ALGEBRA

⏪ **Rewind** – look at page 146 for the human number line
You use one hand for adding and subtracting positive numbers (the natural way) and the other hand for adding and subtracting the negative numbers (the back-to-front way).

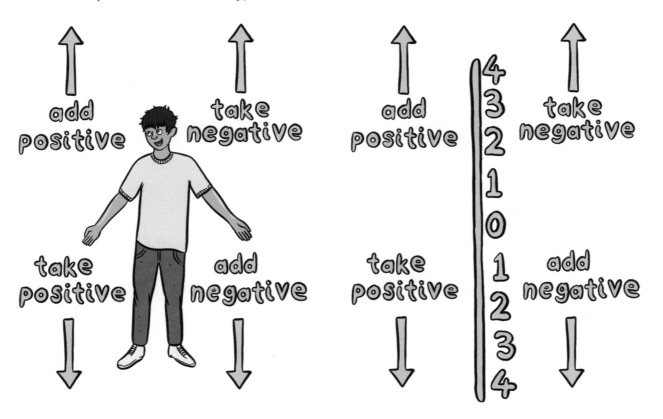

You can add and subtract on your 'human' number line by thinking of each x as a 'jump' up and each 1 as a single step up. Try to make as few moves as possible with the same result.

$2x + 3x - x + -2x$ represents 2 jumps up, another 3 jumps up, 1 jump down and another 2 jumps down, which is 2 jumps up overall.

> *Make sure you either do the movements or draw the movements on a number line.*

So $2x + 3x - x + -2x = 2x$

Where jumps and steps are mixed together, you can switch the order in which they happen. Remember to bring the sign with the term each time you swap the order of terms.

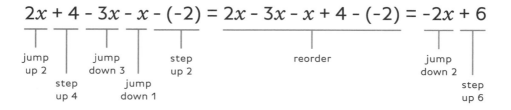

$$2x + 4 - 3x - x - (-2) = 2x - 3x - x + 4 - (-2) = -2x + 6$$

| jump up 2 | step up 4 | jump down 3 | jump down 1 | step up 2 | reorder | jump down 2 | step up 6 |

USING NAPIER'S BONES FOR ADDING AND SUBTRACTING IN ALGEBRA

The letter x is used to represent any number. When x is a whole number, $3x$ is a number in the three times table. $7x$ is the number in the equivalent row of the 7-bone. When you add these two numbers together, you get the number in the equivalent row of the 10-bone.

In the diagram, the numbers in the loop show that (3 lots of 4) + (7 lots of 4) = 10 lots of 4.

$(3 \times 4) + (7 \times 4)$
$= (12 + 28)$
$= 40 = 10 \times 4$

Check that this idea works for all the rows in the diagram. You can write down the whole pattern using algebra; for example, $3x + 7x = 10x$

Investigate what happens when you use different bones. Check there is a similar pattern. Can you explain your pattern in words and in algebra?

SUBSTITUTING VALUES INTO ALGEBRAIC EXPRESSIONS

Everything you have done so far in this chapter works with x representing *any* number.

Sometimes you have more than one x (such as $3x$). Remember that algebra does not contain any multiplication signs. You have to write in the multiplication sign when you replace the letter with a number.

$3x$ means 3 lots of x.

If x is given a value, say 5, then $3x$ means 3 lots of 5 or $3 \times 5 = 15$

> $3x$ is not 35 when $x = 5$

Evaluate 3x - 2 when $x = 5$

Put five yellow counters in three tubes with the yellow end at the top.

Build the expression $3x - 2$ with your tubes and two-colour double-sided counters.

Remove the wrapper from each tube and count how many counters you have all together. Think of a smart way to count them.

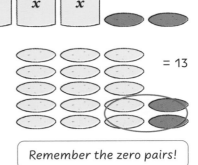

= 13

Answer: When $x = 5$, $3x - 2 = (3 \times 5) - 2 = 15 - 2 = 13$

> Remember the zero pairs!

> Copy the complete expression but take x out and put 5 in its place.

Evaluate 3x - 2 when $x = -5$

When you swap x for -5, you have to put five red counters in three tubes with the yellow end at the top.

Answer: When $x = -5$, $3x - 2 = 3 \times (-5) - 2 = (-15) - 2 = (-17)$

Evaluate 3 - 2x when $x = 4$

Put four yellow counters in each tube with the yellow end at the top.

To build the expression $3 - 2x$, you need to turn the tubes so that the red ends are at the top.

Remove the wrapper from each tube and count how many counters you have all together.

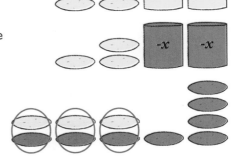

Answer: When $x = 4$, $3 - 2x = 3 - 2 \times 4 = 3 - 8 = -5$

Evaluate 3 - 2x when x = -4

To substitute x = -4, make sure there are four red counters in each tube, yellow edge facing up. Turn the tubes upside down. Count how many counters you have.

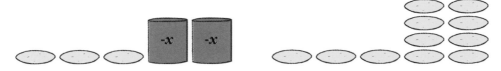

Answer: When x = -4, 3 - 2x = 3 - 2 × (-4) = 3 + 8 = 11

ACTIVITY 9.5

1. Substitute x = 5 into these expressions. Make the expressions with your counters to help you.

    a) x + 3   b) 2x - 1   c) 3 + 3x d) 5 - x e) 12 - 5x

2. Substitute x = -4 into the same expressions.

 Fast forward – look at page 206 for algebra manipulation

Using the Table function on your calculator

Many scientific calculators have a Table function. Press the Menu or Mode key on your calculator to see if it has a Table function. If it does, then your calculator will work out the value of an algebraic expression for a set of values that you can choose.

    You can make a table of values for 2x + 3, with the whole numbers 1 to 5 on the left and the values for the expression on the right. In Table mode, the calculator display shows f(x) =. You type the algebra 2x + 3 and press the equals key. (How you type the x depends on the type of calculator you have.) Then answer the questions start, end and step. If you choose start 1, end 5 and step 1 you'll get the table you want. (These values may already be there – they are called the default values.)

> *Notice the x column starts at 1, ends at 5 and goes up in steps of 1.*

> *f(x) is just a name for the algebra expression with x in it.*

x	f(x)
1	5
2	7
3	9
4	11
5	13

> *Look at the pattern in these answers!*

Go back through the instructions and make tables of values for other expressions with negative as well as positive values for x.

> *Pressing the Mode key again will give you the option of going back to Calculate mode. Some calculators call this Run mode.*

Using the Table function to check your algebra

You may want to find out whether you have correctly substituted a number into an expression.

To substitute the value $x = (-3)$ into the expression $5 - 3x$ you can create a table that includes the row with $x = (-3)$ on it.

For example, type $f(x) = 5 - 3x$, start (-3), end 3 and step 1. Read off the value 14 from row (-3).

x	$f(x)$
-3	14
-2	11
-1	8
0	5
1	2
2	-1
3	-4

ACTIVITY 9.6

Repeat Activity 9.5, but this time, type each expression into Table mode and read off the values you need from the table.

> Make sure your values include (-4) and 5.

 Fast forward – look at page 242 and 246 for expanding and factorizing; page 250 for quadratic equations and page 258 for algebraic graphs

CHAPTER SUM-UP

Reflection

Having worked through this chapter, how do you feel about these skills?

Skill	I have tried this	I need more practice	I am confident with this
Representing a number with x			
Adding and subtracting algebraic expressions			
Collecting like terms together			
Substituting values into algebraic expressions			

Quiz

1. How many of these expressions simplify to just one term?

a) $(x + 2) + (2x - 1)$

b) $(5 - 2x) + x + x$

c) $(5 - 3x) + (7 - 3x)$

d) $(3x - 4) - (x - 4)$

2. Which of the expressions in Question 1 gives the biggest answer when the value $x = (-2)$ is substituted?

10. Equations and Inequalities

AIMS

- To solve simple equations in one step
- To solve more complicated equations in two steps
- To understand what an inequality is
- To solve inequalities

RESOURCES

- Two-colour double-sided counters
- A set of card tubes with yellow and red ends (see page 284)
- A calculator with Table mode

PREVIOUS KNOWLEDGE

- Using letters to represent numbers
- Adding and subtracting algebraic expressions
- Substituting values into algebraic expressions
- Making a table of values using the Table mode on a calculator

 Rewind – look at page 182 for representing expressions with tubes and counters

ACTIVITY 10.1

Represent these expressions with tubes and counters.

a) $x + 3$ b) $2x + 5$ c) $3x - 1$ d) $4 - x$ e) $(-1) - 3x$

SOLVING EQUATIONS: TUBES AND COUNTERS

Solving an equation is finding out the value of x.

> In an **equation**, you are told that two algebraic expressions balance each other.

One-step equations

Solve $x + 3 = 5$

Represent the equation with two equal sets of counters.

Take 3 from both sides.

Simplify and stack the counters to match the tube.

So, there must be two counters in the tube.

> Writing $2 + 3 = 5$ is true but it doesn't answer the question 'What is x?'

Answer: $x = 2$

You could write your answer like this to show your working.

$$x + 3 = 5$$
$$-3 \qquad \qquad -3$$
$$x = 2$$

If you prefer to work with movement, imagine $x + 3$ written on one shoulder and 5 written on the other. They balance, so your shoulders are level. Point to these and move your hands to your hips to take the 3 from both sides.

Solve $x - 2 = 4$

Represent the equation with two equal sets of counters.

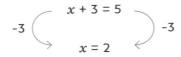

191

Add two yellow counters to each set, to make two zero pairs.

Simplify and stack the counters to match the tube.

So, there must be six counters in the tube.

Answer: $x = 6$

You could write your answer like this to show your working.

$$+2 \quad \overset{x - 2 = 4}{\underset{x = 6}{\big(\qquad\big)}} \quad +2$$

Solve $3x = 12$
Represent the equation with two equal sets of counters.

 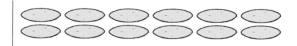

Put the counters into three stacks.

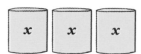 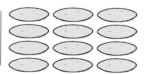

Each stack must be the same.

So, there must be four counters in the tube.

Answer: $x = 4$

You could write your answer as shown overleaf to show your working.

$$3x = 12$$

÷3 ⤵ ⤷ ÷3

$$x = 4$$

Solve $\frac{x}{2} = 3$

The expression $\frac{x}{2}$ means the number of counters in half a tube. You need to know how many counters there are in a whole tube.

Stack two of these together to make a whole tube.

So, there must be six counters in the tube.

Answer: $x = 6$

You could write your answer like this to show your working.

$$\frac{x}{2} = 3$$

×2 ⤵ ⤷ ×2

$$x = 6$$

ACTIVITY 10.2

Solve these equations. Use tubes and counters to help you. Write your answers carefully.

a) $x + 5 = 11$ c) $x - 5 = 2$ e) $5x = 20$ g) $\frac{x}{2} = 9$

b) $x + 12 = 18$ d) $x - 5 = 8$ f) $7x = 49$ h) $\frac{x}{4} = 3$

The answers may not be positive whole numbers

Solve $x + 5 = 3$

Represent the equation with two equal sets of counters.

> You are going to need some zero pairs here.

Take five from both sides.

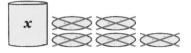

Simplify and stack the counters to match the tube.

So, there must be two red counters in the tube.

Answer: $x = (-2)$

You could write your answer like this to show your working.

$$x + 5 = 3$$
$$-5 \qquad \qquad -5$$
$$x = (-2)$$

Solve $x - 2 = (-4)$
Represent the equation with two equal sets of counters.

Put in two yellow counters to make two zero pairs.

Simplify and stack the counters to match the tube.

So, there must be two red counters in the tube.

Answer: $x = (-2)$

You could write your answer like this to show your working.

$$x - 2 = (-4)$$
$$x = (-2)$$

+2   +2

Solve 2x = 5

Represent the equation with two equal sets of counters.

Put the counters into two stacks. Split the last counter in half.

Each stack must be the same.

So, there must be $2\frac{1}{2}$ counters in the tube.

Answer: $x = 2\frac{1}{2}$ or $x = \frac{5}{2}$

You could write your answer like this to show your working.

> Notice the top-heavy fraction has the number you are dividing on the top and the number you are dividing by on the bottom. You can leave your answer like this.

$$2x = 5$$
$$x = \frac{5}{2} = 2\frac{1}{2}$$

÷2   ÷2

ACTIVITY 10.3

Solve these equations. Write your answers carefully.

a) $x + 7 = 3$

b) $x + 2 = (-8)$

c) $x - 5 = (-7)$

d) $x - 5 = (-4)$

e) $2x = 13$

f) $4x = 9$

g) $\frac{x}{2} = (-9)$

h) $\frac{x}{4} = (-5)$

Multi-step equations

Solve 2x + 5 = 11
Represent the equation with two equal sets of counters.

Your aim is to leave one tube on its own. The 'onion method' peels away layers, starting with the outside layer (+ 5) and then moving onto the inside layer (× 2).

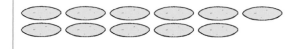

Take five counters from both sides.

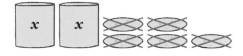
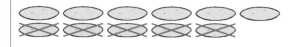

Simplify and stack the counters to match the tubes.

So, there must be three counters in one tube.

Answer: $x = 3$

You could write your answer like this to show your working.

$$2x + 5 = 11$$
$-5 \qquad \qquad -5$
$$2x = 6$$
$\div 2 \qquad \qquad \div 2$
$$x = 3$$

Solve 3x - 1 = 5
Represent the equation with two equal sets of counters.

In the 'onion method', the outside layer is (−1) and the inside layer is (×3).

Add one yellow counter to both sides to create a zero pair.

Simplify and stack the counters to match the tubes.

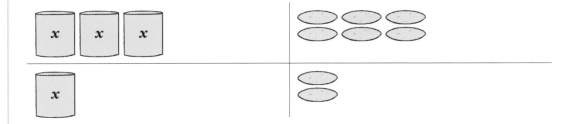

So, there must be two counters in a tube.

Answer: $x = 2$

You could write your answer like this to show your working.

$$3x - 1 = 5$$
$$+1 \qquad \qquad +1$$
$$3x = 6$$
$$\div 3 \qquad \qquad \div 3$$
$$x = 2$$

Solve 7 - 2x = 3

Represent the equation with two equal sets of counters.

> Having 'minus 2x' makes this harder. Deal with that first.

Put two yellow tubes on both sides to make zero pairs. (This is adding 2x.)

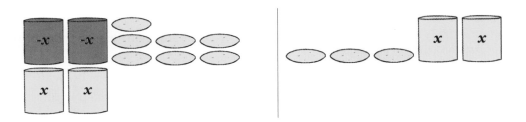

Take three from both sides.

Stack the counters and simplify to match the tubes.

So, there must be two counters in the tube.

Answer: $x = 2$

> Remember that $x = 2$ and $2 = x$ say the same thing.

You could write your answer like this to show your working.

$$7 - 2x = 3$$
$+2x$ $+2x$
$$7 = 3 + 2x$$
-3 -3
$$4 = 2x$$
$\div 2$ $\div 2$
$$2 = x$$

ACTIVITY 10.4

Solve these equations. Use tubes and counters to help you. Write your answers carefully.

a) $2x + 5 = 15$ c) $7x - 5 = 30$ e) $6x - 14 = 46$ g) $12 - 5x = 2$

b) $3x + 1 = 10$ d) $4x - 5 = 11$ f) $10 - x = 8$ h) $5 - 3x = 5$

SOLVING EQUATIONS: BAR MODELS

Some people like to use a bar model to solve equations.

Solve $2x + 9 = 17$

Draw two bars the same length. The top bar represents 17. The bottom bar represents x, another x and an extra 9.

> You might not get the sizes of the bars quite right but it doesn't matter.

17		
x	x	9

When you remove the extra 9, the 17 bar becomes 17 - 9 = 8

8	
x	x

So, you can see that x must be 4.

4	4
x	x

Answer: $x = 4$

> *Remember to write your answer clearly.*

Solve 4x - 11 = 17

Start with a bar for 4x (grey). Underneath, put the subtraction bar (red).
The rest of the bar (blue) represents 17.

x	x	x	x
		11	
17			

You can now see that 4x is the same as 17 + 11 = 28

x	x	x	x
28			

So x must be 28 ÷ 4 = 7

x	x	x	x
7	7	7	7

Answer: $x = 7$

Solve 10 - 3x = 4

Start with a subtraction bar model.

10			
	x	x	x
4			

You could write this as an addition: $4 + 3x = 10$

10			
4	x	x	x

Or you could go straight to this bar for $3x = 6$

6		
x	x	x

2	2	2
x	x	x

Answer: $x = 2$

ACTIVITY 10.5

Use the bar model method to solve these equations. Remember to write your answers clearly.

a) $2x + 5 = 15$ c) $7x - 5 = 30$ e) $6x - 14 = 46$ g) $12 - 5x = 2$

b) $3x + 1 = 10$ d) $4x - 5 = 11$ f) $10 - x = 8$ h) $5 - 3x = 5$

These are the same questions as in Activity 10.4. Which method do you prefer: solving equations using tubes and counters or solving equations using the bar model method?

 Fast forward – look at page 222 for more complicated equations and simultaneous equations

INEQUALITIES

Read < as 'less than'.

Read > as 'more than'.

You can combine an inequality and an equality together.

Read ≤ as 'less than or equal to' or 'at most'.

Read ≥ as 'more than or equal to' or 'at least'.

In an **inequality**, you are told that one algebraic expression is larger or smaller than another.

Drawing inequalities on a number line

Show $x < 4$

Draw a circle at the boundary value, which is 4.

> You can turn this round and say $4 > x$ instead.

Decide which side of the boundary has the numbers that are less than 4. All the numbers less than 4 are on the same side of the boundary.

Draw an arrow above all the numbers that are less than 4. The arrow tells you that the numbers less than 4 continue beyond the end of the number line.

> This includes fractions, decimals and negative numbers.

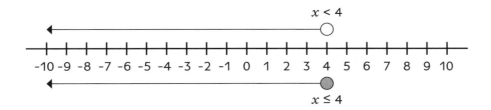

To show the inequality $x \leq 4$ you need to colour in the circle that shows the boundary value 4. The arrow will be the same as before.

> Using empty circles to indicate that the boundary value is not included and filled circles to include the boundary value is a convention that mathematicians have agreed.

ACTIVITY 10.6

1. Draw number lines and arrows for these inequalities. You could draw them with a vertical number line if you prefer.

 a) $x < 6$ b) $x \leq (-1)$ c) $x > 2$ d) $x \geq 3$ e) $2 < x$

2. Which two of the inequalities are the same? Explain in words why.

Combining inequalities to mean 'between'

Sometimes there are two boundary values. If x is between 2 and 7, it means that x is bigger than 2 and less than 7 at the same time. You write $2 < x < 7$

> Notice the inequalities go the same way to make a chain.

 You can draw each inequality separately. Then, draw the inequalities with two circles and a line between them.

> Leave out these two arrows if you prefer.

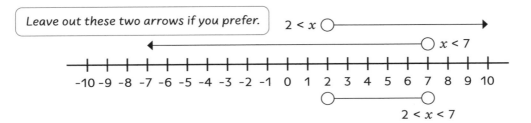

Sometimes you have one or both boundaries included.

The numbers that are more than (-2) and less than or equal to 5 look like this.

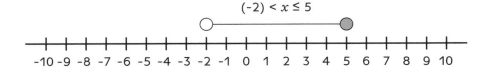

$(-2) < x \leq 5$

LISTS OF WHOLE NUMBERS

When two inequalities together mean 'between', you can make a list of all the whole numbers that are between the boundaries.

List the integers that satisfy the inequality (-3) $< x \leq 4$

Start with a list from (-3) to 4: (-3), (-2), (-1), 0, 1, 2, 3, 4

Decide whether to cross out the boundary values or not. You must not include (-3) but you need 4.

So, the answer is , (-2), (-1), 0, 1, 2, 3, 4

> An **integer** is a whole number. It can be positive or negative or 0.

ACTIVITY 10.7

1. Write a list of integers which satisfy these inequalities.

    a) $2 < x \leq 7$ b) $0 \leq x < 5$ c) $(-2) \leq x \leq 1$ d) $(-6) < x < (-4)$

2. What happens if you try to solve the inequality $6 < x \leq 4$?

◀◀   **Rewind** – look at page 188 for Table mode

INVESTIGATE

When you solve an equation, the solution is a number (or numbers). For an inequality there will be a range of numbers for the answer.

Use the Table mode on your calculator to make a table of values for $2x + 3$ for values of x from (-5) to 5.

The answers go from (-7) to 13. To solve the inequality $2x + 3 \geq 5$ you need to describe the set of values of x which give answers that are 5 or more.

This gives the boundary value.

x	$f(x)$
0	3
1	5
2	7
3	9

This gives the boundary value $\longrightarrow$

You can see that the answer is 5 when $x = 1$ and that for numbers bigger than 1, the answer is bigger than 5. You write $x \geq 1$ for the answer to show you mean 1 as well as the numbers bigger than 1.

You can use this as a method for solving inequalities. You should show the answer and part of the table with headings as evidence that your answer is correct.

Solving inequalities

You can use this idea to solve all inequalities.

- Change the sign to make it an equation.
- Solve the equation to give the boundary value.
- Choose which side of the boundary gives the answers you need.
- Write your answer clearly.
- Explain what you are doing!

Solve the inequality $5x - 1 < 19$

Boundary value when $5x - 1 < 19$

$$5x - 1 = 19$$
$$+1 \qquad \qquad +1$$
$$5x = 20$$
$$\div 5 \qquad \qquad \div 5$$
$$x = 4$$

Notice the < sign in the question has changed to =

You can use tubes and counters or the bar model to solve this equation.

So, the possible answers are $x < 4$, $x \leq 4$, $x > 4$ or $x \geq 4$

The inequality in the question has no equals symbol, so the answer will not include the boundary.

Therefore, $x < 4$ or $x > 4$

Try a number that is not 5. Try $x = 3$

$5x - 1 = 5 \times 3 - 1 = 15 - 1 = 14$

Compare the answer with 19. 14 is less than 19, so 3 is on the correct side of the boundary, 4.

The answer is $x < 4$

Solve the inequality 10 - 2x ≥ 4

Boundary value when 10 - 2x ≥ 4

$$10 - 2x = 4$$

+2x → +2x

$$10 = 4 + 2x$$

-4 → -4

$$6 = 2x$$

÷2 → ÷2

$$3 = x$$

So, the possible answers are $x < 3$, $x \leq 3$, $x > 3$ or $x \geq 3$

The boundary is included, so $x \leq 3$ or $x \geq 3$

Try a value near to 3. When $x = 4$, 10 - 2x = 10 - 2 × 4 = 2

Compare the answer with 4 — it is on the wrong side of 4, so you want the inequality that does not have $x = 4$ in it.

The answer is $x \leq 3$

> Notice the sign is the opposite way round compared with the question.

ACTIVITY 10.8

Find the boundary values and then solve these inequalities.

a) $x + 4 > 10$

b) $8x - 2 < 30$

c) $2 + 3x \geq 26$

d) $2x - 9 > (-13)$

e) $7 - x > 5$

f) $5 - 3x \leq 2$

CHAPTER SUM-UP

Reflection

Having worked through this chapter, how do you feel about these skills?

Skill	I have tried this	I need more practice	I am confident with this
Solving simple equations in one step			
Solving more complicated equations in two steps			
Understanding what an inequality is			
Solving inequalities			

Quiz

Which of these questions has the biggest values of x in the answer?

a) $x + 5 = 13$ b) $2x - 11 = 1$ c) $11 - 3x = 5$ d) $x + 8 < 16$ e) $2x - 1 \geq 7$

11. Algebraic Manipulation

Rewind – look at page 164 for order of operations
look at page 187 for substituting into formulae
look at page 182 for representing algebraic expressions with counters and tubes

HOW BRACKETS ARE USED IN ALGEBRA

There is a convention that mathematicians use about which order operations should be done. The convention is called BIDMAS. The B of BIDMAS stands for brackets, and it means that anything in brackets should be completed first.

It is sometimes useful to write an expression without the brackets. Expanding brackets is the process of removing brackets from an expression.

EXPANDING BRACKETS USING TUBES AND COUNTERS

Expand 2(x + 3)

First, represent the x + 3 part of the expression that is in the brackets.

The digit 2 outside the brackets in 2(x + 3) means you need two of these.

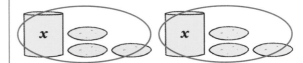

Answer: 2(x + 3) = 2x + 6

Expand 3(x - 1)

First, represent the part of the expression in the brackets, which is (x - 1).

You need three of these for 3(x - 1).

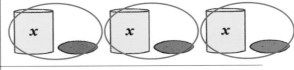

Answer: 3(x - 1) = 3x - 3

Expand 2(3x - 1)

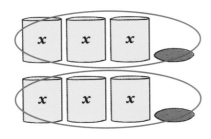

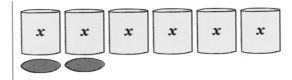

Answer: 2(3x - 1) = 6x - 2

Expand -(x - 3)

This expression can be represented by starting with zero and taking (x - 3). Start with some zero pairs.

Take a tube with the yellow edge at the top and three red counters.

That leaves a red tube and three yellow counters.

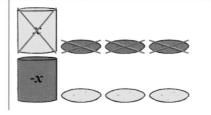

Answer: -(x - 3) = -x + 3

If you compare (x - 3) with -(x - 3) you can see that the negative symbol outside the brackets has the effect of turning reds into yellows and yellows into reds.

Just flip tubes and counters over to change the sign.

(x - 3)

-(x - 3)

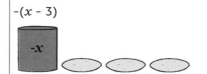

Expand -2(1 - 2x)

You can expand this using the short-cut above. Start by making (1 - 2x).	*If you are not sure, use zero pairs.*

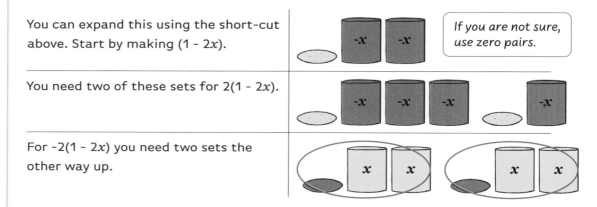

You need two of these sets for 2(1 - 2x).
For -2(1 - 2x) you need two sets the other way up.

Answer: -2(1 - 2x) = -2 + 4x. You can also write this as 4x - 2

Expand and simplify 3(x - 1) - 2(1 - 2x)
The first part of this is the same as 3(x - 1) (see page 207). The second part is the same as -2(1 - 2x) (the example above).

Use the answers to each part separately and put them together.

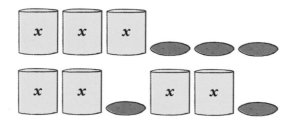

Answer: 3(x - 1) - 2(1 - 2x) = 3x − 3 − 2 + 4x = 7x − 5

ACTIVITY 11.1

1. Expand the brackets. Use counters and tubes to help you.

    a) $2(x + 4)$ c) $3(x - 2)$ e) $-(2x + 1)$

    b) $3(x + 2)$ d) $3(1 - x)$ f) $-2(3x - 1)$

2. Use your answers for Question 1 to simplify these expressions.

    a) $3(x + 2) + 2(x + 4)$ c) $3(1 - x) - (2x + 1)$

    b) $3(x - 2) + 2(x + 4)$ d) $-(2x + 1) - 2(3x - 1)$

EXPANDING BRACKETS USING ALGEBRA TILES

You can use a sketch of a rectangle to represent any multiplication.
    This sketch represents the multiplication 2×3.

$2 \times 3 = 6$

A rectangle that is 4 cm tall and x cm wide could be represented by the following sketch.

> You don't know the exact size of the rectangle unless you know the value for x.

> The answer for the area is $4x$ — this is really just the instruction 'multiply 4 by x'.

In a set of algebra tiles, small squares represent positive 1 (1) or negative 1 (-1).
    Strips represent positive x (x) or negative x (-x).
    The small squares and the strips are the same width.
    You can represent $4x$ with four strips.
    Put the strips together to make a rectangle that is 4 cm high and x cm wide.

> You don't really know how long to make each strip because x can take different values, so don't try to put small 1 squares in a line to make the x strip.

You can use the same idea to expand brackets.

Expand 2(x + 3)

One x strip and three 1 squares represent (x + 3). To represent 2(x + 3) you need two lots of these; that is, two x strips and six 1 squares.

Arrange them into a rectangle like this.

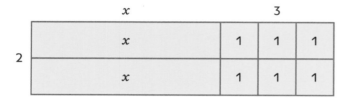

The multiplication is represented by the rectangle that is 2 cm tall and (x + 3) cm wide.

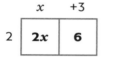   So, the area of the rectangle is 2(x + 3) = 2x + 6

Expand 3(x - 1)

You can represent this multiplication by a rectangle that is 3 cm tall and 1 cm less than x cm wide. If you trace this diagram and fold along the dotted line, you can see that the area is three less than 3x.

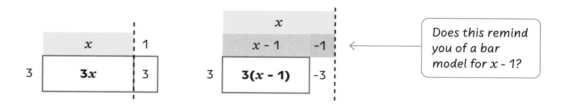

Does this remind you of a bar model for x - 1?

Compare the two rectangles and you can see that 3(x - 1) = 3x - 3

You could just draw this to help you to imagine the folding process. Remember, the sizes are not important in your sketch.

Some people call this a grid method for expanding brackets.

You can use algebra tiles for this too. You need one x strip and one negative 1 tile, three times over.

	x	-1
	x	-1
3	x	-1
	x	-1

Expand 2(3x - 1)

The algebra tiles for this will have two rows, each with three x strips and one -1 tile.

	$3x$			-1
2	x	x	x	-1
	x	x	x	-1

You could draw a simpler diagram like this.

	$3x$	-1
2	**6x**	**−2**

Answer: 2(3x - 1) = 6x - 2

Expand -(x - 3)

Begin with one x strip and three -1 tiles to represent (x - 3)

x	-1	-1	-1

For -(x - 3) you need to flip over the strip and three tiles, giving one -x strip and three 1 tiles.

	x		-3	
-1	-x	1	1	1

So, you can see that -(x - 3) = -x + 3

You can represent this by a rectangle that is -1cm tall and (x - 3)cm wide.

	x	-3
-1	**-x**	**3**

Answer: -(x - 3) = -x + 3

> Remember, two negative numbers multiplied together gives a positive number for the answer.

Expand -2(1 - 2x)

Use the algebra tiles for (1 - 2x)

1	-x	-x

For -2(1 - 2x) you need two sets of these flipped over.

-1	x	x
-1	x	x

Use the grid method for expanding brackets.

	1	-2x
-2	**-2**	**4x**

Answer: -2(1 - 2x) = -2 + 4x. You could also write -2(1 - 2x) = 4x - 2

ACTIVITY 11.2

1. Use algebra tiles or the grid method to expand the brackets.

a) 2(x + 4)   c) 3(x - 2)   e) -(2x + 1)

b) 3(x + 2)   d) 3(1 - x)   f) -2(3x - 1)

2. Use your answers for Question 1 to simplify these expressions.

a) 3(x + 2) + 2(x + 4)   c) 3(1 - x) - (2x + 1)

b) 3(x - 2) + 2(x + 4)   d) -(2x + 1) - 2(3x - 1)

The questions in this activity are the same as in Activity 11.1, where you used tubes and counters to expand the brackets.

Which method do you prefer: using tubes and counters, algebra tiles or the grid method?

EXPANDING BRACKETS WITH x ON THE OUTSIDE

A set of algebra tiles also has larger squares (x^2 tiles). The sides of one larger square match the length of one x strip. The area of one larger square is $x \times x$, which is written as x^2.

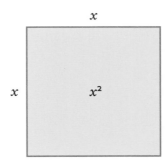

Use algebra tiles to expand $x(x + 1)$
You need a large x^2 square and a strip to make the rectangle.

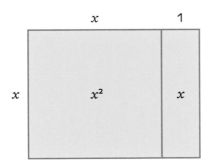

> You cannot use small 1 tiles for this as you don't know how long x is supposed to be. You have to use a strip placed vertically.

You can draw a simple grid like this.

	x	+1
x	x^2	x

Answer: $x(x + 1) = x^2 + x$

Use algebra tiles to expand $x(2x - 3)$ and $3x(2x - 3)$
The part in the bracket ($2x - 3$) can be represented using algebra tiles.

x	x	-1	-1	-1

So, the expression $x(2x - 3)$ is represented like this.

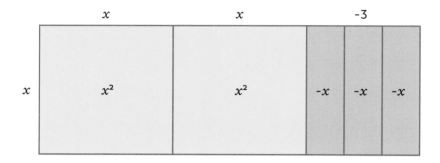

Answer: $x(2x - 3) = x^2 + x^2 - 3x$

You usually write $x(2x - 3) = 2x^2 - 3x$ and you can save time by drawing the grid like this:

	$2x$	-3
x	$2x^2$	$-3x$

You can extend this to $3x(2x - 3)$ by making three rows of algebra tiles, copying the arrangement above for $x(2x - 3)$. The grid looks like this:

	$2x$	-3
$3x$	$6x^2$	$-9x$

Answer: $3x(2x - 3) = 6x^2 - 9x$

EXPRESSIONS WITH MORE THAN ONE VARIABLE

A *variable* is a letter in an expression (often x or y). Its value is not fixed.

A rectangle that is x cm tall and y cm wide has its own algebra tile xy. It can be placed either way round.

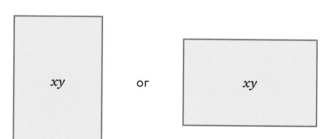

Use algebra tiles to expand $x(x + y)$

The rectangle is x cm tall and $(x + y)$ cm wide, like this.

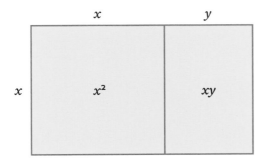

Use the grid method in the same way.

Expand $2x(3x - 2y)$

The grid shows that $2x(3x - 2y) = 6x^2 - 4xy$

Try it with algebra tiles if you have enough!

	x	y
x	x^2	xy

	$3x$	$-2y$
$2x$	$6x^2$	$-4xy$

ACTIVITY 11.3

Expand the brackets.

a) $x(x + 4)$ c) $x(2x + 5)$ e) $3x(x - 8)$ g) $3(2x + y)$ i) $3x(x - 2y)$

b) $x(x - 2)$ d) $x(3x - 4)$ f) $4x(5 - x)$ h) $x(x + 3y)$ j) $y(3x - y)$

If you like the tubes and counters representation of algebra, you can think of the multiplication $x \times x$ as putting x tubes of x counters into a square box. You would count the boxes, the tubes and the counters separately. Try it!

> *This is similar to representing 100, as described in Chapter 2 (see page 80).*

USING YOUR CALCULATOR TO CHECK YOUR ALGEBRA

To check whether $x(x - 5) = x^2 - 5$, create two tables of values in Table mode.

If the tables are the same, then your algebra is correct.

> *Use the same start value, end value and step size.*

Using start 1, end 5, step 1, the tables for $x(x - 5)$ and $x^2 - 5$ are shown on the next page.

> *Some calculators let you type two functions $f(x)$ and $g(x)$ and the two sets of values are shown side by side.*

x	$x(x - 5)$	$x^2 - 5$
1	-4	-4
2	-6	-1
3	-6	4
4	-4	11
5	0	20

These two sets of values are not the same, so there must be a mistake.
Try $x(x - 5) = x^2 - 5x$

x	$x(x - 5)$	$x^2 - 5x$
1	-4	-4
2	-6	-6
3	-6	-6
4	-4	-4
5	0	0

These two sets of values are the same, so there is plenty of evidence that the algebra is correct.

 Fast forward – look at page 224 for solving equations with brackets
look at page 242 for expanding two brackets

FACTORIZING

Factorize $3x + 6$
Begin with three tubes with the yellow edge at the top (to represent $3x$) and six counters (to represent 6).

> *Factorizing* means rewriting a number or expression as a multiplication. In algebra, it means you have to put the brackets in.

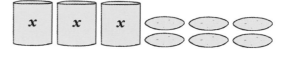

Then, arrange the tubes and the counters into three groups.

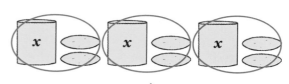

Answer: $3x + 6 = 3(x + 2)$

> If you try to make four groups or six groups, the groups will not be the same.

Factorize $4x - 6y$
Start with these tubes.

Arrange the tubes into two identical groups.

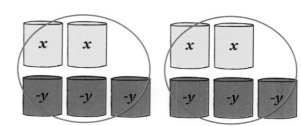

Answer: $4x - 6y = 2(2x - 3y)$

Factorize $x^2 + 4x$

You can solve this problem by using the grid method in reverse.

Put each term of the expression (x^2 and $4x$) into a grid with two boxes.

Notice both terms are multiples of x, so x can go on the left, outside of the grid.

Now ask yourself: 'What must I multiply x by to get x^2?'
Write the answer above the relevant square of the grid.

Repeat for $4x$.

	x	4
x	x^2	$4x$

Answer: $x^2 + 4x = x(x + 4)$

Factorize fully $6xy - 15y^2$

Write the terms in a grid.

> When a question asks you to factorize fully, it is a clue that there will be more than one number or letter on the outside of the bracket.

Notice both terms are multiples of 3 and both terms are multiples of y.
Write $3y$ outside the grid.

Now ask yourself: 'What must I multiply $3y$ by to get $6xy$?'
Write the answer above the relevant square of the grid.

Repeat for $-15y^2$

	$2x$	$-5y$
$3y$	$6xy$	$-15y^2$

Answer: $6xy - 15y^2 = 3y(2x - 5y)$

You might not notice that both terms are a multiple of y, so you might get $3(2xy - 5y^2)$ for your answer. This is not wrong and it is factorized but it is not factorized fully.

	$2xy$	$-5y^2$
3	$6xy$	$-15y^2$

Check what you have in the bracket. Can you factorize again?
Notice both terms are a multiple of y, so you get $3(2xy - 5y^2) = 3 \times y(2x - 5y)$ which you can get to $3y(2x - 5y)$ by this other route.

ACTIVITY 11.4

1. Factorize these expressions.

    a) $5x - 15$ b) $6x - 9$ c) $2 - 8x$ d) $x^2 + 3x$ e) $4x - 3x^2$

Use Table mode to check your algebra.

> Make a table for the expression in the question. Compare it with a table for the answer you get.

2. Factorize these expressions fully.

    a) $4x^2 - 6x$ b) $9xy + 3y$ c) $15xy - 10x^2$ d) $8x^2 - 24xy$ e) $4x^2y + 6xy^2$

SUBSTITUTING VALUES INTO A FORMULA

The formula $v = u + at$ is used in science. To find the value of v when $u = 5$, $a = -10$, $t = 2$, substitute each value into the formula, keeping all the signs the same. Work out the calculation you have written down.

$v = u + at = 5 + (-10) \times 2$

> Remember, *a* and *t* next to each other means multiply.

> Remember the order of operations.

> A **formula** is an equation that links two or more variables together. It contains a set of instructions about how to work out the value of one letter when you know the value of the other letters. The plural of formula is formulae. Formulae are often used in science.

$v = 5 + (-20)$

Answer: $v = (-15)$

ACTIVITY 11.5

1. Find the value of v in each case. Use the formula $v = u + at$

    a) $u = 4$, $a = 10$, $t = 3$ b) $u = (-2)$, $a = 3$, $t = 5$ c) $u = 0.5$, $a = 0.2$, $t = 10$

2. Find the value of s in each case. Use the formula $s = ut + \frac{1}{2}at^2$

    a) $u = 4$, $a = 10$, $t = 3$ b) $u = (-2)$, $a = 3$, $t = 5$ c) $u = 0.5$, $a = 0.2$, $t = 10$

FINDING OTHER VALUES FROM A FORMULA

You can use the formula $v = u + at$ to find the value for t when $v = 20$, $u = 5$, $a = 3$

$$v = u + at$$
$$20 = 5 + 3t$$

You now have to solve the equation.

$$20 = 5 + 3t$$
$$-5 \qquad \qquad -5$$
$$15 = 3t$$
$$\div 3 \qquad \qquad \div 3$$
$$5 = t$$

> Remember the 'onion method'. You remove the outer layer first and the inner layer afterwards.

If the question continued and asked you to find the value for t for other values of *v*, *u* and *a*, you would not have to repeat all the steps in solving the equation. Instead, you could rearrange the formula so that it starts *t* = and then substitute the new values directly into a formula for *t*.

CHANGING THE SUBJECT OF A FORMULA

Look at this formula: $d = s \times t$

d is the subject of the formula.

> The **subject of a formula** is the letter on its own on one side of the formula. It must not be on the other side as well.

For the formula $v = u + at$, *v* is the subject.

But *s* is not the subject of the formula $s = ab + as$ because the *s* appears twice.

You can rewrite a formula so that a different letter is the subject of the formula.

This means you have the instructions for finding a different letter.

Make *t* the subject of the formula $v = u + at$

> In algebra, you write a division as a fraction. The number you divide by goes on the bottom.

$$v = u + at$$
$$-u \qquad \qquad -u$$
$$v - u = at$$
$$\div a \qquad \qquad \div a$$
$$\frac{v - u}{a} = t$$

> Use the 'onion method' again. You remove the outer layer first and the inner layer afterwards.

Make *a* the subject of the formula $A = \frac{1}{2}(a + b)h$

You might like to use a flow diagram to help you with this question.

If you started with *a* and had to find the value of *A*, you would have three steps to do and the order would matter. You would have to add *b* first (because of the brackets).

You would then have to multiply by *h* and halve it. (These two steps could swap round if you prefer.)

Start with *a* → [+b] → *a + b* → [×h] → *(a + b)h* → [÷2] → to get $A = \frac{1}{2}(a + b)h$

You can now start at the end and undo all the changes to work backwards to get *a*.

to get $a = \frac{2A}{h} - b$ ← [-b] ← $\frac{2A}{h}$ ← [÷ h] ← *2A* ← [×2] ← Start with *A*

ACTIVITY 11.6

1. Make R the subject of $V = IR$. Find the value of R when $V = 20$, $I = 4$

2. Make x the subject of $x + 3y = 10$. Find the value of x when $y = 3$

3. Make x the subject of $2x + t = 7$. Find the value of x when $t = 11$

4. Make a the subject of the formula $v = u + at$.
Find the value of a when $v = 7$, $u = 3$, $t = 2$

> Use a flow diagram to help you.

5. Make r the subject of the formula $C = 2\pi r$.
Find the value of r when $C = 25$

> Use π on your calculator.

6. Make u the subject of the formula $s = u - 5a$. Find the value of u when $s = 10$, $a = 3$

7. Make a the subject of the formula $m = \dfrac{(a + b + c)}{3}$. Find the value of a when $m = 8$, $b = 10$, $c = 6$

8. Make h the subject of the formula $A = \frac{1}{2}(a + b)h$.
Find the value of h when $A = 10$, $a = 3$, $b = 2$

> You can keep the bracket together for this one.

CHAPTER SUM-UP

Reflection
Having worked through this chapter, how do you feel about these skills?

Skill	I have tried this	I need more practice	I am confident with this
Understanding how brackets are used in algebra			
Expanding brackets			
Factorizing an expression with two terms			
Expanding and factorizing using a calculator's Table mode			
Substituting values into a formula			
Changing the subject of a formula			

Quiz

1. Expand or factorize each expression to find its partner. Which expression is the odd one out?

a) $3(x - 4)$ c) $4(x - 3)$ e) $3x - 12$ g) $6(x - 2)$ i) $4(x - 2)$

b) $2(3x - 4)$ d) $6x - 8$ f) $4x - 8$ h) $6x - 12$

2. Which gives the biggest answer when $x = 10$ is substituted?

12. Further Equations

◀◀ **Rewind** – look at page 190 for solving equations using tubes and counters, and page 198 for solving equations using the bar model method

▶▶ **Fast forward** – look at page 250 for solving quadratic equations

SOLVING EQUATIONS WHERE THE SOLUTION IS NEGATIVE

How would you solve the equation $2x + 5 = 1$?

The methods are exactly as you have used before.

You don't need to know in advance that the answer is negative.

Using tubes and counters

Use tubes and counters to solve the equation $2x + 5 = 1$

Represent the equation with two equal sets of counters. Use some zero pairs as well.

> Remember, your aim is to leave one tube on its own. The 'onion method' peels away layers, starting with the outside layer (+ 5) and then the inside layer (× 2).

Take five yellow counters from both sides.

Simplify and stack the counters to match the tubes.

Simplify and stack the counters to match one tube.

So, there must be two red counters in one tube.

Answer: $x = (-2)$

You could write your answer like this to show your working.

$$2x + 5 = 1$$

-5 $\quad$ $2x = (-4)$ $\quad$ -5

÷2 $\quad$ $x = (-2)$ $\quad$ ÷2

Using the bar model

If you prefer, you can use the bar model, but the lengths of the bars may not look right.

Solve $2x + 5 = 1$

Draw two bars the same length. The top bar represents 1. The lower bar represents x, another x and an extra 5.

1		
x	x	5

You will not get the sizes of the bars to look right but it doesn't really matter.

223

When you remove the extra 5, the top bar becomes 1 - 5 = (-4)

(-4)	
x	x

So, you can see that x must be (-2)

(-2)	(-2)
x	x

Answer: $x = (-2)$

Remember to write your answer.

If you redraw the bars with x as a negative amount, you can get the bar model to look right.

5		
	$x = (-2)$	$x = (-2)$

1

ACTIVITY 12.1

Solve these equations using the method of your choice. Which question is the only one with a positive answer?

a) $x + 12 = 4$

b) $2x + 7 = 5$

c) $3x - 2 = (-11)$

d) $3x - 17 = 19$

e) $3 - 2x = 13$

SOLVING EQUATIONS WITH BRACKETS

Here is a choice of methods you can use. You can work with the brackets, or you can expand so there are no brackets.

Try them all and see which one you like best. Some methods work better for some questions than others.

Using tubes and counters

Solve the equation $3(x - 1) = 9$

Represent the equation with two equal sets of counters.

Put the counters into three stacks.

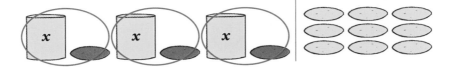

Simplify. You can see that $x - 1 = 3$

Add one yellow counter to both sides.

Use the zero pair.

So, there must be four counters in the tube.

Answer: $x = 4$

You could write your answer like this to show your working.

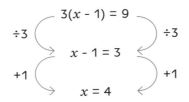

In the 'onion method', the outside layer is the (× 3) and the inside layer is (-1).

$$3(x - 1) = 9$$
$$\div 3 \qquad \div 3$$
$$x - 1 = 3$$
$$+1 \qquad +1$$
$$x = 4$$

Using the bar model
Method 1

Solve the equation 3(x - 1) = 9

The bar for x - 1 looks like this

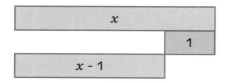

Put three of the x - 1 bars together. The bar model for the equation looks like this.

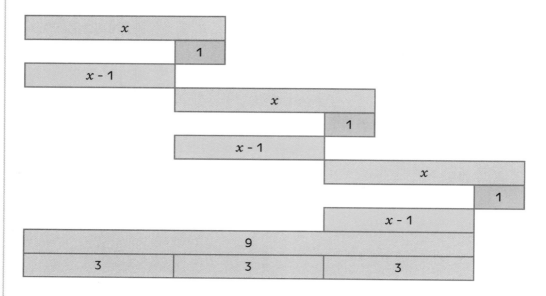

You can see that x - 1 = 3

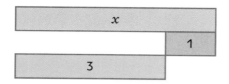

So x = 4

Method 2

The bar model for the same equation gives this.

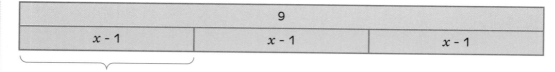

So you know that x - 1 = 3

A new bar model gives this.

So $x = 4$

Using expanding

Solve the equation $3(x - 1) = 9$

If you look at this equation and think the brackets make solving it look difficult, then you can remove the brackets!

The grid method for expanding begins like this...

and gives this...

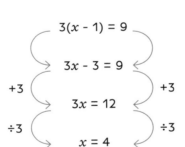

So, you can solve the equation $3x - 3 = 9$ instead.

Using whatever method you prefer, you can see that

$$3(x - 1) = 9$$
$$3x - 3 = 9$$
$$+3 \qquad\qquad +3$$
$$3x = 12$$
$$\div 3 \qquad\qquad \div 3$$
$$x = 4$$

ACTIVITY 12.2

1. Solve these equations. Try out different methods.

a) $7(x - 6) = 14$

b) $8(x + 2) = 56$

c) $9(x - 4) = 36$

d) $6(x + 2) = 540$

e) $3(x + 5) = 12$

f) $2(x - 5) = 17$

Which method do you prefer – can you explain why?

2 Now try these equations. They are a bit harder!

a) $3(4x - 1) = 33$

b) $\frac{1}{2}(x + 5) = 7$

227

SOLVING EQUATIONS WITH x ON BOTH SIDES

Using counters and tubes

Solve the equation $3x - 2 = x + 8$

Represent the equation with two equal sets of counters.

Take a yellow tube from both sides.

Add two yellow counters to both sides to make zero pairs.

Put the counters into two stacks.

So there must be five counters in the tube.

Answer: $x = 5$

You could write your answer like this to show your working.

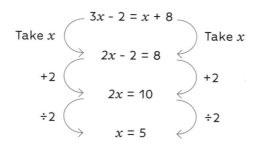

$$3x - 2 = x + 8$$

Take x ⟶ $2x - 2 = 8$ ⟵ Take x

$+2$ ⟶ $2x = 10$ ⟵ $+2$

$\div 2$ ⟶ $x = 5$ ⟵ $\div 2$

Check your answer

You should substitute your answer into each side of the original equation.

If your working is right, then you will get the same answer twice.

When $x = 5$ the left side gives $3x - 2 = 3 \times 5 - 2 = 15 - 2 = 13$

When $x = 5$ the right side gives $x + 8 = 5 + 8 = 13$ so your answer is correct.

Solve the equation $x + 1 = 10 - 2x$

Represent the equation with two equal sets of counters.

Add two yellow tubes to both sides to make zero pairs.

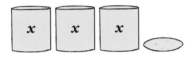   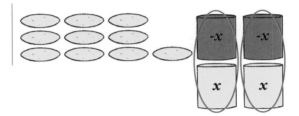

Take a yellow counter from both sides.

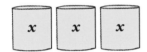   

Put the counters into three stacks.

Split into matching sets.

So there must be three counters in the tube.

Answer: $x = 3$

You could write your answer as shown overleaf to show your working.

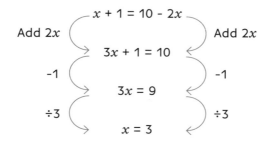

Check your answer

When $x = 3$ the left side gives $x + 1 = 3 + 1 = 4$

When $x = 3$ the right side gives $10 - 2x = 10 - 2 \times 3 = 10 - 6 = 4$ so it is correct.

ACTIVITY 12.3

Solve these equations. Check your answer by working out the value of each side of the equation.

a) $2x + 4 = x + 6$ c) $3x - 2 = 5x - 4$ e) $2x - 4 = 14 - x$

b) $3x - 1 = 2x + 4$ d) $x + 3 = 11 - x$ f) $7x - 15 = 5 - 3x$

Using the bar model

You could use a bar model for these equations if you prefer.

Solve the equation $3x - 2 = x + 8$

The bar model for $3x - 2$ looks like this.

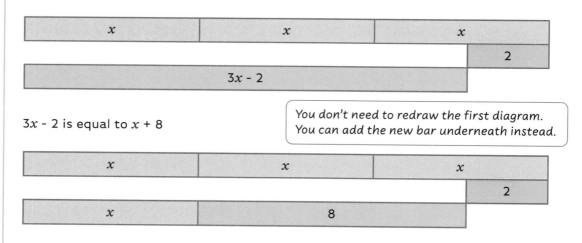

$3x - 2$ is equal to $x + 8$

> You don't need to redraw the first diagram. You can add the new bar underneath instead.

Cover the first x to give you this bar model.

You can see that 8 + 2 = 10

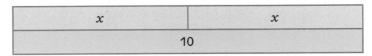

So $x = 5$

Solve the equation $x + 1 = 10 - 2x$

The bar model for $10 - 2x$ looks like this

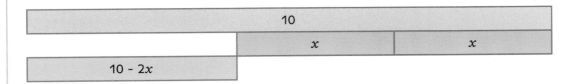

$10 - 2x$ is equal to $x + 1$. It looks neater if you draw $1 + x$

> You don't need to redraw the first diagram. You can add the new bar underneath instead.

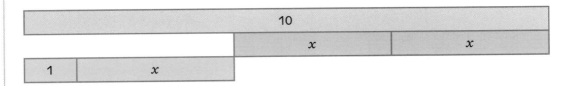

This gives this bar model.

So you can see $x = 3$

ACTIVITY 12.4

Solve these equations using the bar model method. These are the same questions as in Activity 12.3.

a) $2x + 4 = x + 6$

b) $3x - 1 = 2x + 4$

c) $3x - 2 = 5x - 4$

d) $x + 3 = 11 - x$

e) $2x - 4 = 14 - x$

f) $7x - 15 = 5 - 3x$

Did you prefer to solve the equations using the bar model method or counters?

SOLVING SIMULTANEOUS EQUATIONS

Sometimes there are two values to find, usually x and y. You might know two things that link the values at the same time. Simultaneous means at the same time, so you call them simultaneous equations.

> **Simultaneous equations** are typically two equations, each with two unknowns (usually x and y). The value of each unknown is the same in both equations.

Two numbers add up to 12. If you double one of the numbers and add the result to the other number, the answer is 17. What are the two numbers?

Let the numbers be x and y. You know that

$$x + y = 12$$
$$2x + y = 17$$

> Simultaneous equations are usually written one above the other with x, y and $=$ lined up neatly.

Choose one equation and represent it with tubes and counters. It does not really matter which equation you choose but it is often easier if you choose the one with the bigger numbers. Here $2x + y = 17$ has been chosen.

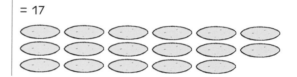

The other equation tells you that $x + y = 12$

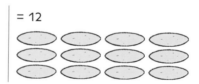

Take $x + y$ from $2x + y$ and take 12 from 17. The two sides will still balance.

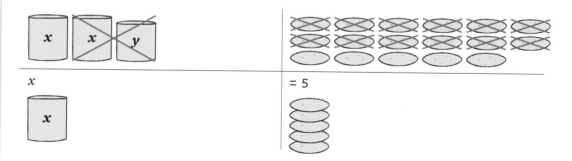

So you know that $x = 5$

> Finding x is only half the answer.

Now, find y.

Look at the equation $x + y = 12$. Replace x with five counters.

 $x + y$

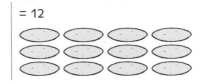 $= 12$

You can see that $y = 7$

Answer: $x = 5$, $y = 7$

You can show your method like this.

$$2x + y = 17$$
$$x + y = 12$$
$$\overline{}$$
$$x + 0 = 5$$

Subtract

So $x = 5$

Substitute into the equation $x + y = 12$

$5 + y = 12$ so $y = 7$

The solution is $x = 5$, $y = 7$

Check with the other equation:

$2x + y = 2 × 5 + 7 = 17$, which is correct.

Solve the simultaneous equations   **$2x + 3y = 14$**

$2x + y = 10$

Represent the first equation $2x + 3y = 14$

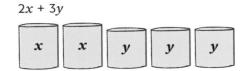 $2x + 3y$

 $= 14$

The other equation tells you that $2x + y = 10$

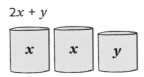 $2x + y$

 $= 10$

If you take $2x + y$ from $2x + 3y$ you can take 10 from 14. The two sides will still balance.

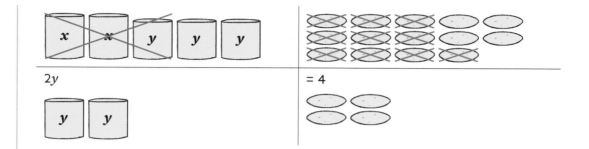

2y   = 4

So you can see that $y = 2$

To find x, look at the equation $2x + y = 10$ with $y = 2$

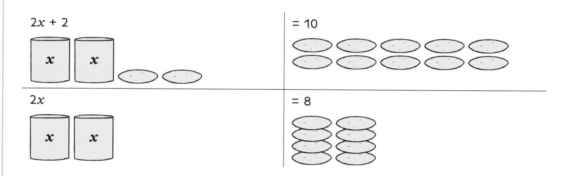

2x + 2   = 10

2x   = 8

So you can see that $2x = 8$ and so $x = 4$

Answer: $x = 4$, $y = 2$

You can show your method like this.

$$2x + 3y = 14$$
$$2x + y = 10$$

Subtract $0 + 2y = 4$
Divide by 2 $y = 2$

Substitute into the equation $2x + y = 10$

$2x + 2 = 10$ so $2x = 8$

So $x = 4$

The solution is $x = 4$, $y = 2$

Simultaneous equations with a minus sign

Solve the simultaneous equations $x + y = 4$

$2x - y = 5$

Represent each of the equations with tubes and counters.

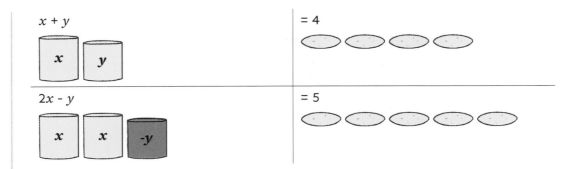

Put the two lots of tubes and counters together.

Remember zero pairs!

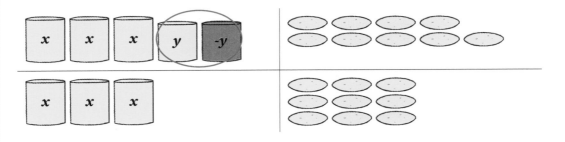

So you can see that $x = 3$

To find y, look at the equation $x + y = 4$ with $x = 3$

So you can see that $y = 1$

Answer: $x = 3$, $y = 1$

Check using the other equation $2x - y = 2 \times 3 - 1 = 5$ so this is correct.

You can show your method like this.

$$x + y = 4$$
$$2x - y = 5$$

Add the equations $\qquad\qquad 3x \quad = 9$

Divide by 3 $\qquad\qquad\qquad\quad x \quad = 3$

When $x = 3$, $3 + y = 4$

So $y = 1$

ACTIVITY 12.5

Solve these simultaneous equations.

a) $3x + 2y = 9$
$x + 2y = 7$

b) $3x - 4y = 0$
$2x + 4y = 20$

c) $5x + 6y = 3$
$5x + 3y = 9$

The bar model for solving simultaneous equations

You might prefer to use the bar model to solve simultaneous equations. You will need to 'add' bars together or stack them underneath each other. Look for places where the equations match.

Solve the simultaneous equations $2x + y = 17$
$x + y = 12$

Draw an addition bar for $2x + y = 17$

Underneath, draw another bar for $x + y = 12$. Line up the parts of the bar that match the first one.

17		
x	x	y

	12	
	x	y

So you can see that $x = 5$

Replace x with 5 in one of the bar models. You can also see that $y = 7$

12	
5	y

The solution is $x = 5$, $y = 7$

Check using the other equation.

17		
5	5	7

So the answer is correct.

Solve the simultaneous equations   **$2x + 3y = 14$**
     $2x + y = 10$

Draw an addition bar for $2x + 3y = 14$

Draw another bar for $2x + y = 10$. Line up the parts of the bar that match the first one.

14				
x	x	y	y	y

10		
x	x	y

4	
y	y

You can see that $2y = 4$

So you know that $y = 2$

Replace y with 2 in one of the bar models.

10		
x	x	2

So you can see that $x = 4$

Check using the other equation

14				
4	4	2	2	2

So the answer is correct.

Using the bar model to solve simultaneous equations with a minus sign

Solve the simultaneous equations   **$x + y = 4$**
     $2x - y = 5$

Draw a subtraction bar model for the equation with the minus sign.

x	x

	y

5	

Draw the bar model for the other equation so it lines up with the first. It is better to draw $y + x = 4$

4	
y	x

So you can see that $3x = 5 + 4 = 9$

5		4
x	x	x
9		

So you can see that $x = 3$

Replace x with 3 in one of the bar models. You can also see that $y = 1$

4	
y	3

The solution is $x = 3$, $y = 1$

Check using the other equation $2x - y = 5$

3	3
	1
5	

So the answer is correct.

Solving simultaneous equations when the numbers do not match

Using a bar model

The simultaneous equations in this book so far have been chosen so that there is a match for either x or y. This means you can then make a new equation with only one letter in it. Where there is no match, you must complete an extra step to make a match.

> There is usually more than one way of doing that.

Solve the simultaneous equations $3x - 2y = 11$

$x + \ y = 7$

Draw a bar model for the more complicated equation.

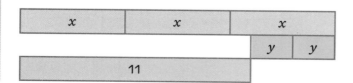

> You might not get the sizes of the bars quite right but it doesn't really matter.

Put bars for the equation $x + y = 7$ side by side.

7		7	
x	y	x	y

> Two bars is enough to get y to match. If you used three bars, then x would match.

Move the parts of the bar to line up with the first equation.

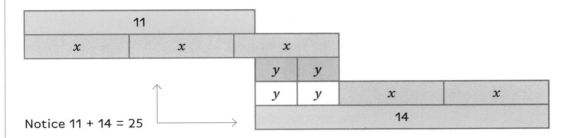

Notice 11 + 14 = 25

25				
x	x	x	x	x

So you can see that $x = 5$

Use the equation $x + y = 7$. Replace x with 5.

7	
5	y

So you can see that $y = 2$

Answer: $x = 5$, $y = 2$

Check using the equation $3x - 2y = 11$

5	5	5	
		2	2

11	

So the answer is correct.

ACTIVITY 12.6

Try to solve the equations $3x - 2y = 11$ and $x + y = 7$ by making the bar model for three lots of $x + y = 7$ and getting the x to match. You should get different working but the same answer.

Using tubes and counters

Solve the simultaneous equations $3x - 2y = 11$

$x + y = 7$

Represent each of the equations with tubes and counters.

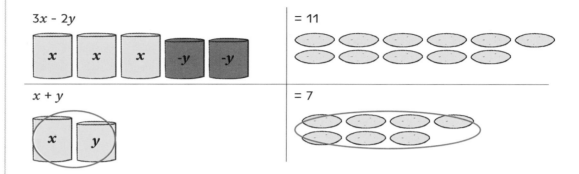

Put the two lots of tubes and counters for the second
equation together with the tubes and counters for the
first equation.

Remember zero pairs!

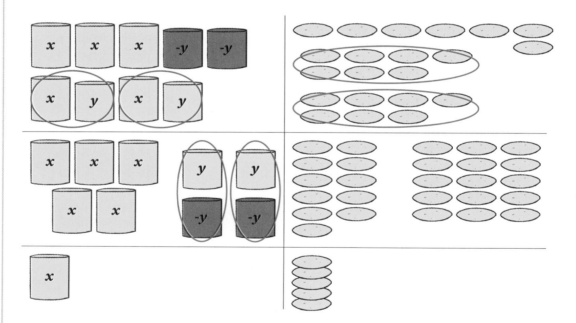

So you can see that $x = 5$

To find y, look at the equation $x + y = 7$

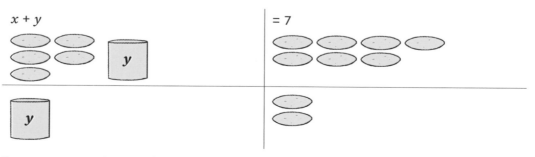

So you can see that $y = 2$

The solution is $x = 5$, $y = 2$

Check using the other equation:

$3x - 2y = 3 \times 5 - 2 \times 2 = 15 - 4 = 11$, so this is correct.

ACTIVITY 12.7

1. Solve these simultaneous equations. You can choose your method.

a) $5x + 2y = 20$
   $2x + y = 9$

b) $4x - 3y = 25$
   $x + y = 8$

c) $2x + 5y = 16$
   $3x + y = 11$

2. For this question, you will need to change both equations to get a match.

$2x + 3y = 17$
$3x + 2y = 13$

CHAPTER SUM-UP

Reflection

Having worked through this chapter, how do you feel about these skills?

Skill	I have tried this	I need more practice	I am confident with this
Solving equations where the solution is negative			
Solving equations with brackets			
Solving equations with x on both sides			
Solving simultaneous equations			

Quiz

Solve these equations. Which one gives a negative number for the answer?

a) $5(x + 3) = 45$
b) $3x + 5 = x + 3$

c) $6x - y = 1$
   $2x + 3y = 1$

13. Quadratics

AIMS

- To expand a pair of brackets
- To factorize a three-term quadratic expression
- To solve a quadratic equation
- To understand how to complete the square (Higher Tier)

RESOURCES

- A set of algebra tiles (see page 285)
- A scientific calculator with Table mode

PREVIOUS KNOWLEDGE

- Grid method for multiplication
- Using algebra tiles for expanding brackets
- Using algebra tiles for factorizing

Rewind – look at page 242 for expanding and factorizing

Fast forward – look at page 258 for drawing quadratic graphs

ACTIVITY 13.1

Use algebra tiles to represent these expressions.

a) $2(x + 2)$ c) $-3(2 - x)$ e) $x(x + 2)$ g) $x(x - 3)$

b) $-(x - 1)$ d) $3(2x - 1)$ f) $x(2x + 1)$ h) $-x(3 - x)$

EXPANDING A PAIR OF BRACKETS

All terms are positive

Represent $(x + 1)(x + 2)$ using algebra tiles and expand the brackets
You need enough algebra tiles to make a rectangle that is $(x + 1)$ cm tall and $(x + 2)$ cm wide.

In your answer, you must show how many of each type of tile you have used, so your answer should have three terms for the three different kinds of tile.

So you can see that $(x + 1)(x + 2) = x^2 + 3x + 2$

The grid for this is shown below.

	x	$+2$
x	x^2	$2x$
$+1$	x	2

You could put the brackets the other way round and the grid would look like this.

	x	$+1$
x	x^2	x
$+2$	$2x$	2

Notice the answer is the same. Check with algebra tiles that this is right.

One term is negative

Expand $(x + 3)(x - 1)$

This expression represents the area of a rectangle that is $(x + 3)$ cm tall and $(x - 1)$ cm wide. You can think of the width as x cm wide with an extra (-1) cm

So, the rectangle for the expression $(x + 3)(x - 1)$ looks like this.

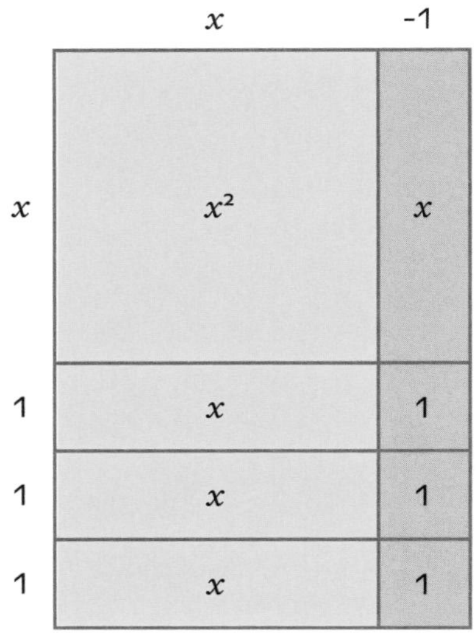

Remember zero pairs. One of the yellow x's makes a zero pair with the red $-x$.

So there are two yellow x's in the answer $(x + 3)(x - 1) = x^2 + 2x - 3$

The grid for this is shown below.

	x	-1
x	x^2	$-x$
$+3$	$3x$	-3

Some people like to write $(x + 3)(x - 1) = x^2 + 3x - x - 3 = x^2 + 2x - 3$

You can go straight from the grid to the answer if you prefer.

Two terms are negative

The expression $(x - 2)(x - 3)$ is represented by these algebra tiles.

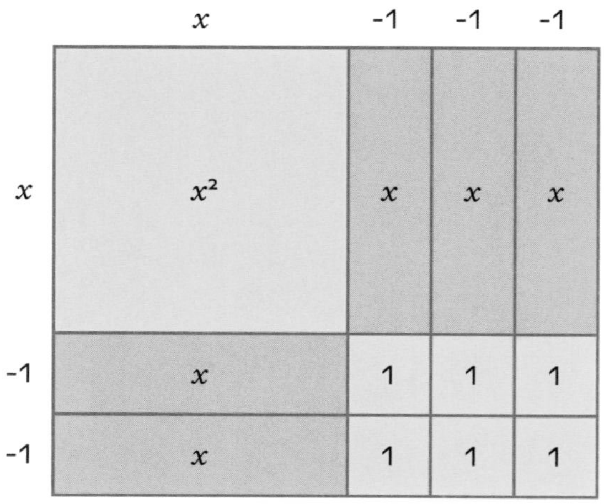

Remember, two negative numbers multiplied together gives a positive number for the answer.

$(x - 2)(x - 3) = x^2 - 5x + 6$

You can just draw the grid and write the answer $(x - 2)(x - 3) = x^2 - 5x + 6$

	x	-3
x	x^2	$-3x$
-2	$-2x$	6

Checking using a calculator

◀◀ **Rewind** – look at page 188 for checking using the Table mode on a calculator

Return to the example $(x - 2)(x - 3)$ and use the Table mode on your calculator to check that you have expanded the brackets correctly. Create a table of values for $(x - 2)(x - 3)$ and $x^2 - 5x + 6$. If they are not the same, then there is a mistake in your algebra.

There is a negative x term

Expand $(2 - x)(1 + x)$

The algebra tiles can be arranged like this.

Putting together the zero pair gives the answer $(2 - x)(1 + x) = 2 + x - x^2$

ACTIVITY 13.2

Expand the brackets. Use algebra tiles or the grid method. Use Table mode on your calculator to check your work.

a) $(x + 1)(x + 3)$

b) $(x + 2)(x + 4)$

c) $(x + 2)(x - 1)$

d) $(x - 3)(x + 2)$

e) $(x - 1)(x - 4)$

f) $(x - 4)(x + 3)$

g) $(1 + x)(1 + 2x)$

h) $(2 - x)(3 - x)$

FACTORIZING A THREE-TERM QUADRATIC EXPRESSION

> **Factorizing** means rewriting a number or expression as a multiplication. In algebra, it means you have to put the brackets in. It is the reverse of expanding brackets.

All terms are positive

Factorize $x^2 + 6x + 8$

Arrange the algebra tiles that represent the expression into a rectangle. The shape and size of the rectangle gives the two factors. Each factor is a bracket with x and a number added to it or subtracted from it.

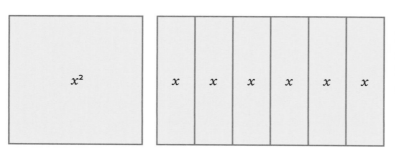

It can be a bit tricky to get the rectangle right. You might find it easiest to put the big square in the top left and arrange the little squares in the bottom right.

Fit the strips to fill the gaps.

So you can see that $x^2 + 6x + 8 = (x + 2)(x + 4)$

You could have made the rectangle the other way round and got the answer $(x + 4)(x + 2)$

> Both $(x + 4)(x + 2)$ and $(x + 2)(x + 4)$ are correct as they are really the same!

You could also write your answers in a grid, using the same order as above to fill it in.

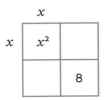

> There are several ways you can get 8. It could be 1×8, 2×4, $(-1) \times (-8)$ or $(-2) \times (-4)$. Which one gives the correct number of x's?

Complete the grid and write down your answer.

> The grid on its own is not the complete answer.

$x^2 + 6x + 8 = (x + 2)(x + 4)$

There is one negative term in the middle

Factorize $x^2 - 9x + 8$

Arrange the algebra tiles that represent the expression into a rectangle.

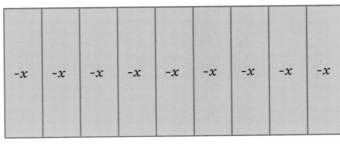

You need to consider all the ways you can arrange the eight small squares.
The arrangement below is the one that works in this example.

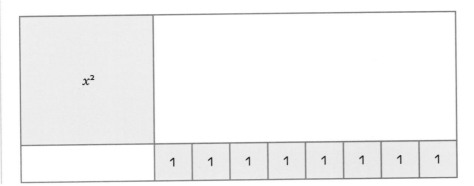

The strips fit in like this. Notice that the small squares are positive when the strips are negative. This means there will be negative numbers in both brackets.

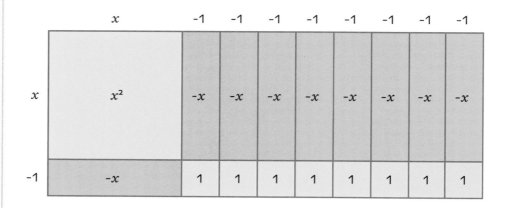

So you can see that $x^2 - 9x + 8 = (x - 1)(x - 8)$

There is a negative term at the end

Factorize $x^2 - x - 2$

Represent the expression with algebra tiles.

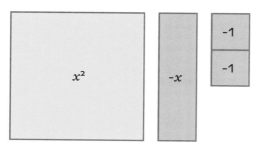

> Remember the sunshine diagrams from page 97? They might be useful here too.

The negative number on the end is a clue that one of the two brackets has a minus sign and the other does not. You only have one negative strip to complete the rectangle. Put in a zero pair.

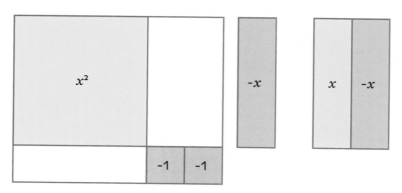

Put the positive and negative strips together.

So you can see that $x^2 - x - 2 = (x + 1)(x - 2)$

Record your answer in a grid and write the algebra.

INVESTIGATE

Arrange a yellow x^2 tile and six red (–1) tiles in as many ways as you can to create the top left and bottom right of a rectangle. Use as many strips as you need to complete the rectangle. In how many ways can you do this? Draw the grid and write the algebra for each one.

Hint: One way gives
$x^2 - 5x - 6 = (x + 1)(x - 6)$

Try to arrange $x^2 + 2x - 6$ into a rectangle. There are some expressions that just cannot be done!

ACTIVITY 13.3

Factorize each of these. Use algebra tiles or a grid to help you.

a) $x^2 + 2x + 1$ c) $x^2 + 8x + 15$ e) $x^2 - 8x + 12$ g) $x^2 + 4x - 5$ i) $x^2 + x - 12$
b) $x^2 + 8x + 7$ d) $x^2 - 6x + 5$ f) $x^2 - 7x + 12$ h) $x^2 - 6x - 7$

Use Table mode on your calculator to check your work.

SOLVING QUADRATIC EQUATIONS

> A **quadratic equation** is formed when a quadratic expression is equal to zero.

Using Table mode to find the roots

Investigate the roots of the quadratic equation $x^2 - 3x - 10 = 0$ using Table mode.

> A **root of an equation** is a value of x for which the expression gives the correct value.

In Table mode, enter $f(x) = x^2 - 3x - 10$. Choose start -10, end 10, step 1. Look through the answers for values that give zero.

You can see that there are two rows that give the answer zero, so $x = -2$ and $x = 5$ are both roots of the equation $x^2 - 3x - 10 = 0$

Factorizing to solve quadratic equations

If you factorize the expression $x^2 - 3x - 10$, you get $x^2 - 3x - 10 = (x + 2)(x - 5)$

If you create a table of values for $(x + 2)(x - 5)$ you can see you get the same roots. Notice that when $x = -2$, the bracket $(x + 2)$ is zero and when $x = 5$, the bracket $(x - 5)$ is zero. This leads to an algebraic way of solving quadratic equations. The values of x for which the brackets are zero are the roots of the equation.

Solve the equation $x^2 + 5x - 14 = 0$ algebraically

Using the grid method for factorizing, you start with this.

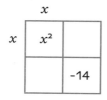

The choice of numbers to give (-14) are $(-1) \times 14$, $1 \times (-14)$, $(-2) \times 7$ and $2 \times (-7)$. Choose the pair that gives the correct middle term.

	x	$+7$
x	x^2	$7x$
-2	$-2x$	-14

So $(x - 2)(x + 7) = 0$

> The only way to get zero for a multiplication is when one of the numbers is zero.

Either $(x - 2) = 0$ or $(x + 7) = 0$

> You replace one complicated equation with two easier ones. People who skip this step of writing often get positive and negative signs back to front.

So either $x = 2$ or $x = -7$

> Write the words 'either... or' in your answer.

Check your answer by typing the original equation into Table mode and searching for the zeros.

You can also check without a calculator by substituting each value in turn into the equation.

When $x = 2$, the equation becomes $2^2 + 5 \times 2 - 14 = 4 + 10 - 14 = 0$ so it is correct.

When $x = (-7)$, the equation becomes $(-7)^2 + 5 \times (-7) - 14 = 49 - 35 - 14 = 0$ so it is correct.

ACTIVITY 13.4

Factorize each expression to help you to solve these quadratic equations. Check your answers.

a) $x^2 + 11x + 10 = 0$ c) $x^2 - 6x + 8 = 0$ e) $x^2 - 4x - 12 = 0$

b) $x^2 - 6x + 5$ d) $x^2 + 3x - 4 = 0$ f) $x^2 - 6x - 16 = 0$

 Fast forward – look at page 267 for using graphs to solve quadratic equations that do not factorize

COMPLETING THE SQUARE

Completing the square is a way of rewriting a quadratic expression so that it begins with brackets squared and ends with adding or subtracting a number.

ACTIVITY 13.5

Look at these expressions.

a) $(x + 3)^2$ b) $(x + 1)^2$ c) $(x - 2)^2$ d) $(x - 5)^2$

1. Rewrite each expression as two identical brackets multiplied together.

2. Use algebra tiles to represent each expression. What do you notice about the shapes of the rectangles?

3. Expand the brackets. Write in words any patterns in the numbers that you notice.

4. How do you think you could represent $(x + 0.5)^2$?

Write the expression $x^2 + 4x$ in completed square form

Arrange the algebra tiles for $x^2 + 4x$ like this.

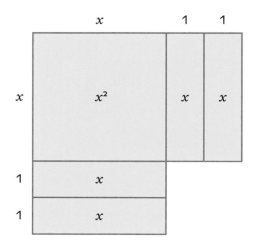

To complete the square, you need to fill in the corner with four yellow tiles. Bring in 4 zero pairs to keep the expression the same.

| 1 | -1 | 1 | -1 | 1 | -1 | 1 | -1 |

So you can see that $x^2 + 4x = (x + 2)^2 - 4$

Create a table of values for each of these expressions to check they are always equal.

You can say that $x^2 + 4x = (x + 2)^2 - 4$ is an identity.

An **identity** is an equation that is true for all values of x. You can rewrite one side to get the other.

ACTIVITY 13.6

1. Complete the square with algebra tiles for these expressions.

Write in words any patterns that you notice.

a) $x^2 + 2x$ b) $x^2 + 6x$ c) $x^2 - 4x$ d) $x^2 - 8x$

2. Can you use your pattern to rewrite $x^2 + 20x$ without tiles?

Completing the square for a three-term expression (using algebra tiles)

Write the expression $x^2 + 2x + 7$ in completed square form

Represent the expression with algebra tiles.

Use the large square and the strips to make a square with the corner missing.

Use the remaining tiles to complete the square.

	x	1
x	x^2	x
1	x	1

(tiles: 1, 1, 1, 1, 1, 1)

So you can see that $x^2 + 2x + 7 = (x + 1)^2 + 6$

Write the expression $x^2 - 6x + 1$ in the form $(x + a)^2 + b$

Represent the expression with algebra tiles.

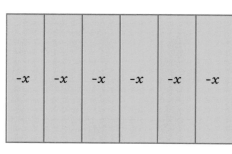

(x^2 | $-x$ $-x$ $-x$ $-x$ $-x$ $-x$ | 1)

Use the large square and the strips to make a square with the corner missing.

	x	1	1	1
x	x^2	$-x$	$-x$	$-x$
1	$-x$			
1	$-x$			
1	$-x$			

1

1	-1	1	-1
1	-1	1	-1
1	-1	1	-1
1	-1	1	-1

This is just another way of saying 'in completed square form'. You do not need to work with a and b here.

Use the remaining tile and eight zero pairs to complete the square.

So you can see that $x^2 - 6x + 1 = (x - 3)^2 - 8$

ACTIVITY 13.7

1. Use algebra tiles to complete the square for these expressions.

a) $x^2 + 6x + 10$ b) $x^2 + 4x + 2$ c) $x^2 - 2x - 3$ d) $x^2 - 8x + 11$

Use Table mode on your calculator to check that your algebra is correct.

2. For each table, find the minimum value in the $f(x)$ column and the value of x for which it happens. What do you notice?

Completing the square for a three-term expression (without using algebra tiles)

All the examples you have seen of completing the square using algebra tiles can also be done using the patterns you might have identified in Activity 13.7. The number in the bracket with the x is half the number of the coefficient of x in the expression.

> The **coefficient** of x is the number that multiplies x in the expression.

Write the expression $x^2 - 6x + 1$ in completed square form

Look at the first two terms of $x^2 - 6x + 1$. You can see that you will need -3 in the bracket with x.

> Use half of the -6 in the bracket.

Draw the grid to expand the bracket.

	x	-3
x	x^2	$-3x$
-3	$-3x$	9

The bracket has an extra 9 that the two terms on their own do not.

So $x^2 - 6x = (x - 3)^2 - 9$

So you can write $x^2 - 6x + 1 = (x - 3)^2 - 9 + 1$, which gives the answer
$x^2 - 6x + 1 = (x - 3)^2 - 8$

Here is an example with an odd number of x's.

Write $x^2 + x - 4$ in completed square form

Put half the coefficient of x in the bracket. Use a grid to work out $(x + 0.5)^2$

	x	0.5
x	x^2	$0.5x$
0.5	$0.5x$	0.25

Swap the first two terms for $(x + 0.5)^2$ and remember to keep the -4 on the end.

$$x^2 + x - 4$$
$$(x + 0.5)^2 - 0.25 - 4$$

Combine the numbers $(x + 0.5)^2 - 4.25$

You can do this with tiles if you split one of the x strips lengthways, and cut a small square into quarters.

MINIMUM VALUES

Completed square form gives a method for finding the minimum value of a quadratic expression. When the bracket is zero, the number on the end is the value of the expression. For other values of x, the bracket adds a positive amount, so the value is bigger. So the smallest value happens for the value of x for which the bracket is zero.

Find the minimum value of $x^2 - 5x + 10$ and the value of x for which it occurs

Completed square form begins with $(x - 2.5)^2$

	x	-2.5
x	x^2	$-2.5x$
-2.5	$-2.5x$	6.25

> There's a quick way to work out 2.5^2
> Round 2.5^2 down to 2. Round 2.5^2 up to 3.
> Multiply 2 by 3 and add 0.25
> This method works for the squares of all numbers ending point five. Why does it work?

So $x^2 - 5x + 10 = (x - 2.5)^2 - 6.25 + 10 = (x - 2.5)^2 + 3.75$

Answer: When $x = 2.5$ the minimum value is 3.75

> Check: Use Table mode with $f(x) = x^2 - 5x + 10$, start -5, end 5 and step 0.5 to create a table of values.
>
> 3.75 is the smallest answer in the second column. It happens on the row with $x = 2.5$

ACTIVITY 13.8

Find the minimum values for these expressions and the value for x for which they happen. Use your calculator Table mode to show that you are correct.

a) $x^2 - 2x - 8$ b) $x^2 - 6x + 20$ c) $x^2 + 4x - 7$ d) $x^2 - 5x + 3$

CHAPTER SUM-UP

Reflection

Having worked through this chapter, how do you feel about these skills?

Skill	I have tried this	I need more practice	I am confident with this
Expanding a pair of brackets			
Factorizing a three-term quadratic expression			
Solving a quadratic equation			
Understanding how to complete the square			

Quiz

1. Which one of these expressions never goes below zero?

a) $(x - 4)(x + 2)$ c) $x^2 + 7x + 13$
b) $x^2 + 4x + 3$

> Hint: Find the minimum value! Check using Table mode.

2. For the other two expressions, find the roots of the equation formed when the expression equals zero.

14. Algebraic Graphs

COORDINATES USING POSITIVE AND NEGATIVE NUMBERS

You can describe the position of a point on a surface using coordinates. You need to draw two number lines that cross at zero, and this point is called the origin. The horizontal number line is called the x-axis and the vertical number line is called the y-axis.

As you move from the origin to another point, you can go across to the right or left and then up or down to get there.

The point in this diagram is 4 squares across to the right and 2 squares up from the origin, so is called the point (4, 2)

You can use algebra for a point, using x for the distance to the right and y for the distance up: (x, y)

If you want to go to the left or down from the origin, you have to use negative numbers for x and y.

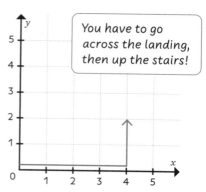

You have to go across the landing, then up the stairs!

Remember, positive numbers for right and up; negative numbers for left and down.

ACTIVITY 14.1

The triangle on this grid has vertices at

   (2, -1), (-1, 3) and (0, -2)

1. Where would the point (-2, 0) be?

2. Where could a point with two negative coordinates be?

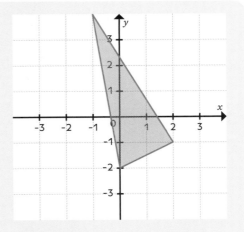

If you like to use movement to help with your learning, put both arms out horizontally. That is the x-axis. The points to your right have positive x-coordinates and the points to your left have negative x-coordinates. The points above your arms have positive y-coordinates and the points below your arms have negative y-coordinates.

   Stand in front of a mirror and point to (-2, -1), (2, 2), (-2, -2) and (1, -2). The diagrams show you how the points will look in the mirror.

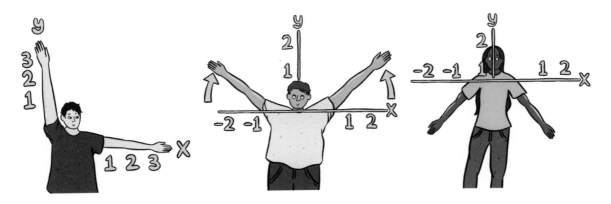

Which coordinate would be zero for these points? Is the other coordinate positive or negative?

   a) Points vertically above your head
   b) Points vertically below your head
   c) Points on your right arm when horizontal
   d) Points on your left arm when horizontal

Points and lines

When points are joined to make a straight line, there is a pattern in the coordinates. You can use algebra to describe the pattern. This is called the equation of the line. For GCSE Maths, you need to be able to draw a line from the equation and find the equation of a line from the graph.

ACTIVITY 14.2

Print a copy of the blank coordinate grids (see page 286). Follow the instructions below to create six graphs.

Graph 1
Plot the points (3, 4), (3, 2), (3, 0) (3, -2). Join them to make a straight line.
All these points have the same x-coordinate, so the equation of the line is $x = 3$.
Label the line with the equation.

To draw the line $x = 2$ on the same axes, plot some points where the first coordinate is 2. Join them and label the line.

Draw and label the line $x = -3$. What do you notice about the three lines?

Graph 2
Plot the points (4, 2), (2, 2), (0, 2) (-2, 2). Join them to make a straight line.
All these points have the same y-coordinate, so the equation of the line is $y = 2$.
Label the line with the equation.

To draw the line on the same axes, plot some points where the second coordinate is 1. Join them and label the line.

Draw and label the line $y = -3$. What do you notice about the three lines?

Graph 3
Plot the points (4, 4), (2, 2), (0, 0) (-2, -2). Join them to make a straight line.
These points all have the first coordinate the same as the second coordinate, so the equation of the line is $y = x$. Label the line with the equation.

On the same axes, draw the line $y = -x$ by plotting (4, -4) and (-3, 3). Look at the other points on the line. Do they fit the same pattern? Can you explain the pattern in words?

> You can also use the equation $x + y = 0$ for this.

Graph 4
Draw the line $y = x$

Draw another line by plotting all the points where the second coordinate is one more than the first coordinate. Label the line $y = x + 1$

Draw another line by plotting all the points where the second coordinate is one less than the first coordinate. Label the line $y = x - 1$.

What do you notice about these lines?

Graph 5

To draw the line $y = 2x$, use your calculator to work out the points.

Go to Table mode and enter $f(x) = 2x$

> The $f(x)$ is already displayed. You only need to type $2x$. There is a key for x.

To match the graph, you need to set the start value as -10, the end value as 10 and the step as 1.

The table you get gives the coordinates (without the brackets!) This table shows part of your display and the points you need to plot.

x	$f(x)$	coordinate
-2	-4	(-2, -4)
-1	-2	(-1, -2)
0	0	(0, 0)
1	2	(1, 2)
2	4	(2, 4)

Notice these points have the second coordinate twice as big as the first.

Plot the points that fit on the graph. Ignore the rest.

Join the points and label the line $y = 2x$

Draw the lines $y = 2x + 3$, $y = 2x + 7$, $y = 2x - 4$ using Table mode to get the points. Label each line with its equation.

What do you notice about the lines?

Graph 6

Use Table mode to help you to draw the lines $y = 3 - x$, $y = 3 - 2x$, $y = 3 - 3x$. Label each line with its equation. What do you notice about these lines?

THE CONNECTION BETWEEN ALGEBRA AND GRAPHS

You have seen in Activity 14.2 that vertical lines have the equation $x = $ constant. You can see the value of the constant from the graph.

> A **constant** is a number in an expression that does not change from one point to another.

You have also seen that horizontal lines have the equation $y = $ constant. You can see the value of the constant from the graph.

The lines through (0, 0) which go diagonally through the grid have the equations $y = x$ and $y = -x$

Other lines can be written in the form $y = mx + c$ where m and c are constants.

> Using these letters is another convention that mathematicians have agreed.

There is a link between the values of m and c and what the graph looks like.

Look at the table of values for the graph $y = 2x - 3$

This is of the form $y = mx + c$ with $m = 2$ and $c = -3$

x	$f(x)$
-4	-11
-3	-9
-2	-7
-1	-5
0	-3
1	-1
2	1
3	3
4	5

Notice that the y-coordinates go up in twos when the x-coordinates go up in ones. You could change the 3 in the equation and this would still happen.

The y-intercept is the point where the graph crosses the y-axis.

The gradient is the amount that y increases every time x increases by one. It measures how steep the line is.

Notice that when $x = 0$, $y = 2 \times 0 - 3 = -3$

You could change the 2 in the equation and this would still happen.

You can see the same things on the graph.

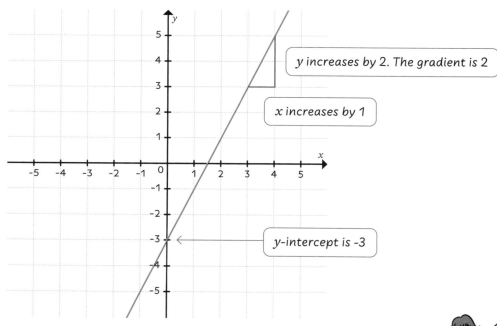

y increases by 2. The gradient is 2

x increases by 1

y-intercept is -3

Gradient

Use movement to help you to understand gradient.

What dance move is this to you?

In the equation $y = 2x - 3$, $m = -3$ and $c = 4$

For the graph $y = 4 - 3x$ you can predict what the graph will look like before plotting the points.

The y-intercept is 4, so the graph goes through the point (0, 4)

The gradient is (-3), so y will decrease by three every time x increases by one.

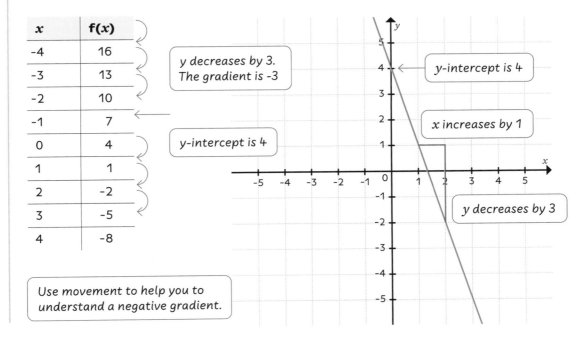

x	$f(x)$
-4	16
-3	13
-2	10
-1	7
0	4
1	1
2	-2
3	-5
4	-8

y decreases by 3. The gradient is -3

y-intercept is 4

y-intercept is 4

x increases by 1

y decreases by 3

Use movement to help you to understand a negative gradient.

You can use this connection to find the equation of a line that has been drawn for you.

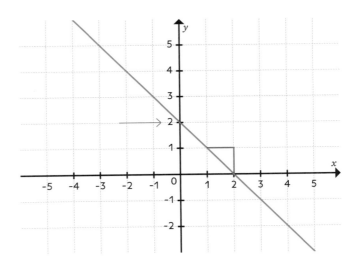

The equation of a line is
$y = mx + c$

The y-intercept is at (0, 2)
so $c = 2$

For every one that x increases, y decreases by one, so the gradient is -1. Therefore, $m = -1$

The equation of the line is
$y = -1x + 2$

You can rewrite this as
$y = 2 - x$

Some mathematicians prefer not to start an equation with a negative if they can help it!

Check this is right by making a table of values in Table mode and compare with the graph.

Find the gradient of the line

For every one that x increases, y increases by 0.5, so the gradient is $\frac{1}{2}$

You could also say for every two that x increases, y increases by one, so the gradient is $\frac{1}{2}$

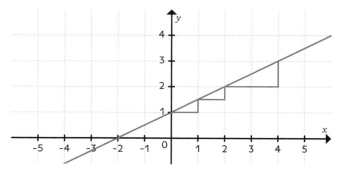

ACTIVITY 14.3

1. Make a calculator table of values for these lines. Write down the y-intercept and gradient for each.

a) $y = 3x + 5$

c) $y = 7x - 4$

e) $y = \frac{1}{2}x - \frac{1}{2}$

b) $y = 2 + 5x$

d) $y = -1 - 2x$

f) $y = 3(x + 2)$

Can you see a way of getting your answers directly from the equation?

Look back at the graphs in Activity 14.2. What do you notice about the gradients when the lines are parallel?

2. This graph has three lines drawn for you.

a) Write down the gradient and y-intercept of these lines.

b) Write down the equation of these lines.

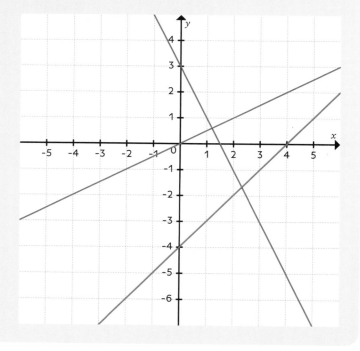

REARRANGING AN EQUATION

When the equation of a line is $y = mx + c$, the gradient is m and the y-intercept is c.

Sometimes the equation of the line is given in a rearranged form. You must rewrite it in the form $y = mx + c$ to use Table mode and to use the equation to write down the gradient and y-intercept.

⏪ **Rewind** – look at page 207 for expanding brackets
look at page 219 for rearranging formulae

$y = 4(x + 2)$. Write down the gradient and the y-intercept
Expand the brackets: $y = 4x + 8$

So, the gradient is 4 and the y-intercept is 8

$y = \dfrac{(x - 1)}{2}$. Write down the gradient and the y-intercept
Write as two separate fractions: $y = \frac{1}{2}x - \frac{1}{2}$

So, the gradient is $\frac{1}{2}$ and the y-intercept is $-\frac{1}{2}$

$x + y = 7$. Write down the gradient and the y-intercept
Subtract x from both sides to give $y = 7 - x = -1x + 7$

So, the gradient is -1 and the y-intercept is 7

> To check your work, make a calculator table of values. Choose a row and see if the two numbers added together make 7.

$3y - 4x = 12$. Write down the gradient and the y-intercept
Rearrange the equation in two steps

$$3y - 4x = 12$$
$+4x$ $\qquad$ $+4x$
$$3y = 4x + 12$$
$\div 3$ $\qquad$ $\div 3$
$$y = \tfrac{4}{3}x + 4$$

> Check your work using a calculator table of values. Substitute the values for x and y into the formula. You should get the answer 12.

So the gradient is $\frac{4}{3}$ and the y-intercept is 4

What to do if you don't have a calculator

Plot the line $y = 3x - 1$
If you don't have a calculator, you must complete your own table of values.

Substitute each value for x into the equation. Write the answer in the table.

When $x = 3$, $y = 3 \times 3 - 1 = 9 - 1 = 8$

When $x = 2$, $y = 3 \times 2 - 1 = 6 - 1 = 5$

x	$f(x)$
-2	
-1	
0	
1	
2	
3	

When $x = 1$, $y = 3 \times 1 - 1 = 3 - 1 = 2$

When $x = 0$, $y = 3 \times 0 - 1 = 0 - 1 = -1$

When $x = -1$, $y = 3 \times (-1) - 1 = (-3) - 1 = -4$

When $x = -2$, $y = 3 \times (-2) - 1 = (-6) - 1 = -7$

> To make it easier, start with the positive numbers.
>
> Check your answers for the negative numbers using the patterns.
>
> The intercept should be -1
>
> The y-values should go up in threes.

x	$f(x)$
-2	-7
-1	-4
0	-1
1	2
2	5
3	8

> *y increases by 3*
> *The gradient is 3*

> *y-intercept is –1*

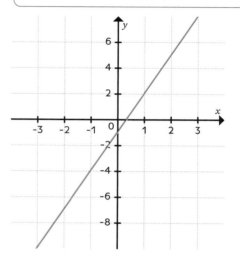

DRAWING A CURVED GRAPH FROM ITS EQUATION

If the equation contains an x^2 term, the points will not line up, so you need to join them with a smooth curve.

Draw the graph of $y = x^2$

Use Table mode to make the table of values. Plot the points, then join them with a smooth curve.

> Remember, the square of a negative number is not negative!

x	$f(x)$
-4	16
-3	9
-2	4
-1	1
0	0
1	1
2	4
3	9
4	16

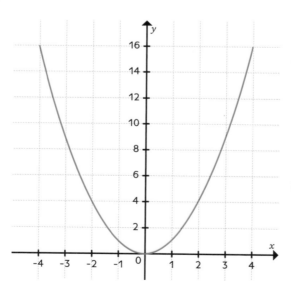

> Notice the curve has a line of symmetry.

> A **parabola** is the name of the shape of the graph of $y = x^2$ Other quadratic graphs are parabolas too.

Draw the graph of $y = x^2 - 3x - 2$ and use it to estimate the roots of the equation $x^2 - 3x - 2 = 0$ (do not use a calculator)

> The roots of the equation are the points where the graph crosses the x-axis.

To make the table of values without a calculator, you could work out each term of the equations separately and add them together to find the answer. So, to find the value for $x = -4$, add 16, 12 and -2.

Some people prefer to write out each calculation and collate the answers in a table. Starting with positive numbers can make that easier. It's up to you!

x	-4	-3	-2	-1	0	1	2	3	4
x^2	16	9	4	1	0	1	4	9	16
$-3x$	12	9	6	3	0	-3	-6	-9	-12
-2	-2	-2	-2	-2	-2	-2	-2	-2	-2
$y = x^2 - 3x + 2$	26	16	8	2	-2	-4	-4	-2	2

> Notice the table has a symmetric pattern.

> Where two identical values are next to each other, continue to draw a curve. Don't join these points with a straight line.

To find out what happens between 1 and 2, you can look at $x = 1.5$

When $x = 1.5$, $y = 1.5^2 - 3 \times 1.5 - 2 = 2.25 - 4.5 - 2 = -4.25$

So the curve goes lower than -4 between $x = 1$ and $x = 2$

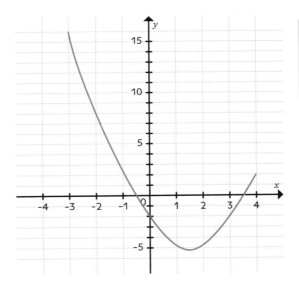

> Which dance move do you think of to help you remember the shape of a parabola?

The curve crosses the axis between -1 and 0 and between 3 and 4. So the roots of the equation are approximately -0.6 and 3.6

ACTIVITY 14.4

a) $y = -x^2$

b) $y = x^2 - 2$

c) $y = x^2 - x - 3$

d) $y = 3 - 2x - x^2$

e) $y = x^2 + 2x - 8$

f) $y = 5 + 4x - x^2$

1. Use Table mode to make a table of values for equations a) to d). For parts e) and f) do not use a calculator; instead work out the values yourself and write them in a table. Use values of x from -5 to 5.

2. Print another copy of the blank grids from page 286 and plot the graphs. Ignore any points that do not fit on the axes.

3. Write down the values of x where each curve crosses the x-axis.

4. Which of these graphs give a u-shaped graph and which give an n-shaped graph?

CHAPTER SUM-UP

Reflection

Having worked through this chapter, how do you feel about these skills?

Skill	I have tried this	I need more practice	I am confident with this
Understanding coordinates using positive and negative numbers			
Understanding the connection between algebra and graphs			
Drawing a line from its equation			
Understanding the gradient of a line			
Finding the y-intercept of a line			
Drawing a curved graph from its equation			
Using a graph to answer questions			

Quiz

1. Plot the graphs of $y = x + 3$ and $y = 5x - x^2$. Where do the lines cross?

2. Use Table mode to draw these graphs. Draw the matchstick people to go with each. Which famous dance moves does the set of graphs represent?

a) $y = x^2$

b) $y = 4x^2 - x^4$

c) $y = \frac{1}{x}$ for positive values of x

d) $y = 3 - x^2$

Part 3

Getting Ready for Your Exams

HOW TO REVISE EFFECTIVELY

Three best bits of advice for preparing for a maths exam – do the sums, do the sums, do the sums! Past paper questions are best.

We all learn in different ways and so we all need to revise in different ways. Some people prefer to have complete silence when revising and others prefer to listen to music. Be aware of what works for you and consider the following techniques. The important thing is to use 'active' techniques. Just copying out procedures and formulae will be very ineffective.

Here are some active revision techniques.

- Talk about what you are learning. Discuss it with other people or, even better, try and teach it to someone else.
- Source instructional videos and make notes while you are watching them. Pause the videos to give you time to practise some examples.
- Use mind maps, colour coding or highlighting to give you a strong visual image.
- Create a bank of memory cards that detail aspects of maths you find hard to recall. This may be terminology, times table facts, formulae or algorithms; anything that you feel you need to try to remember better. Review these cards for a few minutes every day to help transfer the information from your short-term to your long-term memory.
- Draw pictures and diagrams to help you understand mathematical concepts.
- Complete as many past papers as you can.
- Plan your revision on a large sheet of A3 paper, divided into three columns. Write on sticky notes the topics you need to revise and then place the sticky notes accordingly on the paper.

I don't know much	I am beginning to understand	Test me now!

As you revise, you can start to move your sticky notes from one column to the next. This will help you to plan your time and will also help you to see the progress that you are making.

- Take frequent breaks. Try to concentrate hard on your revision for 20–30 minutes and then take a short, 5-minute break. This will help you to remember better what you have been working on.
- Go over the same thing many times. The more often you revisit something, the more likely you will be to remember it.
- Don't panic! Give yourself plenty of time to revise. Make revision part of your daily routine and talk about it, draw it, explain it and teach it to someone else – or even the dog! – as much as you can.

IN THE EXAM

Starting out

If you get nervous, use the minutes waiting for the exam to start to calm yourself down. Practise deep breathing (see page 53).

If you normally use Napier's bones in class, spend the first few minutes of an exam drawing a multiplication square, or write a list of times table facts. Doing so will continue to calm your nerves and you can refer to these resources as many times as you like during the exam.

Understanding the question

There is a technique called the 'three read technique', which unsurprisingly asks you to read each question three times. Now this may seem like a waste of time but if it stops you from misunderstanding a question, then it is well worth it. You have probably often said 'Oh I didn't realize it meant that, I didn't read the question properly'.

The first read is to understand the context. What is the problem all about? The second is to understand the maths, and the third is to read the question, thinking about your plan for answering it.

Hints for problem solving

- Ask yourself: 'What would I need to know to answer this question?'
- Ask yourself: 'What could I try doing with the information in the question?'

Can you get the first two strategies to meet in the middle?

Do something, even if it does not lead to a final answer. Your jottings might be worth marks or they might spark another idea. You know for certain you get no marks if you don't answer a question at all.

Know when to move on – let the number of marks tell you how many minutes to spend on a question. You can always come back to a question if you have time at the end.

Managing without manipulatives

Use counters and Napier's bones for as long as they are useful to you, but you cannot take them into your exams. Use the advice in Part 1 for moving on to a pictorial method instead.

- Practise filling in a multiplication square so you can manage without Napier's bones.
- Practise drawing coloured dots instead of using coloured counters.

Draw the diagrams

You are allowed to draw as many diagrams as you like in your exam. You could add a few words to help the person marking your work to understand what your diagram is showing. There are no extra marks for getting the right answer by another method.

- Use dots and tally marks if they help.
- Draw number lines or graphs.
- Bar diagrams are evidence of a method – use them if they help.

Write lists

For questions such as finding the highest common factor, write lists of factors and look for the largest in both lists. For questions about catching buses, you can write lists of buses and the times they arrive.

Make use of your smart calculator

Don't forget that your calculator has a Table mode. You can use it to help plot graphs by giving the table of values. To solve equations, you can work out algebra expressions for a whole set of numbers and see which one gives the right answer. You can compare two tables of values to check your algebra rewriting.

Careless mistakes and checking strategies

Everyone makes mistakes, so develop checking strategies to help you to find and correct them. There are no extra marks for getting a question right the first time. Be aware of the types of mistake you make and check specifically for them. For example:

- interchanging digits
- repeating digits.

If you have no time to make any corrections, save more time by leaving out the checking!

When you are checking a calculation, try to check it by a different method than the one you first used, then you are less likely to repeat the error.

Try estimating what you think the answer will be and then be alert to any answers that you get that are very different from your original estimation.

FINALLY

Remember you do not need to get all the marks to get the grade you want! If you can get all the marks on questions you know you can do, and some marks on some of the other questions by trying something, you will have quite a lot of marks in the end. Good luck!

Glossary

ADHD   People with ADHD have difficulty with focusing and holding their attention.

ASD   People with ASD may have difficulty with communication and social interaction.

coefficient   The coefficient of x is the number that multiplies x in the expression.

commutative   Commutative means the answer is the same regardless of the order in which you multiply (or add) the numbers. Multiplication and addition are commutative, but division and subtraction are not.

completing the square   Completing the square is a way of rewriting a quadratic expression so that it begins with brackets squared and ends with adding or subtracting a number.

concrete materials   Concrete materials are physical manipulatives, such as cubes and counters, used to model maths concepts.

constant   A constant is a number in an expression that does not change from one point to another.

convention   A convention is an agreed way of doing things that everyone accepts.

denominator   The denominator of a fraction tells you into how many equal parts a whole has been divided. It is written below the horizontal line.

discount   Discount is an amount that is taken off a price when an item is in a sale.

dyscalculia   People with dyscalculia have difficulty with understanding numbers.

dyslexia   People with dyslexia have difficulty with reading, writing and spelling.

dyspraxia   People with dyspraxia have difficulty with movements and coordination.

equation   In an equation, you are told that two algebraic expressions balance each other.

equivalent fractions   Equivalent fractions may look different but they represent the same value.

expression   An expression is a combination of letters and numbers with no equals sign.

factorizing   Factorizing means rewriting a number or expression as a multiplication. In algebra, it means you have to put the brackets in. It is the reverse of expanding brackets.

factors   Factors are numbers you multiply together to make another number. For example, 3 and 5 are factors of 15.

formula   A formula is an equation that links two or more variables together. It contains a set of instructions about how to work out the value of one letter when you know the value of the other letters. The plural of formula is formulae. Formulae are often used in science.

highest common factor   The highest common factor (HCF) of two numbers is the largest number which is a factor of both numbers.

identity   An identity is an equation that is true for all values of x. You can rewrite one side to get the other.

index   An index (plural: indices) is positioned above and to the right of the base number. It indicates how many times the base number is multiplied by itself when the index is a positive number.

inequality   In an inequality, you are told that one algebraic expression is larger or smaller than another.

integer   An integer is a whole number. It can be positive or negative.

interest   Interest is money that the bank adds to your account at the end of a year.

inverse   Inverse means the opposite. In maths, the inverse of an operation reverses the effect of another operation.

kinaesthetic learning   Kinaesthetic learning is learning through physical activity.

long-term memory   Long-term memory is used for storing information over an extended period.

lowest common multiple (LCM)   The lowest common multiple (LCM) of two numbers is the smallest multiple that is common to both.

metacognition   Metacognition is thinking about one's thinking.

mixed number   A mixed number is a whole number and a fraction. The whole number and the fraction are added together. A mixed number is a top-heavy fraction that has been split into whole numbers and fractions.

multiples   The multiples of a number are all the numbers that are products of the number and any other integer.

multisensory   A multisensory approach uses more than one sense at the same time.

Napier's bones   Napier's bones are a tool for multiplying. They are made from a multiplication square cut into vertical strips; each vertical strip is a 'bone'.

neurodiversity   Neurodiversity refers to differences in the human brain.

number sense   Number sense is the ability to understand our number system and the relationships between numbers and number operations.

numerator   The numerator of a fraction tells you how many of the parts indicated by the denominator you have. It is written above the horizontal line.

over-learning   Over-learning involves revisiting information again and again.

parabola   A parabola is the name of the shape of the graph of $y = x^2$. Other quadratic graphs are parabolas too.

pelmanism   Pelmanism is a card game in which matching pairs must be selected from memory from cards laid face down.

percentages   Percentages are equivalent to fractions where the denominator is 100. 1% means 1 part in every 100.

phonological awareness   Phonological awareness is how well we can process individual sounds in words.

power   A power is used to write a multiplication where a number is multiplied by itself many times.

prime number   A prime number has only two factors, 1 and itself.

product   Multiply numbers to work out the product.

quadratic equation   A quadratic equation is formed when a quadratic expression is equal to zero.

root of an equation   A root of an equation is a value of x for which the expression gives the correct value.

short-term memory   Short-term memory is used to hold information in the mind for a short period of time.

significant figure   The first significant figure is the first non-zero digit needed to write the number. Zeros that are only included as place-fillers are not significant (e.g. 0.05), but trapped zeros are significant (e.g. 205).

simultaneous equations   Simultaneous equations are typically two equations, each with two unknowns (usually x and y). The value of each unknown is the same in both equations.

square numbers   Square numbers are made by multiplying a number by itself. A square number of counters can be arranged in a square.

standard form   A number is in standard form when it is written as a number between one and ten multiplied by a power of ten.

subitizing   Subitizing is the ability to state how many items are in a set without counting them.

subject of a formula   The subject of a formula is the letter on its own on one side of the formula. It must not be on the other side as well.

term   A term is the part of an expression between the + or - signs.

top-heavy fraction   A top-heavy fraction is a fraction where the numerator is bigger than the denominator. There are more parts than you need to make a whole.

variable   A variable is a letter in an expression (usually x and y) that changes from one point to another.

verbal memory   Verbal memory is how well we can remember what we have heard.

verbal processing speed   Verbal processing speed is how long it takes us to make sense of the information that we hear.

working memory   Working memory is the ability to manipulate information being held in the short-term memory.

zero pair   Adding 1 and (-1) gives zero. They are called a zero pair. Other zero pairs include x and $(-x)$.

Resources

All of the templates from this section are available to download and print from **www.jkp.com/catalogue/book/9781787757004**.

GAMES TO IMPROVE LONG-TERM MEMORY

Shopping game

For example: I went shopping and I bought a TV.

    Next player: I went shopping and I bought a TV and a banana.

    Next player: I went shopping and I bought a TV and a banana and a cat.

    Play continues until the list is so long that items are missed out.

    Think about how you remember the list. Do you make up a story that connects all the items? Do you picture the items – maybe you are watching TV, while eating a banana with a cat on your lap? Figuring out how you can remember the list will help you when you are trying to remember facts and procedures in maths.

Kim's game

For this game you will need a tray of items.

    Take some time to look at all the items and try to remember them. Be aware of what strategy you are using to remember them. Then, ask someone to remove one of the items when you are not looking. Now look at the tray again. Can you tell what items are missing?

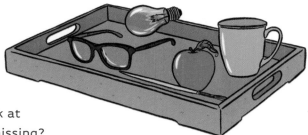

Pelmanism or pairs memory games

You probably know this game. There are endless versions of it! Here we show you how to play it with a pack of playing cards.

    Remove all the picture cards from the pack and place the remaining cards face down on the table. The game might work better if you arrange the cards in rows and columns. A player selects two cards. If the cards are a matching pair, then the player keeps the cards and has another go. If the two cards do not match, then they are replaced in the same position and play passes to the next player. The player with the most pairs is the winner.

Here are just a few ideas for different versions of the game:

- Number match – A pair of cards match if they have the same number.
- Multiplication match – The cards match if they multiply to a certain number. Again, the set of cards used will need to be carefully selected.
- Fraction/decimal/percentage match – For this game, you will need to make your own set of cards, showing fractions decimals and percentages. The cards will match if they show the equivalent numerical amount. For example, $\frac{1}{2}$ would match with 0.5.

Napier's bones

1	2	3	4	5	6	7	8	9	0
0/1	0/2	0/3	0/4	0/5	0/6	0/7	0/8	0/9	0/0
0/2	0/4	0/6	0/8	1/0	1/2	1/4	1/6	1/8	0/0
0/3	0/6	0/9	1/2	1/5	1/8	2/1	2/4	2/7	0/0
0/4	0/8	1/2	1/6	2/0	2/4	2/8	3/2	3/6	0/0
0/5	1/0	1/5	2/0	2/5	3/0	3/5	4/0	4/5	0/0
0/6	1/2	1/8	2/4	3/0	3/6	4/2	4/8	5/4	0/0
0/7	1/4	2/1	2/8	3/5	4/2	4/9	5/6	6/3	0/0
0/8	1/6	2/4	3/2	4/0	4/8	5/6	6/4	7/2	0/0
0/9	1/8	2/7	3/6	4/5	5/4	6/3	7/2	8/1	0/0
1/0	2/0	3/0	4/0	5/0	6/0	7/0	8/0	9/0	0/0

Grid of numbers 1-100

1	2	3	4	5	6	7	8	9	10
11	12	13	14	15	16	17	18	19	20
21	22	23	24	25	26	27	28	29	30
31	32	33	34	35	36	37	38	39	40
41	42	43	44	45	46	47	48	49	50
51	52	53	54	55	56	57	58	59	60
61	62	63	64	65	66	67	68	69	70
71	72	73	74	75	76	77	78	79	80
81	82	83	84	85	86	87	88	89	90
91	92	93	94	95	96	97	98	99	100

Multiplication square

×	1	2	3	4	5	6	7	8	9	10
1										
2										
3										
4										
5										
6										
7										
8										
9										
10										

Base-10 tiles

Place-value slider

Print the template onto card.

Cut out and laminate the place-value grid and the slider strip. Alternatively, cover them with sticky transparent plastic, leaving spare plastic at either end to act as a tab to pull the slider strip through.

Make vertical slits on the place-value grid using a craft knife or sharp scissors, but only on the row containing zeros.

Thread the slider strip through the place-value grid. Write the number you are working with on the strip. Use a dry wipe pen so that you can erase the number later.

You can now slide the number to the left or right depending on whether you are multiplying or dividing. The number of places that you move the slider strip will be determined by the multiples of 10 that you are working with.

HTh	TTh	Th	H	T	O	.	$\frac{1}{10}$	$\frac{1}{100}$
				0	0	.	0	0

HTh	TTh	Th	H	T	O	.	$\frac{1}{10}$	$\frac{1}{100}$
				0	0	.	0	0

Rounding viewer

Use a viewer to remember which digit is to be rounded and which digit is to be checked.

Make the viewer from a piece of card. You can copy this image onto the card and then carefully cut out the centre of the oval and the centre of the rectangle. You will need to make these quite small so that only one digit is seen in each window.

Place the viewer over the number to be rounded.

For example: Rounding to 1 decimal place

12.3657

Is this digit 5 or more? —Yes→ Round up → 12.4

Fraction grids

Print or trace the fraction grids onto acetate or tracing paper.

$\frac{1}{2}$	0.5

$\frac{1}{2}$	0.5

$\frac{1}{3}$		0.133̇3̇

$\frac{1}{4}$			0.25

$\frac{1}{5}$				0.2

$\frac{1}{6}$					0.166̇6̇

$\frac{1}{7}$						0.143

$\frac{1}{8}$							0.125

$\frac{1}{9}$								0.1̇1̇

$\frac{1}{10}$									0.1

$\frac{1}{10}$									0.1

$\frac{1}{100}$									0.01

Nets for algebra tubes

Join the left and right edges to make a tube that your counters will fit inside.

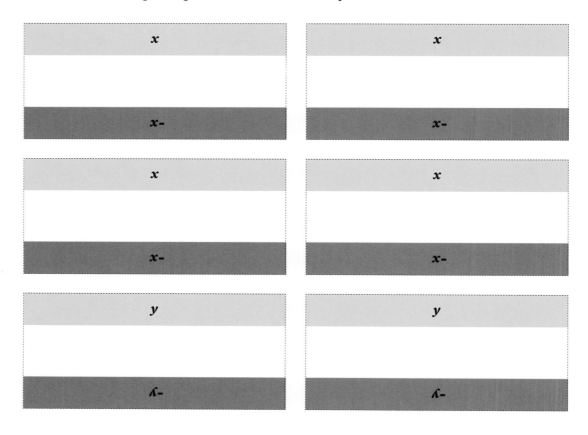

Counters

Algebra tiles

| x^2 | x | x | x | x | x | x | 1 | 1 | 1 | 1 |
| | | | | | | | 1 | 1 | 1 | 1 |

| x^2 | x | x | x | x | x | x | 1 | 1 | 1 | 1 |
| | | | | | | | 1 | 1 | 1 | 1 |

| $-x^2$ | $-x$ | $-x$ | $-x$ | $-x$ | $-x$ | $-x$ | -1 | -1 | -1 | -1 |
| | | | | | | | -1 | -1 | -1 | -1 |

| $-x^2$ | $-x$ | $-x$ | $-x$ | $-x$ | $-x$ | $-x$ | -1 | -1 | -1 | -1 |
| | | | | | | | -1 | -1 | -1 | -1 |

Axes for algebraic graphs

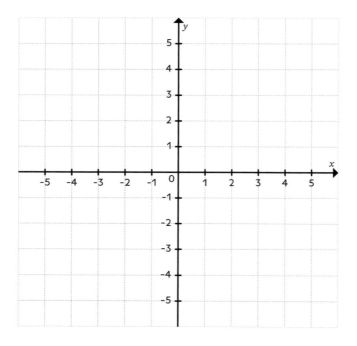

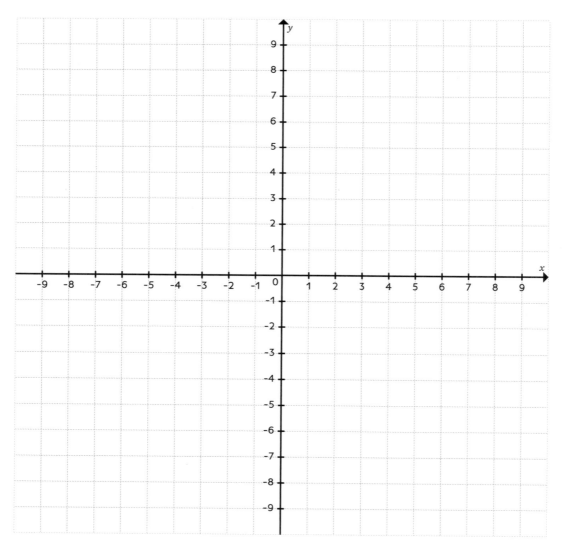

Answers

1. MULTIPLICATION AND DIVISION

Activity 1.1 (page 68)

1. a) 1368

b) 956

c) 4278

d) 5859

e) 8478

2. a) 1368 ÷ 3 = 456   1368 ÷ 456 = 3

b) 956 ÷ 4 = 239   956 ÷ 239 = 4

c) 4278 ÷ 6 = 713   4278 ÷ 713 = 6

d) 5859 ÷ 7 = 837   5859 ÷ 837 = 7

e) 8478 ÷ 9 = 942   8478 ÷ 942 = 9

Activity 1.2 (page 69)

1. a) 1112

b) 5124

c) 2328

d) 6651

e) 3192

2. a) 1112 ÷ 4 = 278   1112 ÷ 278 = 4

b) 5124 ÷ 6 = 854   5124 ÷ 854 = 6

c) 2328 ÷ 8 = 291   2328 ÷ 291 = 8

d) 6651 ÷ 9 = 739   6651 ÷ 739 = 9

e) 3192 ÷ 7 = 456   3192 ÷ 456 = 7

Activity 1.3 (page 70)

1. a) 2754

b) 1633

c) 1935

d) 1938

e) 2835

2. a) 2754 ÷ 34 = 81   2754 ÷ 81 = 34

b) 1633 ÷ 23 = 71   1633 ÷ 71 = 23

c) 1935 ÷ 45 = 43   1935 ÷ 43 = 45

d) 1938 ÷ 57 = 34   1938 ÷ 34 = 57

e) 2835 ÷ 63 = 45   2835 ÷ 45 = 63

3. a) 4891

b) 4648

c) 4524

d) 2565

e) 2136

4. a) 4891 ÷ 73 = 67   4891 ÷ 67 = 73

b) 4648 ÷ 83 = 56   4648 ÷ 56 = 83

c) 4524 ÷ 58 = 78   4524 ÷ 78 = 58

d) 2565 ÷ 57 = 45   2565 ÷ 45 = 57

e) 2136 ÷ 24 = 89   2136 ÷ 89 = 24

5. All the multipliers have two digits where the second digit is one more than the first.

Activity 1.4 (page 72)

1. a) 2886   2886 ÷ 74 = 39   2886 ÷ 39 = 74

b) 1435   1435 ÷ 41 = 35   1435 ÷ 35 = 41

c) 1368   1368 ÷ 57 = 24   1368 ÷ 24 = 57

d) 2494   2494 ÷ 43 = 58   2494 ÷ 58 = 43

e) 1786   1786 ÷ 38 = 47   1786 ÷ 47 = 38

f) 1599   1599 ÷ 39 = 41   1599 ÷ 41 = 39

g) 884   884 ÷ 17 = 52   884 ÷ 52 = 17

h) 4464   4464 ÷ 62 = 72   4464 ÷ 72 = 62

i) 7990   7990 ÷ 85 = 94   7990 ÷ 94 = 85

j) 4698   4698 ÷ 87 = 54   4698 ÷ 54 = 87

2. a) 1612   1612 ÷ 62 = 26   1612 ÷ 26 = 62

b) 2916   2916 ÷ 81 = 36   2916 ÷ 36 = 81

c) 3481   3481 ÷ 59 = 59

d) 3552   3552 ÷ 74 = 48   3552 ÷ 48 = 74

e) 2232   2232 ÷ 93 = 24   2232 ÷ 24 = 93

Investigate (page 73)

Every answer divides exactly by 121 to give the product of the two digits.
For example: 55 × 33 = 5 × 11 × 3 × 11 = 15 × 121, and 11 × 11 = 121

Activity 1.5 (page 73)

1. a) 18,585

b) 5124

c) 57,821

d) 42,247

e) 692,636

Activity 1.6 (page 76)

a) 32

b) 412

c) 32

d) 54

e) 812

f) 111 rem 2 or 111.4 or $111\frac{2}{5}$

g) 247 rem 1 or 247.25 or $247\frac{1}{4}$

h) 4878 rem 1 or 4878.5 or $4878\frac{1}{2}$

i) 1542 rem 5 or 1542.8333... or $1542\frac{5}{6}$

j) 8657 rem 1 or 8657.333... or $8657\frac{1}{3}$

Activity 1.7 (page 77)

1. a) 708

b) 439

c) 1459

d) 269

e) 125

f) 34 rem 3

g) 736 rem 4

h) 687 rem 2

i) 788 rem 1

j) 2789 rem 5

Quiz question (page 79)

a) 1576

b) 1554

c) 1578

d) 1551

So c 6312 ÷ 4 gives the largest answer.

2. PLACE VALUE AND DECIMALS

Investigate (page 81)

Possible whole numbers: 752, 725, 572, 527, 275, 257, 75, 72, 57, 52, 27, 25, 7, 5, 2

Five of the numbers are in the five times table (end in 5).

Activity 2.1 (page 82)

All the whole numbers from 100 to 149 round down and all the whole numbers from 151 to 200 round up. There is a convention that 150 rounds up to 200 to the nearest hundred.

It is the size of the number in the tens column that matters; the ones do not make any difference.

Activity 2.2 (page 82)

a) 170

b) 140

c) 220

d) 0

e) 70

f) 1250

Activity 2.4 (page 87)

1. a) 0.50; 0.505; 0.55; 5.5

b) 0.075; 0.570; 0.705; 0.75

c) 0.099; 0.0999; 0.1; 0.99

2. a) 007 = 7

b) 0.750 = 0.75

c) 0.45 > 0.045

d) 00.02 < 0.2

e) 001.1000 = 1.1

f) 0.03 > 0.000 300

Activity 2.5 (page 89)

1. a) 0.3 to 1dp

b) 0.56 to 2 dp

c) 2.61 to 2dp

d) 6.052 to 3dp

e) 0.150 to 3dp

2. 0.15 to 2 dp rounds to 0.2 to 1 dp. Rounding 0.149 to 1 dp is 0.1, which is not the same answer.

Activity 2.6 (page 91)

1. a) 160

b) 2.5

c) 0.06

d) 0.021

e) 0.01

f) 0.08

g) 0.42

h) 0.063

Activity 2.3 (page 86)

÷ 100	÷ 10	Number	× 10	× 100
0.16	1.6	16	160	1600
0.0152	0.152	1.52	15.2	152
0.4643	4.643	46.43	464.3	4643
0.006 05	0.0605	0.605	6.05	60.5
0.000 087	0.000 87	0.0087	0.087	0.87

i) 42

j) 720

2. a) 160 ÷ 2 = 80   160 ÷ 80 = 2

b) 2.5 ÷ 5 = 0.5   2.5 ÷ 0.5 = 5

c) 0.06 ÷ 3 = 0.02   0.06 ÷ 0.02 = 3

d) 0.021 ÷ 3 = 0.007   0.021 ÷ 0.007 = 3

e) 0.01 ÷ 5 = 0.002   0.01 ÷ 0.002 = 5

f) 0.08 ÷ 0.2 = 0.4   0.08 ÷ 0.4 = 0.2

g) 0.42 ÷ 0.6 = 0.7   0.42 ÷ 0.7 = 0.6

h) 0.063 ÷ 0.7 = 0.09   0.063 ÷ 0.09 = 0.7

i) 42 ÷ 60 = 0.7   42 ÷ 0.7 = 60

j) 720 ÷ 8000 = 0.09   720 ÷ 0.09 = 8000

Activity 2.7 (page 92)

1. a) 2.43

b) 1.9

c) 26.6

d) 16.9

e) 6.351

Activity 2.8 (page 93)

a) 12.8

b) 2.5

c) 0.666... (rounds to 0.67 or 0.667 or 0.6667, etc)

d) 2.6

e) 0.91

f) 2.1285714... (the set of numbers 12,857 recurs)

g) 0.125

h) 0.055

i) 0.2095

j) 0.20202

Activity 2.9 (page 94)

a) 2

b) 31

c) 13

d) 26.4

e) 250

Quiz (page 94)

a) 0.025

b) 0.24

c) 0.1996

d) 0.214

e) 0.196

f) 1.9

In order of size a, e, c, d, b, f

3. MULTIPLES, FACTORS AND PRIMES

Activity 3.1 (page 95)

a) 3, 6, 9, 12, 15

b) 8, 16, 24, 32, 40

c) 12, 24, 36, 48, 60

d) 20, 40, 60, 80, 100

e) 21, 42, 63, 84, 105

f) 240, 480, 720, 960, 1200

Activity 3.2 (page 96)

a) 12

b) 96

c) 300

d) 100

e) 84

f) 170

Activity 3.3 (page 99)

1. a) {1, 2, 3, 4, 6, 8, 12, 24}

b) {1, 2, 3, 6, 7, 14, 21, 42}

c) {1, 2, 4, 8, 16, 32, 64}

d) {1, 2, 3, 4, 6, 7, 12, 14, 21, 28, 42, 84}

e) {1, 7, 11, 77}

f) {1, 3, 5, 9, 15, 45}

2. All the factors of odd numbers are odd. When learning your times tables, the only answers that are odd are when both numbers being multiplied are odd.

Activity 3.4 (page 100)

1	2	3	4	5	6	7	8	9	10
2	4	6	8	10	12	14	16	18	20
3	6	9	12	15	18	21	24	27	30
4	8	12	16	20	24	28	32	36	40
5	10	15	20	25	30	35	40	45	50
6	12	18	24	30	36	42	48	54	60
7	14	21	28	35	42	49	56	63	70
8	16	24	32	40	48	56	64	72	80
9	18	27	36	45	54	63	72	81	90
10	20	30	40	50	60	70	80	90	100

The square numbers are on the diagonal of the square.

Activity 3.5 (page 100)

a) 2

b) 8

c) 25

d) 20

e) 7

f) 1

Investigate (page 100)

Start numbers	Lowest common multiple	Highest common factor	Product
4 and 6	12	2	24
24 and 32	96	8	768
75 and 100	300	25	7500
20 and 100	100	20	2000
21 and 28	84	7	588
17 and 10	170	1	170

The HCF multiplied by the LCM also gives the same product as the original numbers.

Activity 3.6 (page 101)

1	2	3	4	5	6	7	8	9	10
11	12	13	14	15	16	17	18	19	20
21	22	23	24	25	26	27	28	29	30
31	32	33	34	35	36	37	38	39	40
41	42	43	44	45	46	47	48	49	50
51	52	53	54	55	56	57	58	59	60
61	62	63	64	65	66	67	68	69	70
71	72	73	74	75	76	77	78	79	80
81	82	83	84	85	86	87	88	89	90
91	92	93	94	95	96	97	98	99	100

The prime numbers up to 100 are 2, 3, 5, 7, 11, 13, 17, 19, 23, 29, 31, 37, 41, 43, 47, 53, 59, 61, 67, 71, 73, 79, 83, 89, 97.

Activity 3.7 (page 103)

There are four different versions of the factor tree starting with 3 × 40.

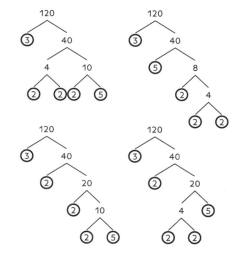

There are other factor trees that start with 10 × 12 like the example. There are even more if you start with 2 × 60, 4 × 30, 5 × 24, 6 × 20 or 8 × 15.

Activity 3.8 (page 104)

a) $70 = 2 \times 5 \times 7$

b) $72 = 2 \times 2 \times 2 \times 3 \times 3 = 2^3 \times 3^2$

c) $80 = 2 \times 2 \times 2 \times 2 \times 5 = 2^4 \times 5$

d) $88 = 2 \times 2 \times 2 \times 11 = 2^3 \times 11$

e) $375 = 3 \times 5 \times 5 \times 5 = 3 \times 5^3$

Quiz (page 105)

a) 97

b) 90

c) 96

So, the biggest is answer 97 (part a)

4. FRACTIONS

Activity 4.1 (page 107)

1. $\frac{1}{3} = \frac{2}{6} = \frac{3}{9} = \frac{4}{12} = \frac{5}{15} = \frac{6}{18} = \dots$

2. $\frac{2}{3} = \frac{4}{6} = \frac{6}{9} = \frac{8}{12} = \frac{10}{15} = \frac{12}{18} = \dots$

Investigate (page 107)

You can multiply or divide the numerator and denominator of a fraction by the same number and get an equivalent fraction.

Activity 4.2 and Activity 4.3 (pages 111 and 112)

a) $\frac{1}{2}$

b) $\frac{1}{2}$

c) $\frac{1}{3}$

d) $\frac{2}{3}$

e) $\frac{4}{9}$

f) $\frac{3}{7}$

g) $\frac{1}{5}$

h) $\frac{7}{8}$

i) $\frac{5}{8}$

j) $\frac{5}{15} = \frac{1}{3}$

Investigate (page 111)

Adding and subtracting numbers to the numerator and denominator changes the fractions.

Activity 4.4 (page 113)

1. a) $1\frac{1}{2}$

b) $1\frac{3}{4}$

c) $2\frac{2}{5}$

d) $1\frac{7}{10}$

e) $4\frac{4}{9}$

2. a) $\frac{7}{2}$

b) $\frac{7}{3}$

c) $\frac{23}{4}$

d) $\frac{27}{10}$

e) $\frac{47}{8}$

Activity 4.5 (page 115)

a) 9

b) 6

c) 12

d) 18

e) 24

f) 28

g) 63

h) 8

i) 14

j) 7.5

Investigate (page 116)

$\frac{1}{8}$ is the same answer

Activity 4.6 (page 117)

1. a) $\frac{1}{6}$

b) $\frac{1}{16}$

c) $\frac{3}{10}$

d) $\frac{3}{20}$

e) $\frac{7}{90}$

f) $\frac{4}{15}$

g) $\frac{21}{32}$

h) $\frac{4}{10} = \frac{2}{5}$

i) $\frac{12}{40} = \frac{3}{10}$

j) $\frac{15}{120} = \frac{1}{8}$

2. The numerator is the product of the numerators, and the denominator is the product of the numerators. The fractions simplify when one of the numbers on the numerators has a common factor with one of the numbers in the denominators.

Activity 4.7 (page 119)

1. a) 2

b) 5

c) 12

d) 4

e) 6

f) $4\frac{1}{2}$

2. a) $1 \times 2 = 2$

b) $1 \times 5 = 5$

c) $4 \times 3 = 12$

d) $\frac{1}{2} \times 8 = 4$

e) $\frac{2}{3} \times 9 = 6$

f) $\frac{3}{4} \times 6 = 4\frac{1}{2}$

Activity 4.8 (page 120)

a) There are 8 pieces in 6 whole ones so
$6 \div \frac{3}{4} = 8$

6					
1	1	1	1	1	1
$\frac{1}{4}$ $\frac{1}{4}$ $\frac{1}{4}$	$\frac{1}{4}$ $\frac{1}{4}$ $\frac{1}{4}$	$\frac{1}{4}$ $\frac{1}{4}$ $\frac{1}{4}$	$\frac{1}{4}$ $\frac{1}{4}$ $\frac{1}{4}$	$\frac{1}{4}$ $\frac{1}{4}$ $\frac{1}{4}$	$\frac{1}{4}$ $\frac{1}{4}$ $\frac{1}{4}$
$\frac{3}{4}$	$\frac{3}{4}$	$\frac{3}{4}$	$\frac{3}{4}$	$\frac{3}{4}$	$\frac{3}{4}$

b) There are 6 pieces in 4 whole ones
so $4 \div \frac{2}{3} = 6$

4			
1	1	1	1
$\frac{1}{3}$ $\frac{1}{3}$ $\frac{1}{3}$	$\frac{1}{3}$ $\frac{1}{3}$ $\frac{1}{3}$	$\frac{1}{3}$ $\frac{1}{3}$ $\frac{1}{3}$	$\frac{1}{3}$ $\frac{1}{3}$ $\frac{1}{3}$
$\frac{2}{3}$ $\frac{2}{3}$	$\frac{2}{3}$ $\frac{2}{3}$	$\frac{2}{3}$ $\frac{2}{3}$	

c) There are 2 pieces in three quarters
so $\frac{3}{4} \div \frac{3}{8} = 2$

1			
$\frac{1}{4}$	$\frac{1}{4}$	$\frac{1}{4}$	$\frac{1}{4}$
$\frac{3}{4}$			$\frac{1}{4}$
$\frac{1}{8}$ $\frac{1}{8}$ $\frac{1}{8}$	$\frac{1}{8}$ $\frac{1}{8}$	$\frac{1}{8}$	$\frac{1}{8}$ $\frac{1}{8}$

d) Only a quarter of a piece is needed for one tenth so $\frac{1}{10} \div \frac{2}{5} = \frac{1}{4}$

1									
$\frac{1}{10}$	$\frac{1}{10}$	$\frac{1}{10}$	$\frac{1}{10}$	$\frac{1}{10}$	$\frac{1}{10}$	$\frac{1}{10}$	$\frac{1}{10}$	$\frac{1}{10}$	$\frac{1}{10}$
$\frac{2}{5}$									

e) One piece plus one seventh of a piece is needed to make a whole one so $1 \div \frac{7}{8} = 1\frac{1}{7}$

1							
$\frac{1}{8}$	$\frac{1}{8}$	$\frac{1}{8}$	$\frac{1}{8}$	$\frac{1}{8}$	$\frac{1}{8}$	$\frac{1}{8}$	$\frac{1}{8}$
$\frac{7}{8}$							$\frac{1}{8}$

Activity 4.9 (page 121)

a) $\frac{2}{4} = \frac{1}{2}$

b) $\frac{4}{5}$

c) $\frac{3}{7}$

d) $\frac{8}{8} = 1$

e) $\frac{3}{6} = \frac{1}{2}$

Activity 4.10 (page 123)

a) $\frac{4}{8} + \frac{1}{8} = \frac{5}{8}$

b) $\frac{5}{8} - \frac{2}{8} = \frac{3}{8}$

c) $\frac{5}{6} - \frac{2}{6} = \frac{3}{6} = \frac{1}{2}$

d) $\frac{7}{10} - \frac{4}{10} = \frac{3}{10}$

e) $\frac{7}{9} + \frac{3}{9} = \frac{10}{9} = 1\frac{1}{9}$

f) $\frac{5}{10} + \frac{2}{10} = \frac{7}{10}$

g) $\frac{2}{6} + \frac{3}{6} = \frac{5}{6}$

h) $\frac{21}{70} + \frac{20}{70} = \frac{41}{70}$

i) $\frac{15}{24} - \frac{8}{24} = \frac{7}{24}$

j) $\frac{14}{20} + \frac{15}{20} = \frac{29}{20} = 1\frac{9}{20}$

Investigate (page 123)

$\frac{1}{2} - \frac{1}{3} = \frac{1}{6}$, $\frac{1}{3} - \frac{1}{4} = \frac{1}{12}$, $\frac{1}{4} - \frac{1}{5} = \frac{1}{20}$, $\frac{1}{5} - \frac{1}{6} = \frac{1}{30}$

... The answer is a fraction with numerator 1 and denominator which is the product of the two denominators.

$\frac{1}{2} - \frac{1}{4} = \frac{2}{4}$, $\frac{1}{3} - \frac{1}{5} = \frac{2}{15}$, $\frac{1}{4} - \frac{1}{6} = \frac{2}{24}$, $\frac{1}{5} - \frac{1}{7} = \frac{2}{35}$ ... The answer is a fraction with numerator 2 and denominator which is the product of the two denominators.

Quiz (page 124)

a) $\frac{1}{2}$

b) $\frac{9}{8}$

c) $\frac{17}{12}$

d) $\frac{1}{12}$

Answer c is the biggest. You get a different operation giving the biggest answer depending on sizes of the fractions.

5. PERCENTAGES, DECIMALS AND FRACTIONS

Activity 5.1 (page 129)

1.

	Fraction	Decimal	Percentage
a)	$\frac{1}{2}$	0.5	50%
b)	$\frac{1}{4}$	0.25	25%
c)	$\frac{7}{10}$	0.7	70%
d)	$\frac{3}{10}$	0.3	30%
e)	$\frac{15}{100} = \frac{3}{20}$	0.15	15%
f)	$\frac{9}{10}$	0.9	90%
g)	$\frac{4}{5}$	0.8	80%
h)	$\frac{73}{100}$	0.73	73%
i)	$\frac{1}{8}$	0.125	12.5%
j)	$\frac{11}{20}$	0.55	55%

2. $\frac{1}{4}$, 0.4, 44%, $\frac{4}{5}$

Investigate (page 129)

Fractions in their simplest form where the denominator goes exactly into 10 or 100 or 100 or 10,000, etc. do not give recurring decimals. All the others give recurring decimals. The denominator in simplified form has only 2s and 5s as prime factors.

Activity 5.2 (page 130)

a) Maths 92%

b) English 72%

c) German 70%

d) History 80%

Antonio did best in Maths.

Investigate (page 131)

All are correct to give 15.

Activity 5.3 and Activity 5.4 question 1 (page 132)

a) £5

b) £18

c) £8

d) £35

e) £5

f) £2

g) £3

h) £1.60

Activity 5.4 question 2 (page 132)

a) £1.84

b) £27.30

c) £34

d) £21.39

Activity 5.5 (page 134)

a) £880

b) £720

c) £84

d) £56

e) £75

f) £45

g) £147

h) £133

i) £9.75

j) £ 5.25

Activity 5.6 (page 136)

1. a) £2531.25

b) £304.175 (£304.18)

c) 97.2

d) 33.5% decrease

e) 12% decrease

2. a) £1157.625 (£1157.63)

b) £224.9728 (£224.97)

c) £1023.046084 (£1023.05)

3. a) 459.27

b) 1,200,500

Activity 5.7 (page 138)

a) £80

b) £50

c) £100

d) £10

e) £42

f) £65

Quiz (page 138)

a) £175

b) £160

c) £180

d) £177

So, part b gives the smallest amount

6. DIRECTED NUMBER

Activity 6.1 (page 140)

(-3) is 3 red counters, (-2) is 2 reds, (-1) is 1 red, 0 is no counters, 1 is 1 yellow, 2 is 2 yellows, 3 is 3 yellows.

Activity 6.2 (page 141)

2. a) 3

b) 0

c) 2

d) 4

e) (-3)

f) 2

g) (-1)

h) (-4)

i) 2

j) 1

Class Game (page 141)

It is impossible to get all 22 points. Any set of counters gives all odd numbers or all even numbers.

Investigate (page 142)

Answers are all even or all odd. With one extra counter, you get the opposite. You will get zero sometimes if you have an even number of counters so you can have the same number of reds as yellows, so all the counters make zero pairs.

Activity 6.3 (page 142)

a) 1

b) 9

c) 5

d) (-1)

e) (-2)

f) (-12)

Activity 6.4 (page 143)

1. a) (-2)

b) (-5)

c) 6

d) 10

e) 3

Activity 6.5 (page 144)

1. a) 10

b) (-8)

c) (-8)

d) (-15)

e) (-15)

2. The product of two positive numbers is positive. The product of a positive and a negative number is negative.

Activity 6.6 (page 144)

1. a) (-10)

b) (-10)

c) 8

d) 8

e) 15

f) 15

2. The product of two negative numbers is positive. The product of a positive and a negative number is negative.

3. Use a multiplication square or Napier's bones to multiply the numbers as if they were both positive, then decide whether the answer should be positive or negative. If one number is positive and the other negative the answer is negative, if both are negative the answer is positive.

4. For $(-1)^2 = 1$, $(-1)^3 = (-1)$, $(-1)^4 = 1$, $(-1)^5 = (-1)$, $(-1)^6 = 1$, the signs alternate. The answer is positive if the power is even. $(-1)^{99} = (-1)$

5. $(-1)^2 = (-1) \times (-1) = 1$; $-1^2 = -(1)^2 = -1$

Activity 6.7 (page 146)

a) (-2)

b) 3

c) (-3)

d) (-4)

e) 4

f) 6

g) 3

h) (-5)

i) (-15)

j) 15

Activity 6.8 (page 146)

a) (-5), (-2), 0, 5, 9

b) (-45), (-23), (-9), 15, 32

c) (-12), (-8), (-7.5), 1.5, 2.5

Activity 6.9 (page 148)

a) (-5)

b) 4

c) 4

d) (-4)

e) 3

f) (-1)

g) 1

h) (-5)

i) (-3)

j) 3

Activity 6.10 (page 149)

a) (-15)

b) 14

c) (-6)

d) (-45)

e) 13

f) (-15)

g) 11

h) 15

i) (-16)

j) 0

Quiz (page 152)

a) 51

b) (-90)

c) (-67)

d) 21

In order of size, largest first: a, d, c, b

7. USING INDICES

Activity 7.1 (page 154)

a) 9

b) 8

c) 343

d) 216

e) 3125

Investigate (page 155)

$2^3 = 8$	$3^3 = 27$	$4^3 = 64$	$5^3 = 125$
$2^2 = 4$	$3^2 = 9$	$4^2 = 16$	$5^2 = 25$
$2^1 = 2$	$3^1 = 3$	$4^1 = 4$	$5^1 = 5$
$2^0 = 1$	$3^0 = 1$	$4^0 = 1$	$5^0 = 1$
$2^{-1} = \frac{1}{2}$	$3^{-1} = \frac{1}{3}$	$4^{-1} = \frac{1}{4}$	$5^{-1} = \frac{1}{5}$
$2^{-2} = \frac{1}{4}$	$3^{-2} = \frac{1}{9}$	$4^{-2} = \frac{1}{16}$	$5^{-2} = \frac{1}{25}$
$2^{-3} = \frac{1}{8}$	$3^{-3} = \frac{1}{27}$	$4^{-3} = \frac{1}{64}$	$5^{-3} = \frac{1}{125}$

Any number to the power zero gives the answer 1.

Activity 7.2 (page 155)

a) $\frac{1}{36}$

b) $\frac{1}{10000}$ = 0.0001

c) $\frac{1}{7}$

d) $\frac{1}{64}$

e) 1

Investigate (page 156)

a) 10^5

b) 10^4

c) 10^6

d) 10^2

e) 10^{-5}

Law 3: To multiply powers of the same number, you can add the powers.

Investigate (page 156)

a) 10^2

b) 10^1

c) 10^{-1}

d) 10^{-4}

e) 10^{-1}

Law 4: To divide powers of the same number, you can subtract the powers.

Investigate (page 156)

a) 10^4

b) 10^8

c) 10^6

d) 10^9

e) 10^{-3}

Law 5: To work out the power of a power, multiply the powers together.

Activity 7.3 (page 157)

a) $4^3 = 64$

b) $8^1 = 8$

c) $3^6 = 729$

d) $3^3 = 27$

e) $5^2 = 25$

f) $5^4 = 625$

g) $6^0 = 1$

h) $2^5 = 32$

i) $3^9 = 19683$

j) $1^4 = 1$

Activity 7.4 and Activity 7.5 (page 160)

1. a) 3.472×10^3

b) 7.78899×10^5

c) 3.68×10^2

d) 5.7×10^{-2}

e) 2.43×10^{-4}

f) 4.99×10^{-1}

2. a) 59

b) 3470

c) 6,020,000

d) 0.5

e) 0.0051

f) 2.8

Activity 7.6 (page 162)

a) 9×10^5

b) 5.4×10^7

c) 3×10^5

d) 5×10^{-3}

e) 7×10^4

f) $50500 = 5.05 \times 10^4$

g) $6800 = 6.8 \times 10^3$

h) $0.37 = 3.7 \times 10^{-1}$

Activity 7.7 (page 163)

1. a) 6000

b) 400

c) 80

d) 0.7

e) 0.04

2. a) 530

b) 6700

c) 0.12

d) 0.49

e) 0.20 (must have the final zero)

3. a) 2.14

b) 350

c) 476

d) 0.00391 (3.91×10^{-3})

e) 309

Activity 7.8 (page 164)

a) C

b) E

c) D

d) F

e) C

f) D

g) A

h) B

i) A

j) F

Quiz (page 165)
a) 24.5 Yes
b) 24.3 No
c) 24.75 Yes
d) 25.53 No
e) 256 No
f) 32 No

8. RATIO AND PROPORTION

Activity 8.1 (page 167)
a) 3:1
b) 3:2
c) 4:1
d) 1:3
e) 2:1
f) 5:2

Activity 8.2 (page 169)
a) 1:1
b) 6:1
c) 1:3
d) 1:4
e) 3:2
f) 7:3

Activity 8.3 (page 170)
a) 18
b) 3
c) 8
d) 5
e) 20
f) 12
g) 28
h) 9

Activity 8.4 (page 171)
1. a) 2 red, 8 yellow
b) 18 red, 9 yellow
c) 16 red, 20 yellow
d) 15 red, 9 yellow
e) 8 red, 8 yellow
f) 15 red, 3 yellow
g) 20 red, 8 yellow
h) 9 red, 21 yellow
2. No. 3 red + 1 yellow (4); 6 red + 2 yellow (8); 9 red + 3 yellow (12)

Activity 8.5 (page 172)
a) 10 red, 20 yellow
b) 9 red, 3 yellow
c) 12 red, 20 yellow
d) 40 red, 35 yellow

Activity 8.6 (page 172)
a) 15 yellow and 25 blue
b) 6 red and 9 yellow, so 30 counters
c) 8 red, 12 yellow and 20 blue
d) 4 red, 6 yellow and 10 blue

Activity 8.7 (page 174)
a) £20:£10
b) £150:£300
c) £120:£480
d) £220:£330
e) £450:£300
f) £2040:£1530
g) £3372:£5620

Activity 8.8 (page 177)
a) Alex has £10, Ben has £30
b) Alex has £150, Ben has £120
c) Alex has £14, Ben has £49

Activity 8.9 (page 179)
1. a) 12.7 cm
b) 30.48 cm
2. a) 10 inches
b) 31.5 inches
3. a) $65
b) $16.12
4. a) £38.46
b) £0.77 (77p)

Quiz (page 180)
Manjinder £30, Natalie £50
Xander $20, Yolande $30, Zoe $50.
Probably Natalie – check exchange rate!

9. INTRODUCTION TO ALGEBRA

Activity 9.1 (page 182)

a) (-6)

b) 2

c) (-2)

d) (-7)

e) 7

f) 6

Activity 9.2 (page 183)

a) $x + 3$

b) $x - 1$

c) $-x - 2$

d) $2 - x$ or $-x + 2$

e) $-3 - x$ or $-x - 3$

f) $-x$ or $-x + 0$

Activity 9.3 (page 184)

1. a) $4x - 2$

b) $-x + 3$ or $3 - x$

c) $-4x - 3$ or $-3 - 4x$

Activity 9.4 (page 185)

1. a) $-2x - 4$

b) $5x - 9$

c) $2x - 5$

**Activity 9.5 and Activity 9.6
(pages 188 and 189)**

1. a) 8

b) 9

c) 18

d) 0

e) (-13)

2. a) (-1)

b) (-9)

c) (-9)

d) 9

e) 32

Quiz (page 189)

1. a) $3x + 1$

b) 5

c) $-6x + 12$

d) $2x$

Expressions b and d simplify to one term

2. a) (-5)

b) 5

c) 24

d) (-4)

Expression c gives biggest answer

10. EQUATIONS AND INEQUALITIES

Activity 10.1 (page 190)

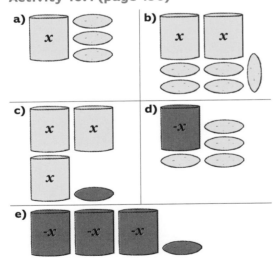

Activity 10.2 (page 193)

a) $x = 6$

b) $x = 6$

c) $x = 7$

d) $x = 13$

e) $x = 4$

f) $x = 7$

g) $x = 18$

h) $x = 12$

Activity 10.3 (page 195)

a) $x = (-4)$

b) $x = (-10)$

c) $x = (-2)$

d) $x = 1$

e) $x = \frac{13}{2} = 6.5$

f) $x = \frac{9}{4} = 2.25$

g) $x = (-18)$

h) $x = (-20)$

**Activity 10.4 and Activity 10.5
(pages 198 and 200)**

a) $x = 5$

b) $x = 3$

c) $x = 5$

d) $x = 4$

e) $x = 10$

f) $x = 2$

g) $x = 2$

h) $x = 0$

Activity 10.6 (page 201)

1. a)

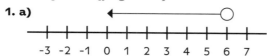

b)

c)

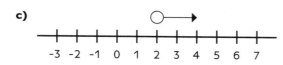

d)

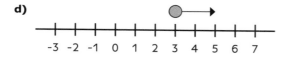

e)

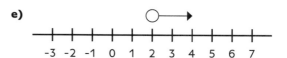

2. c and e are the same, both mean x is greater than 2.

Activity 10.7 (page 202)

1. a) 3, 4, 5, 6, 7

b) 0, 1, 2, 3, 4

c) (-2), (-1), 0, 1

d) (-5)

2. $6 < x \leq 4$ is impossible

Activity 10.8 (page 204)

a) $x > 6$

b) $x < 4$

c) $x \geq 8$

d) $x > (-2)$

e) $x < 2$ or $2 > x$

f) $x \geq 1$

Quiz (page 205)

a) $x = 8$

b) $x = 6$

c) $x = 2$

d) $x < 8$

e) $x \geq 4$

Inequality e has the biggest values, as it includes all numbers greater than 4

11. ALGEBRAIC MANIPULATION

**Activity 11.1 and Activity 11.2
(pages 209 and 212)**

1. a) $2x + 8$

b) $3x + 6$

c) $3x - 6$

d) $3 - 3x$

e) $-2x - 1$

f) $-6x + 2$

2. a) $5x + 14$

b) $5x + 2$

c) $2 - 5x$

d) $-8x + 1$

Activity 11.3 (page 215)

a) $x^2 + 4x$

b) $x^2 - 2x$

c) $2x^2 + 5x$

d) $3x^2 - 4x$

e) $3x^2 - 24x$

f) $20x - 4x^2$

g) $6x + 3y$

h) $x^2 + 3xy$

i) $3x^2 - 6xy$

j) $3xy - y^2$

Activity 11.4 (page 217)

1. a) $5(x - 3)$

b) $3(2x - 3)$

c) $2(1 - 4x)$

d) $x(x + 3)$

e) $x(4 - 3x)$

2. a) $2x(2x - 3)$

b) $3y(3x + 1)$

c) $5x(3y - 2x)$

d) $8x(x - 3y)$

e) $2xy(2x + 3y)$

Activity 11.5 (page 220)

1. a) $v = 4 + 10 \times 3 = 34$

b) $v = (-2) + 3 \times 5 = 13$

c) $v = 0.5 + 0.2 \times 10 = 2.5$

2. a) $s = 4 \times 3 + \frac{1}{2} \times 10 \times 3^2 = 12 + 45 = 57$

b) $s = (-2) \times 5 + \frac{1}{2} \times 3 \times 5^2 = (-10) + 37.5 = 27.5$

c) $s = 0.5 \times 10 + \frac{1}{2} \times 0.2 \times 10^2 = 5 + 10 = 15$

Activity 11.6 (page 220)

1. $R = \frac{V}{I} = \frac{20}{4} = 5$

2. $x = 10 - 3y = 10 - 9 = 1$

3. $x = \frac{7 - t}{2} = \frac{7 - 11}{2} = (-2)$

4. $a = \frac{v - u}{t} = \frac{7 - 3}{2} = 2$

5. $r = \frac{C}{2\pi} = \frac{25}{2\pi} = 3.979$ (to 3 dp)

6. $u = s + 5a = 10 + 5 \times 3 = 25$

7. $a = 3m - b - c = 3 \times 8 - 10 - 6 = 8$

8. $h = \frac{2A}{(a+b)} = \frac{2 \times 10}{3 + 2} = \frac{20}{5} = 4$

Quiz (page 220)

1. a and e, b and d, f and i, g and h. c is the odd one out.

2. a and e give 18, b and d give 52, f and i give 32, g and h give 48, and c gives 28, so b and d give the biggest answer.

12. FURTHER EQUATIONS

Activity 12.1 (page 224)

a) $x = (-8)$

b) $x = (-1)$

c) $x = (-3)$

d) $x = 12$

e) $x = (-5)$

Question d is the only one with a positive answer.

Activity 12.2 (page 227)

1. a) $x = 8$

b) $x = 5$

c) $x = 8$

d) $x = 88$

e) $x = (-1)$

f) $x = 13.5$

2. a) $x = 3$

b) $x = 9$

Activity 12.3 and Activity 12.4 (pages 230 and 231)

a) $x = 2$ (left = right = 8)

b) $x = 5$ (left = right = 14)

c) $x = 1$ (left = right = 1)

d) $x = 4$ (left = right = 7)

e) $x = 6$ (left = right = 8)

f) $x = 2$ (left = right = (-1))

Activity 12.5 (page 236)

a) $x = 1$, $y = 3$

b) $x = 4$, $y = 3$

c) $x = 3$, $y = (-2)$

Activity 12.6 (page 239)

$x = 5$, $y = 2$

Activity 12.7 (page 241)

1. a) $x = 2$, $y = 5$

b) $x = 7$, $y = 1$

c) $x = 3$, $y = 2$

2. $x = 1$, $y = 5$

Quiz (page 241)

a) $x = 6$

b) $x = (-1)$

c) $x = 0.2$, $y = 0.2$

Equation b gives a negative answer.

13. QUADRATICS

Activity 13.1 (page 242)

a) $2x + 4$

b) $-x + 1$

c) $-6 + 3x$

d) $6x - 3$

e) $x^2 + 2x$

f) $2x^2 + x$

g) $x^2 - 3x$

h) $-3x + x$

Activity 13.2 (page 245)

a) $x^2 + 4x + 3$

b) $x^2 + 6x + 8$

c) $x^2 + x - 2$

d) $x^2 - x - 6$

e) $x^2 - 5x + 4$

f) $x^2 - x - 12$

g) $1 + 3x + 2x^2$

h) $6 - 5x + x^2$

Investigate (page 249)

$x^2 + 5x - 6 = (x - 1)(x + 6)$

$x^2 + x - 6 = (x + 3)(x - 2)$

$x^2 - x - 6 = (x - 3)(x + 2)$

Activity 13.3 (page 249)

1. a) $(x + 1)(x + 1)$

b) $(x + 1)(x + 7)$

c) $(x + 3)(x + 5)$

d) $(x - 1)(x - 5)$

e) $(x - 6)(x - 2)$

f) $(x - 3)(x - 4)$

g) $(x + 5)(x - 1)$

h) $(x - 7)(x + 1)$

i) $(x + 4)(x - 3)$

Activity 13.4 (page 251)

a) $(x + 1)(x + 10) = 0$ so $x = (-1)$ or $x = (-10)$

b) $(x - 5)(x - 1) = 0$ so $x = 5$ or $x = 1$

c) $(x - 4)(x - 2) = 0$ so $x = 4$ or $x = 2$

d) $(x + 4)(x - 1) = 0$ so $x = (-4)$ or $x = 1$

e) $(x - 6)(x + 2) = 0$ so $x = 6$ or $x = (-2)$

f) $(x - 8)(x + 2) = 0$ so $x = 8$ or $x = (-2)$

Activity 13.5 (page 251)

1. a) $x^2 + 6x + 9$

b) $x^2 + 2x + 1$

c) $x^2 - 4x + 4$

d) $x^2 - 10x + 25$

4. You would need to split the x tiles lengthways and cut a 1 square into quarters.

$x^2 + x + 0.25$

Activity 13.6 (page 252)

1. a) $(x + 1)^2 - 1$

b) $(x + 3)^2 - 9$

c) $(x - 2)^2 - 4$

d) $(x - 4)^2 - 16$

2. $(x + 10)^2 - 100$

Activity 13.7 (page 255)

1. a) $(x + 3)^2 + 1$

b) $(x + 2)^2 - 2$

c) $(x - 1)^2 - 4$

d) $(x - 4)^2 - 5$

2. a) When $x = (-3)$ minimum value = 1

b) When $x = (-2)$ minimum value = (-2)

c) When $x = 1$ minimum value = (-4)

d) When $x = 4$ minimum value = (-5)

Activity 13.8 (page 257)

a) When $x = 1$, minimum value is (-9)

b) When $x = 3$, minimum value is 11

c) When $x = (-2)$, minimum value is (-11)

d) When $x = 2.5$, minimum value is (-3.25)

Quiz (page 257)

1. c has a minimum of 0.75 when $x = (-3.5)$

2. a has zeros when $x = 4$, (-2)

b has zeros when $x = (-3)$, (-1)

14. ALGEBRAIC GRAPHS

Activity 14.1 (page 259)

1. $(-2, 0)$ is on the x-axis to the left of the origin.

2. If both coordinates are negative, the point is in the bottom left part of the graph.

Activity 14.2 (page 260)

Graph 1: The lines are vertical.

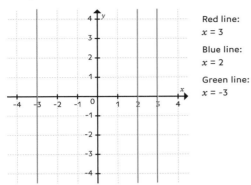

Red line:
$x = 3$

Blue line:
$x = 2$

Green line:
$x = -3$

Graph 2: The lines are horizontal.

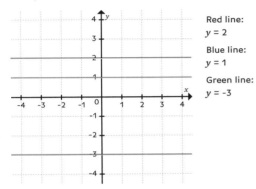

Red line:
$y = 2$

Blue line:
$y = 1$

Green line:
$y = -3$

Graph 3: The diagonal lines pass through (0, 0).

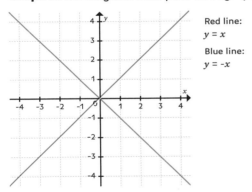

Red line:
$y = x$

Blue line:
$y = -x$

Graph 4: Parallel lines cross the y-axis at a value which matches the number in the equation.

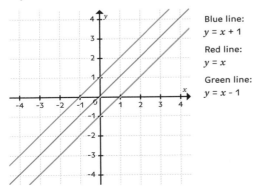

Blue line:
$y = x + 1$

Red line:
$y = x$

Green line:
$y = x - 1$

Graph 5: Steeper parallel lines cross the y-axis at a value which matches the number in the equation.

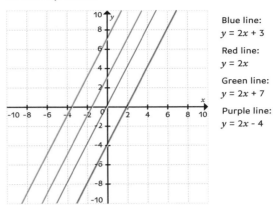

Blue line:
$y = 2x + 3$

Red line:
$y = 2x$

Green line:
$y = 2x + 7$

Purple line:
$y = 2x - 4$

Graph 6: Downhill graphs cross y-axis at (0, 3).

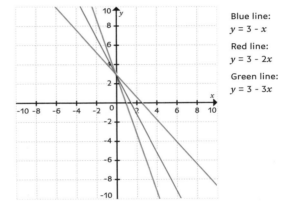

Blue line:
$y = 3 - x$

Red line:
$y = 3 - 2x$

Green line:
$y = 3 - 3x$

Activity 14.3 (page 264)

1. a) The y-intercept is (0, 5) and gradient is 3

b) The y-intercept is (0, 2) and gradient is 5

c) The y-intercept is (0, -4) and gradient is 7

d) The y-intercept is (0, -1) and gradient is -2

e) The y-intercept is (0, $-\frac{1}{2}$) and gradient is $\frac{1}{2}$

f) The y-intercept is (0, 6) and gradient is 3

The y-intercept is the number on its own and the gradient is the coefficient of x (multiplying number)

Parallel lines have the same gradient.

2. a) Blue line: gradient $\frac{1}{2}$ and intercept (0, 0)

Green line: gradient 1 and intercept (0, -4)

Red line: gradient -2 and intercept (0, 3)

b) Blue line: $y = \frac{1}{2}x$

Green line: $y = x - 4$

Red line: $y = -2x + 3$

Activity 14.4 (page 268)

1. a)

x	-5	-4	-3	-2	-1	0	1	2	3	4	5
y	-25	-16	-9	-4	-1	0	-1	-4	-9	-16	-25

b)

x	-5	-4	-3	-2	-1	0	1	2	3	4	5
y	23	14	7	2	-1	-2	-1	2	7	14	23

c)

x	-5	-4	-3	-2	-1	0	1	2	3	4	5
y	27	17	9	3	-1	-3	-3	-1	3	9	17

d)

x	-5	-4	-3	-2	-1	0	1	2	3	4	5
y	-12	-5	0	3	4	3	0	-5	-12	-21	-32

e)

x	-5	-4	-3	-2	-1	0	1	2	3	4	5
y	7	0	-5	-8	-9	-8	-5	0	7	16	27

f)

x	-5	-4	-3	-2	-1	0	1	2	3	4	5
y	-40	-27	-16	-7	0	5	8	9	8	5	0

2. a) $y = -x^2$

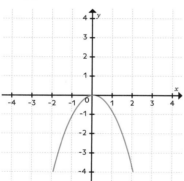

b) $y = x^2 - 2$

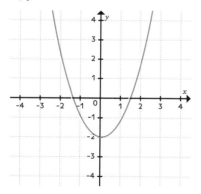

c) $y = x^2 - x - 3$

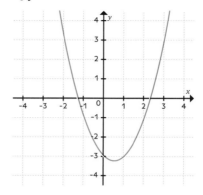

d) $y = 3 - 2x - x^2$

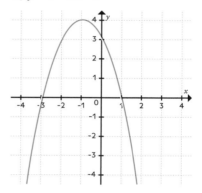

e) $y = x^2 + 2x - 8$

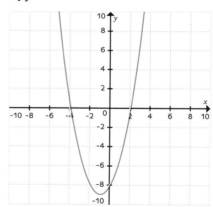

f) $y = 5 + 4x - x^2$

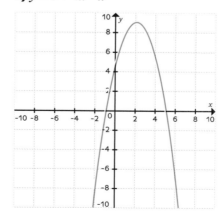

3. a) The curve touches the x-axis when $x = 0$

b) The curve crosses the x-axis when $x = -1.4$ and $x = 1.4$ (to 1 decimal place)

c) The curve crosses the x-axis when $x = -1.3$ and $x = 2.3$ (to 1 decimal place)

d) The curve crosses the x-axis when $x = -3$ and $x = 1$

e) The curve crosses the x-axis when $x = -4$ and $x = 2$

f) The curve crosses the x-axis when $x = -1$ and $x = 5$

4. Graphs b, c and e are u-shaped. Graphs a, d and f are n-shaped. The n-shaped ones have a negative x^2 term.

Quiz (page 268)

1. The lines cross at (1, 4) and (3, 6).

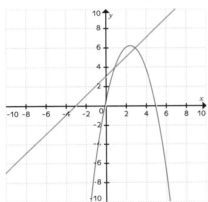

2. a) $y = x^2$

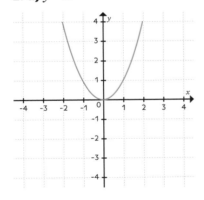

b) $y = 4x^2 - x^4$

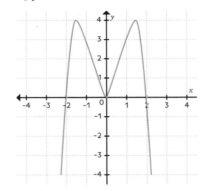

c) $y = \frac{1}{x}$

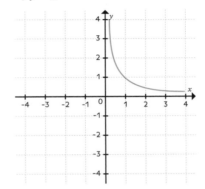

d) $y = 3 - x^2$

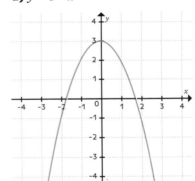

Index

Notes

Notes

Notes

Notes